KENNETH REXROTH

·CLASSICS· REVISITED

BOOKS BY KENNETH REXROTH

POEMS
The Collected Shorter Poems
The Collected Longer Poems
Sky Sea Birds Trees Earth House Beasts Flowers
New Poems
The Phoenix and the Tortoise
The Morning Star
Selected Poems

PLAYS

Beyond the Mountains

CRITICISM & ESSAYS

The Alternative Society
American Poetry in the Twentieth Century
Assays
Bird in the Bush
Classics Revisited
Communalism, from the Neolithic to 1900
The Elastic Retort
With Eye and Ear

TRANSLATIONS

100 Poems from the Chinese
100 More Poems from the Chinese: Love and the Turning Year
Fourteen Poems of O. V. Lubicz-Milosz
Seasons of Sacred Lust: The Selected Poems of Kazuko Shiraishi
    (with Ikuko Atsumi, John Solt, Carol Tinker, and
    Yasuyo Morita)
The Burning Heart: Women Poets of Japan
    (with Ikuko Atsumi)
The Orchid Boat: The Women Poets of China
    (with Ling Chung)
100 French Poems
Poems from the Greek Anthology
100 Poems from the Japanese
100 More Poems from the Japanese
30 Spanish Poems of Love and Exile
Selected Poems of Pierre Reverdy
Li Ch'ing-chao: Complete Poems (with Ling Chung)

AUTOBIOGRAPHY

An Autobiographical Novel

EDITOR

The Continuum Poetry Series

KENNETH REXROTH

·CLASSICS· REVISITED

Afterword by Bradford Morrow

A NEW DIRECTIONS BOOK

Manufactured in the United States of America
Originally published by Avon Books, 1969
First published clothbound and as New Directions Paperbook 621 in 1986
Published simultaneously in Canada by Penguin Books Canada Limited

Library of Congress Cataloging-in-Publication Data

Rexroth, Kenneth, 1905–1982
    Classics revisited.
    (A New Directions Book)
    Reprint. Originally published: New York : Avon, 1968.
    1. Literature—History and criticism—Addresses,
essays, lectures.   I. Title.
PN511.R57   1986   809   85-31088
ISBN 0-8112-0987-3
ISBN 0-8112-0988-1 (pbk.)

New Directions Books are published for James Laughlin
by New Directions Publishing Corporation,
80 Eighth Avenue, New York 10011

Contents

Introduction

Men have been writing for over five thousand years and have piled up a vast mass of imaginative literature. Some of it is just writing that happens to have lasted physically. There are, however, a small number of books that are something more. They are the basic documents in the history of the imagination; they overflow all definitions of classicism and, at the same time, share the most simply defined characteristics. It is usually said that they deal with the archetypes of human experience, with characters at once concrete and universal, and with events and relationships that are invariant in the lives of all men.

The archetypes of individual psychology are nodes, or *foci*, in the structure of each developing personality. Archetypes in this sense are characteristic of the greatest works of the human imagination as well. The unity of human experience is determined by the narrowness of the range of action and interaction of organisms and environments, for all men everywhere. Eskimos, Polynesians, Romans, Chicagoans—all men have the same kind of bodies and the same kind of brains and cope with an environment in ways that would seem more uniform than not to an observer from another planet.

This concentration on human individuals and their interrelationships distinguishes great literature from myth. Myths subjectivize the objective world. They put man into nature. The questions of man's relationship to his environment are answered by dramatic tableaux that are embodied in ritual. The greatest works of imaginative literature are mirror-images of myth. They objectify the crucial history of the subjective life. They make reality, nature, out of man. Their dramas are real, not formal. That is, dramatic tension is inherent in their materials, their elements. It does not depend on an overlying structure. Therefore, dramatic intensity springs from the very fact of relationships, and it reveals the fundamental dynamism of human life in the way, for instance, in which the operation of a power plant reveals the laws of physics.

In contrast, the interrelationships in myth tend to grow static as they are resolved—for instance, the interrelationship of the Olympian gods in *The Iliad* and *The Odyssey* never rises above a kind of frozen busyness. The drama is in the relationships of men.

It might be imagined that the history of the greatest literature would be a history of the evolution of an ever-deepening process of individuation. Certainly throughout history the symbolic patterns of myth increase in efficiency by becoming etherealized. They encompass ever wider, more profound, more intense means. Myth in this way parallels science, of which in a sense it is the metaphorical vesture, or substitute. Man fills the gap between technology and environment with myth and ritual. Mystery is resolved by being embodied.

Notoriously, the great dramatic fictions of mankind have not progressed as has science or even religious insight. Art is not improved by technology. The bisons in the cave at Altamira are not inferior to the best paintings in the last Biennale—and so with literature. James Joyce's *Ulysses* does not improve Homer. At one time it was believed that the mid-nineteenth century had witnessed a revolution of sensibility and insight. The poetry of Baudelaire, the novels of Dostoievsky were imagined to be different in kind from what had preceded them. Only the very young, and few of them, believe this any more. In fact, it would be easier today to muster cogent arguments on the other side.

The perils of the soul and its achievements are constant. From his earliest literary efforts man does not seem to have advanced in his comprehension of them, and may well have declined. Above all others, this is the area where novelty seems to be of no importance whatsoever, yet its lack never results in tedium. Quite the reverse: the contemporary novel that embodies paradigms of the great tragic commonplaces of human life seems precisely "novel," fresh, and convincing, while literature that deals with contemporaneity on its own terms is hackneyed before it appears in print.

The fundamental relationships of man to man, man to his environment, man to himself do not have to be presented as especially grandiose. The murder of Agamemnon and the long-drawn-out resolution of vengeance are only one aspect of the human condition. There are quiet and idyllic classics, even inconspicuous ones.

The most obvious classics are tragic because life is tragic in its very structure. There are no optimistic classics that tell us all is for the best in the best of all possible worlds, and besides, everything is getting better and better. There are no classics that are untrue. But certainly there are many that are powerful, though, it may be, very quiet, affirmations of life. The human race endures because millions of people have gone on inconspicuously affirming their existence, including aspects too tragic for literature.

Life may not be optimistic, but it certainly is comic, and the greatest literature presents man wearing the two conventional masks: the grinning and the weeping faces that decorate theater prosceniums. What is the face behind the double mask? Just a human face—yours or mine. That is the irony of it all—the irony that distinguishes great literature: it is all so ordinary.

The Epic of Gilgamesh

The first surviving work of fiction may well be the first in fact. *The Epic of Gilgamesh* dates from the beginnings of civilization in Mesopotamia. Gilgamesh was the fifth king of the Sumerian city of Uruk after the Great Flood. Under his rule, about 2,500 B.C., Uruk conquered the surrounding city-states and established something like a small nation. For two thousand years Gilgamesh survived in the Near East as an epic hero. There are versions of his story in Hittite, Hurrian, Canaanite, Sumerian, and Assyrian, and the dim memory of his fame in the *Koran*. The most complete text comes from Assurbanipal's library, formed just before the destruction of Nineveh in the seventh century B.C. The story seems to have taken form almost two thousand years before that. Considering the disparity of cultures and languages, the great stretch of time, the means of reproduction and communication, *The Epic of Gilgamesh* is one of the most popular stories ever told.

Rightly so. It may be the first, but it is a highly developed fictional narrative. It is not a myth. Even to call it an epic requires a stretching of the definition. It is more like a novel of a modern, individualistic hero than it is like Homer's *Iliad*. It is a spiritual adventure, a story of self-realization, the discovery of the meaning of the personality, of a type that would never change down the four-thousand-year-long history of human imagination. Its figures have the cogency of symbols that will never alter. It is modern because it is like a dream of a modern man.

Gilgamesh is not a demigod. In spite of his divine ancestry and the concern of the gods of Mesopotamia with his adventures, in spite of those adventures' wondrous character, he remains as secular as Stephen Dedalus. True, critics have taken the twelve tablets, or chapters, of the Assyrian story as standing for the twelve houses of the Zodiac and Gilgamesh as the sun moving through the drama of the year. May be; but this is a symbolic substructure as remote from the human problems of Gilgamesh as the identical substructure is from the adventures of Stephen Dedalus in James Joyce's *Ulysses.* It would be possible to develop a convincing argument that *Tom Jones* is a sun myth; such symbolic patterns seem to be determinants of the imagination. What is important about Gilgamesh is that, like Tom Jones, he is a man.

As King of Uruk, Gilgamesh has too much power for the good of his community. He deflowers the virgins, consumes the young men in war, works the elders to death building the city walls. The people appeal to the gods, who make him a companion of clay, the wild man Enkidu, as a foil for his energy. Enkidu is tamed and brought to the city by a temple prostitute. As Gilgamesh comes in the night to claim the *droit du seigneur* from a new-wedded bride, Enkidu grapples with him and they fight a mighty battle. Enkidu at last is thrown; whereupon he and Gilgamesh embrace and swear eternal friendship. They set off for the Land of Cedars to bring back the great trees guarded by the fearful giant Humbaba. They are protected by the prayers of Gilgamesh's mother, the priestess-goddess Ninsun; watched over by Shamash, the sun god; and aided by the storm winds to defeat Humbaba. When they return to Uruk in victory, the goddess Ishtar falls in love with Gilgamesh and offers herself to him. He rejects and insults her. She appeals to the gods for vengeance. Her father sends down the Bull of Heaven to destroy Gilgamesh. The companions kill the Bull, cut out his heart, and offer it to Shamash, the sun god, and Enkidu throws the thigh of the Bull in the face of Ishtar. The gods in council decide that one of the two heroes must die—more for killing the Bull of Heaven and Humbaba and cutting the sacred cedars than for insulting Ishtar. They smite Enkidu with a fatal disease. Enkidu's death and Gilgamesh's lament over his body are the finest poetry of the whole story.

Gilgamesh sets off across the world in quest of immortality. Eventually he comes to Utnapishtim, the survivor of the Deluge, far away in the Western Ocean in the Garden of the Sun. Utnapishtim says that with the exception of himself, the gods have kept immortal life for themselves and allotted death to man. He tells Gilgamesh the story of the Deluge, a narrative that has many points in com-

mon with the later tale of Noah. Then he demonstrates that Gilgamesh cannot hold off sleep, much less death. However, Utnapishtim
shows him how to find an underwater plant that will restore youth.
Gilgamesh dives down and gets the plant, but loses it to a serpent on
his way home.

At last he comes back to Uruk and realizes that the mighty walls,
the temples, and the gardens that he had built are all the immortality he will ever know. And so he dies, and the citizens bury him with
many offerings, and mourn his death. In the twentieth century,
archeologists find the remnants of the walls of Gilgamesh's Uruk
still enduring, and the "Gilgamesh motif," a man throttling two
beasts, far away in time and place, on Anglo-Saxon jewelry at Sutton
Hoo, above the North Sea.

One reason why *The Epic of Gilgamesh* still has great power to
move us is a poetic style that does not depend on elements like
rhyme or meter but on rhetorical devices, parallelism and antithesis,
and the antiphonal organization of short and long phrases, all of
which are translatable and which are worked into emotive patterns
in the originals with consummate skill. These are characteristics
The Epic of Gilgamesh shares with much Near Eastern poetry,
notably with the *Psalms, The Song of Songs,* the great Canticles of
the Old Testament, the Song of Deborah in the book of *Judges.*

This solemn style, like the words of some great ritual, is the direct
embodiment of a vision and judgment of the human condition that
is permanent and universal. The absurdity of life and death, heroic
wistfulness, nostalgia for lost possibilities, melancholy of missed
perfection were as meaningful five thousand years ago to the Su-
merians as they are to us. We look at them today in museum
cases—round heads, curly hair, immense eyes and noses, plump
hands folded over plump chests, cloaks like leaves or feathers—and
they look out at us, and we know that they knew that the love of
comrades cannot prevail against the insult of death, that erotic
women destroy men with impossible demands, that nothing endures, that the memory of heroic action lasts a little while and
sometimes the walls of empire a little longer, that the meaning of
life can be revealed but never explained, and that the realization of
these truths constitutes the achievement of true personality. From
the first narrative in the world's literature Gilgamesh emerges as the

first conscious self. In the course of four thousand years of fiction, self-consciousness will be achieved in many different and more elaborate ways, but it will in fact and essence vary not at all.

Since the discovery of the Assyrian tablets in the last century there have been several English versions of *The Epic of Gilgamesh*. The best is the one by N. K. Sandars in the Penguin Classics. It is in natural English, devoid of false archaisms; all the known texts have been woven into the narrative with taste and skill; and the fifty pages of introduction are as helpful and informative as could be desired.

Homer
The Iliad

The best-qualified critics have always agreed that the first work of Western European literature has remained incomparably the greatest. In itself this is a revelation of the nature of the human mind and of the role of works of art. This is a popular judgment as well as a critical one. Today, over twenty-five centuries old, Homer competes successfully with current best sellers and detective stories and the most sensational and topical nonfiction.

Modern Americans may be the heirs of Western Civilization, but all the elements of that civilization have changed drastically since Homer's day. The office worker who reads Homer on the subway on the way to work bears little superficial resemblance to either Homer's characters or his audience. Why should two long poems about the life of barbaric Greece have so great an appeal?

It was the fashion in the nineteenth century to deny the existence of Homer and to break up *The Odyssey* and *The Iliad* into collections of folk ballads. Nothing disproves those theories more than this public reception. *The Iliad* and *The Odyssey* have been read by such a vast diversity of men because they are unitary works of art and deal with universal experience with unsurpassed depth, breadth, and intensity. Each poem shows the powerful insight and organization that come from the artistic craft of a complete person.

Men have argued about *The Iliad* for so long and raised so many side issues that it is easy for a critic to forget that it is formally a tragedy, saturated with a tragic sense of life and constructed with the inevitability of the tragedy of Orestes or Macbeth. It is a double tragedy—of Achilles and the Greeks and of Hector and the Trojans, each reinforcing the other. To modern taste, the heroes are not the Greeks, who are portrayed as quarreling members of a warrior band, but the Trojans, men of family united in the community of the city-state.

Homer, like most later writers of epic, Teutonic, Irish, or Icelandic, portrays heroic valor as fundamentally destructive, not just of social order, but of humane community. The Greeks are doomed by their characteristic virtues. Achilles sulks in his tent; Agamemnon has stolen his girl. The Greek camp is beset with a disorder that wastes all good things. Underlying disorder is violence. Violence is not approved of in itself by the Greeks, but all the values that they most admire—the nobility, pride and power, glamour and strength of barbaric chieftains—flourish only in the context of violence and must be fed by it continuously. Failure of these values provokes shame, the opposite of the assumption of responsibility, and shame provokes disaster.

On the other side of the wall, the Trojans go their orderly and dignified ways. None of them approves of the crime of Paris, but he is a member of the family of the King of Troy, and the citizens of Troy are members one of another. So they assume his guilt in an act of collective responsibility. When the Greeks arrived before the walls of Troy, the Trojans could have thrown Paris and Helen out of the city. The invaders would have gone their way. When *The Iliad* opens, the Greeks have been fighting for ten years and are worn out with the moral attrition of war, while the Trojans have grown ever closer together in the consciousness of doom. "Our lot is best, to fight for our country," says Hector; and Homer implies a contrast with the Greeks, who are fighting for themselves, each for his own valor and pride.

Greeks and Trojans are not the only protagonists of this tragedy. There is another community—the gods of Olympus. In the vast literature of Homeric criticism, I have never read a mention of what kind of community this was, of where in Homer's day he could have found an earthly parallel to such a group of people. The court of Zeus is precisely a court, like those to be found in the great empires of the ancient Near East—in Egypt, Babylon, or Persia. After Homer, for a few hundred years, Greek society strove to rise above the tyrant and the court of the tyrant. The Greeks of the Classical period looked on the rulers of Persia or Egypt and their provincial imitators in the Greek world as at once frivolous and dangerous, because, in Greek opinion, they were motivated not by the moral consensus of a responsible community, but by the whims of what today we would call a collection of celebrities.

Homer contrasts the societies of the Greeks, the Trojans, and the Olympian gods as the three forms of political association that prevailed in the Heroic Age (a time that in fact, four hundred years before, must have seemed almost as remote to him as his age does to us): the barbaric war band; the ancient, Bronze Age, pre-Greek city-state; and the imperial court. He also contrasts men and gods as two disparate orders of being. The gods may behave like painted and perfumed courtiers of the Persian King of Kings, but they function also as conceptual forms of the forces of nature and of the forces that operate within the human personality on nonhuman levels. In this role, too, the tragedy of *The Iliad* reveals them as frivolous, dangerous, and unpredictable.

True, Homer speaks worshipfully at times of the gods, and especially of Zeus—but in terms of standardized flattery, empty of moral content. Utterly unlike that of the Jew or Muslim or Christian, Homer's view of the supernatural is devoid of value altogether. Value arises only in the relations of men. He contrasts two different systems of relationships: the epic chivalry of the Heroic Age war band of the Greeks, and the Trojan community of mutual respect and responsibility. The conflicts and resolutions and tragedies that beset the interactions of these human beings are all the good and evil there is to be found in *The Iliad*. The gods contribute only chance, fate, doom—as amoral as so many roulette wheels.

Homer has been read for almost three thousand years, and is read today by millions, because he portrayed men in the night-bound world of insensate circumstance, as being each man to his fellow the only light there is, and all men to one another—as the source of the only principle of order. This, says Homer, is the human condition. Out of it in *The Iliad* he constructed a dramatic architecture of a cogency never to be surpassed.

Each time I put down *The Iliad*, after reading it again in some new translation, or after reading once more the somber splendor of the Greek, I am convinced, as one is convinced by the experiences of a lifetime, that somehow, in a way beyond the visions of artistry, I have been face to face with the meaning of existence. Other works of literature give this insight, but none so powerfully, so uncontaminated by evasion or subterfuge. If the art of poetry is a symbolic criticism of value, *The Iliad* is the paramount classic of that art. Its purity, simplicity, definition, and impact reveal life and expose it to irrevocable judgment, with finality and at the beginning of European literature.

Homer
The Odyssey

In all the melee on the Trojan plain, there is one person who always takes the common-sense point of view. He is cunning, prudent, imperturbable. He always seeks the greatest return for the least expenditure of blood or spirit. This is Odysseus. Amongst the Levantine Trojans and the Viking-like Greeks, caught up in the irrationality of circumstance and broken against their own contradictions, he seems an intruder from another time. And so he is.

The Iliad is a symphonic work of art. The double theme with its intense polarity is modulated, retarded, and quickened, yet moves relentlessly to climax and recapitulation. The only devices in *The Odyssey* are flashbacks in time, the narratives within the narrative. They complicate the structure; they do not compound it. The episode with Nausikaa is self-sufficient and is written with such poignancy and clarity that it led Samuel Butler to "prove" that *The Odyssey* was written by Nausikaa herself.

Only a few stories of the various Heroic Ages, those we think of as preëminently epic, are concerned with the working out of an inexorable doom, the consequence of sin, folly, and flaws of character in the protagonists. These few are tragedies—the *Nibelungenlied*; several Icelandic sagas, but especially *Burnt Njal*; the tale of Tristram and Iseult; the story of Arthur, Launcelot, and Guinevere; and the Irish Cuchulain cycle.

Epics like *The Ramayana, Gilgamesh*, the story of the Holy Grail are quests. Others are adventure stories like *Sinbad the Sailor*. When the latter possess a dramatic structure, it is of the sort we would call comic.

The Odyssey is a collection of adventures, of little melodramas like the earliest English and Scots Ballads, and of folktales like those in Grimm. The supernatural appears not from Olympus, but on the level of fairy stories and superstitions. In contrast, there is nothing folkloristic about *The Iliad*. Its legendary materials are myths. *The Iliad* never falters in its vision of the gods as personifications of nonhuman forces herding men to their doom. In *The Odyssey*, Poseidon is only the unruly and unpredictable sea; Athena, the virtues of Odysseus himself projected on the heavens.

The virtues of Odysseus are not those of a warrior, but those of a merchant-adventurer who has wandered the ancient seas from Gibraltar to the Crimea and the Caucasus and has survived and profited: agility, inventiveness, courage, prudence, and persistence. They include neither heroic valor nor civic duty. Odysseus knows neither shame nor guilt.

In *The Odyssey*, man is a part of nature. He can outwit nature, learn its secrets, use it. Its personifications are less than human and succumb to human wisdom or cunning. The heroes of *The Iliad* are shaken and thwarted in their courses by vast powers. In *The Odyssey*, men are continually tricked and tempted by *daimons*, by malicious spirits, or by "some god." Odysseus blames a malicious devil when he forgets to wear his cloak on a chilly night. The enchantresses of *The Odyssey* are not archetypes of the grandeur, misery, and enervation of lust like Helen. They are witches; above all, they are the extravagantly satisfying whores that sailors wander the surface of the planet seeking to this day. Even Nausikaa bears an uncanny resemblance to that good girl the old bo'sun met once in his far-off youth when he wandered into a church social and who took him home to meet the folks.

It is home that haunts *The Odyssey*, as it has haunted men in fo'c'sles before and since. Although, like all sailors, Odysseus thinks he wants to get home, again like all sailors, he spends an inordinate time doing it. The keystone lines in *The Odyssey* which compare with Hector's last interview with his wife and child, or Achilles' with Priam, are in praise of marriage, yet they sound suspiciously ironic.

The adventures of *The Odyssey* are fantastic, but their denouement is pure fantasy. Odysseus' return and slaughter of the suitors is the most outlandish thing in Greek literature. No custom like it is known in the mercantile Levant of Homer's time, nor in the similar societies of the South Seas in the recent past. We have no reason to believe that a wife whose husband had abandoned her for twenty years would remain faithful, that she would be persecuted by a mob of suitors who would move into her home and struggle with one another for her hand and consume her substance. Nor has there ever been any legal code or custom that would justify the husband in mercilessly slaughtering them all when he showed up incognito after twenty years.

Something the story does resemble: the ever-recurring dream in the barren hotel rooms, crowded barracks, and fo'c'sles of traveling men, soldiers and sailors, long away. "Is my wife true to me? What is she doing now? Do they think of me at home? Will my son recognize me when I get back? Are those fellows still pestering my wife? Has she given in to them? Do they hang around the house? Wait till I get back; I'll fix them." As dream and daydream, the climax of *The Odyssey* has been a universal experience of wandering husbands; as fact, it has not existed. Any seafaring society with such a custom would have exterminated itself.

All *The Odyssey* has a character of dream unlike the stark objectivity of *The Iliad*. The events of *The Iliad* follow one another, bright, swift, sure, and dramatically necessary. The events of *The Odyssey* fade and dissolve; the narrative wanders in time; the pictures are brilliant, but they glitter through a mist of reverie—an old sailor musing over the glamour of his past. The texture of the verse is

light in *The Odyssey*; the imagery sparkles; but it never loses both its
decorative delicacy of detail and its melancholy tone. *The Iliad* is
full of the thunder and lightning of the king of gods and men. When
there is thunder in *The Odyssey*, it is that of some foolish one-eyed
giant whose fellows laugh at him.

The Odyssey is entertainment. It is entertainment of the highest
order, but it is difficult to imagine anyone saying, "Reading *The
Odyssey* changed my life fundamentally." *The Iliad* can be read
only superficially as entertainment. If we make ourselves available
to it, it confronts us with a vision of the nature of reality and the
being of man. *The Iliad* says: "This is life. It is tragic, and if it has
meaning, that meaning is an incommunicable mystery; it can be
presented, but never explained." *The Odyssey* says: "This is life. It is
comic, and it is full of meanings. These meanings are all the
multiform techniques for living; they can be learned by work,
intelligence, and a canny conscience."

Tragedy is a posture; comedy is an activity. If one read enough
comedies, they might change one's life fundamentally. Life as
comedy can be learned; as tragedy it can only be assumed. Most
men are predominantly one type or the other; an individual's view
of life is seldom equally balanced between tragedy and comedy.
However, the dramatic artists of the world's literature have usually
written both; they have realized that there are two faces of the coin
of life: on one side, the head of an implacable and beautiful god; on
the other, a curious animal.

Beowulf

Like the more hardy and noble fish, the kinds of men that we heirs
of the Anglo-Saxon tradition think most heroic thrive best amidst
the colder seas. The figures of the Norse, Welsh, and Irish Heroic
Ages possess a magnanimity, courage, and contempt for triviality
that we do not find in the heroes of Homer. Nor do our heroes come

to their doom because they have pushed their normal endowment of great pride to the point of existential conceit; nor are they haunted by irresponsible fate or plagued by the frivolities of the gods.

For these reasons, *Beowulf* seems essentially heroic in a way in which the epics of the Mediterranean do not; its hero fulfills our insistence upon a moral heroism. His legend is one with those of Gordon, Florence Nightingale, and Wellesley, or of Jesse W. Lazear and other martyrs of Public Health. Modern criticism has devalued our nineteenth-century heroes. But Beowulf is far away; all we know of him is a single document; so he stands as a mythic paradigm of the brave, generous, self-sacrificing aristocrat.

Beowulf, nephew of Hygelac, King of the Geatas in Southern Sweden, sails with fourteen companions to Denmark and offers to rid the hall of Hrothgar, King of the Danes, of a devouring monster in human shape called Grendel. After a feast, the Danes withdraw. Grendel enters and kills one of the Swedes. Beowulf wrestles with the monster and tears off his arm. Grendel, mortally wounded, escapes to die at the bottom of the aweful mere that is his home. The next night Grendel's mother kills and carries off one of the Danish nobles. In full armor Beowulf plunges into the water and, after a terrible fight, kills her with a mysterious sword that he finds under the waves. After the death of Hygelac and his son, Beowulf becomes King of the Geatas. In his extreme old age, a dragon ravages his country; Beowulf destroys it but dies of his wounds, and the poem ends with his funeral. Hrothgar and Hygelac were historical persons, and Beowulf may have actually existed.

The most unexpected quality in *Beowulf* is its abiding communication of joy. In contrast with the Mediterranean glitter of *The Odyssey*, plagued by fatigue and melancholy, *Beowulf* takes place in an atmosphere of semidarkness—the gloom of fire-lit halls, stormy wastelands, and underwater caverns. It is full of blood and fierceness. Its rhythms have the tone of peremptory challenge and the clang of iron. Men exult in their conflict with one another and the elements. The sea is not a jealous, cantankerous, senile deity. It is a cold, thrilling antagonist.

Even Grendel and his mother are serious in a way in which Greek demons never are. They may be horrors survived from the pagan Norse world of frost, giants, wolf men, and dragons of the waters, but nobody would ever dream of calling them frivolous. They share Beowulf's dogged earnestness; what they lack is his joy, which suffuses the book in spite of a countersuffusion, a doom that haunts the far background of the narrative, like a few drops of ink and milk spreading into water from opposite directions.

Though they glory in themselves as successful animals, always we feel that *Beowulf* is a tale of men at the end of their tether. Not only does life end and splendor fall to ruin, but a hand is writing, *"Mene, mene, tekel upharsin"* in the firelight on the walls of Hrothgar's banqueting hall. This civilization is almost over. The onrushing Twilight of the Gods is ominous in the distance. The refrain of another great Anglo-Saxon poem: *"Thaes ofereode, thisses swa maeg!"*—"That passed away, this will too"—might as well have occurred every twenty lines or so in *Beowulf*; or again, "Mood be the more as our might lessens."

This sense of doom we can feel simply reading the poem in adequate translation. If we read the notes or introduction, we learn that *Beowulf* takes place not only against the imminent end of the Heroic Age of the Teutonic peoples; in addition, a tragedy is unfolding in the background. The immediate personal future of Hrothgar's family was filled with treachery and disaster. The author knew this, and so did his audience: foreboding echoes as a counter-pattern of rhythm and symbolism against all the poem's exultation.

This is a specifically Northern epic theme. Arnold Toynbee, quoting John Knox, calls it "the monstrous regimen of women." Both Helen and Penelope determine the Homeric epics only by the passive exercise of their femininity. The queens and enchantresses of the North interfere actively. It is their machinations that bring disaster.

Grendel and his mother—devourers of men, inhabitants of sub-terranean depths—embody the demonic past whose claims can be destroyed with the facility of only courage and strength. But the future cannot be destroyed. Its doom depends on the deliberate evil acts of its participants—not on *karma*, not on myth, not on the unconscious. It will be played out in treachery, the murder of kinsmen, and civil war. All through the poem the poet inserts carefully muted ambiguous references to the dynastic ruin that is about to overwhelm all the participants except Beowulf himself. It is this tension between the easily subjugated occult and the inchoate and ungovernable overt fact of human destiny that gives the poem its irony, its pathos, and its structure. Once this tension is understood, *Beowulf* ceases to seem a folkloristic collection of Scandinavian legends and emerges as a strictly organized but muted tragedy—an elegiac drama.

Beowulf dies and is buried "above the battle," overlooking the pale, cold sea—the perfect example of heroic transcendence. His grave must have been much like the ship burial discovered in our own generation at Sutton Hoo in England, on the western shore of the same sea of adventure. Amongst the surviving treasures of that anonymous hero are the enameled clasps of his sporran, ornamented with a figure of a man strangling two beasts: the Gilgamesh motif come to the far North across four thousand years.

There are many contemporary translations of *Beowulf* in verse and prose: several paperbacks, amongst them the Penguin, Mentor, and Everyman, and a number of elaborate scholarly editions. The best as modern poetry is Edwin Morgan's, published in 1952 in England by the Hand and Flower Press and in the United States by the University of California.

Njal's Saga

Njal's Saga is one of the most complex and dramatic novels ever written. It teems with characters: each sharply, however briefly, drawn; all presented in the most dramatic contexts. The narrative is carried by dialogue and by action of maximum concreteness. It is the story of the life of a man of great wisdom and spiritual strength in the early days of the colonization of Iceland. Much of it is concerned with the development of barbaric blood feuds and the struggle of Njal as a leader of the community to reduce them to the workings of civilized justice. With others he is usually successful; but his closest friend, Gunnar, has a wife, Hallgerd, whose malevolent pride endlessly clashes with the imperious temper of Njal's wife, Bergthora, and sets in train a series of vendettas in which first Gunnar and then Njal himself and his wife and all his sons are destroyed. Yet in spite of murders, battles, ambushes, ghosts, and Viking raids, the thing that most amazes the modern reader about *Njal's Saga* is the unparalleled maturity of its characters. These yeomen on their bleak island at the end of the earth are adult in a fashion unknown to Homer's Agamemnon or Proust's Swann.

We think of Icelandic Saga literature as the expression of a Heroic Age with its disorder, its lack of all clearly defined and accepted values except those necessary to animal survival, its conflict between shame and guilt, and its political instability, all resulting in the comparative simplicity of the typical epic plot. Nothing could be less true. The heroic characters of the finer sagas are not members of a barbaric war band gathered from the homeless men of collapsing and emerging civilizations. Like the Greek city-state before Alexander, Icelandic society in its early days is a convincing proof of the Malthusian argument. Here is an isolated society, the result of a demanding selective process—even to go to Iceland from Scandinavia a man had to be something of a hero—kept pruned biologically by an equally demanding ecology, small enough so that the members acted upon one another intensely and personally. Islanding produces rapid evolutionary change and demands full use of all the potentialities of a species, whether it be the alpine flora of a mountain range separated by thousands of miles from similar environments or the exclusive good families of Henry James's Boston or New York or the Japanese court of *The Tale of Genji*. Such closed communities are not just inbred: they are social, moral, intellectual, and ultimately spiritual, as well as biological, forcing beds, self-isolating and concentrating. It is because of such islanding that a work like *Njal's Saga* is as complex as *The Wings of the Dove* or *Remembrance of Things Past*.

The objection to overpopulation is aesthetic, not economic. Kropotkin was right. It would be possible to feed Manhattan with hydroponic vegetables and protein-rich algae, raised in the windows of the glass-steel-and-concrete barracks. But humane values diffuse and drain away amongst too many people, and too many is a rather small number—not much more than the population of the Florence of the Medicis, the Athens of Sophocles, the Iceland of the sagas.

Mass man is man without responsibility. *Njal's Saga* is an epic of ever-mounting crises of conscience, the steady intensification of the moral interaction of a very limited number of human beings whose relationships are governed by a continuously and spontaneously evolving law. It is possible to play many thousands of games with thirty-two chessmen. It is impossible to play any if the pieces are increased to millions. The order of the electrons in the universe is a statistical order. Only in single, limited objects is it a real one, and only in very small objects is it actually determinable.

Throughout the saga Njal is the focus of the contending social forces. He is the knot that holds the complex tensions of his society together. What brings him down is, first, simply the passage of time. If one makes a life habit of unlimited liability, the accumulated responsibilities of a lifetime may become too complex and, at the same time, too poignantly focused to be borne. One man might sustain so complicated an architecture of stresses and balances as long as there was no unaccountable interference from outside.

Njal is a professional "Law Speaker," one of the creators of a structure of decency and order amongst independent but co-operating yeomen. Such a structure can be made self-sustaining, but it cannot be made self-perpetuating. It is perpetuated by child-bearing and children are borne by women. Once again the monstrous regimen of women works behind the scenes with its own intestinal vindictiveness that brings all noble superstructures to ruin. Njal, after a lifetime of unparalleled nobility and relentless education of the conscience, ends, like the Nibelungs, in fire. His home and his family are destroyed with him, and all for an impetuous spite. A vector of tension unaccounted for in his careful system of checks and balances of moral liability smashes a lifetime's husbandry, like an arrow shot from outside into a web of glass.

Although the narrative of *Njal's Saga* is complicated with psychological subtleties and constantly shifting minor motivations unsurpassed in fiction, the major confrontation is stated with clarity and simplicity. It is the womb against law and order, what contemporary slang calls the struggle of Id and Superego. Perhaps this is why the masses prefer mass society. Amongst millions, this destructive electrical charge does not leap between positive and negative like lightning but is grounded out in the asexual anonymous mass. It is so powerful in *Njal's Saga* because of the superlative beauty of the structure of conflicting conscience and liability—and because from this structure there shines forth an inescapable embodied realization: the knowledge that life is more powerful than order. Existence is orderly; the individual and his related fellows persist only as long as they are so; but it is vital disorder that endures throughout time and from which organization emerges into temporary significance and into which it washes away.

Most people of my generation read *Njal's Saga* in the Everyman's Library edition, in which it is called *Burnt Njal*. There is now a new scholarly translation in vigorously idiomatic English: *Njal's Saga*, translated by Carl F. Bayerschmidt and Lee M. Hollander, published by New York University Press, 1955.

Job

Of all the Hebrew Scriptures, *The Book of Job* is the most provocative of meditation. It is concerned with the fundamental confrontation, the ultimate mystery of man's existence, the irreconcilability of absolute and contingent in the natural order. Why does evil exist? Whether God exists or not, there is still the inexplicable waste of value in the world of facts. The law of the conservation of energy may be substantiated by experiment, but there is no demonstrable principle of the conservation of good. From this mystery all the other dilemmas of the moral life depend. What is the meaning of Auschwitz, or the pains and betrayals of the most commonplace life? Was Dostoievsky's character right? "It's all not worth the tears of one child. I respectfully hand Him back my ticket."

This is the subject of the dramatic poem of Job. There is nothing specifically Jewish about it, and an ancient Talmudic tradition says it was written in another language. Job and his friends are not Jews but what we would call Bedouins. Their conflicting wisdoms were learned from the mystery of the desert, the cruelty of nature, the impassivity of the constellations. Like most of the wisdom literature of the Bible, *The Book of Job* is the product of an international literary elite, the reflection of the highly developed sensibility and intellectual life of empires that stretched from the Crimea to the Indus and the cataracts of the Nile. Yet, like *The Iliad*, it is a careful reconstruction of a world five hundred or more years gone.

Job is a patriarchal herdsman, like Abraham, and there are no ideas in the book that might not have occurred to primitive man as philosopher. The form—a *flyting, tenzone,* disputation—is found in all the literatures of the ancient Near East, as is the subject—the suffering of the just and innocent. The prologue in the court of heaven and the epilogue, the just man justified, are obviously folkloristic, and the body of the poem uses universal legendary materials. Yet all reference to cult, rite, law, specific religious practice is avoided. It is as though the author had deliberately set out to create a moral drama of the greatest possible ecumenical acceptance. He certainly succeeded, for his poem is as meaningful today as it ever was.

Gregory the Great founded the Medieval tradition of treating *Job* as a charade of Christian prophecy and Catholic doctrine and rite. Before him Origen, philosophically more sophisticated, had said that since the being of God is by definition incomprehensible, so necessarily His justice is incomprehensible. This extraordinary *non sequitur* would come down through Duns Scotus to Luther to Kierkegaard, and be secularized in our own day by the Existentialists. In its final atheistic form, it is the philosophic obsession of the mid-twentieth century. We no longer ask if existence has meaning but, "Does meaning exist?"

The evils that afflict Job are purely physical and negative— deprivations, pains, and destructions. In life he never meets with positive, active moral evil, wrong done consciously in full will by person to person. The question debated by Job and his friends is not whether natural disasters are unmerited. They are aware that they do not occur in a context in which merit has meaning, unless they emanate from the will of a person. The entire debate assumes that they do—that the Creator is a person with personal knowledge of the consequences, omniscient as well as omnipotent. If the creative principle of the universe is a person, why are not the destruction and waste of good in time just as malevolent as any interpersonal evil? In the dialogue God is called *Shaddai*, the utterly self-sufficient power. Had he known of it, the poet would have asked, "Does Lord Acton's epigram extend all the way to omnipotence, or is that the point at which it turns into its opposite?" Does *The Book of Job* move as Whitehead said: from God the Void, to God the Enemy, to God the Friend?

Job's friends are like the liberal clergy of so short a time ago. They believe that creation is demonstrably conservative of good, that justice eventually triumphs and the good man reaps his reward. They deny evil as such. In one way or another they argue that the evils of the world are really goods: they are privative, educative, disciplinary, deserved, misunderstood, illusory; but never gratuitous, much less malevolent. The poet underlines every speech of the "comforters" with irony like the mounting bass notes of an organ.

Job answers simply, "I have been just and harmless in heart and deed, and I have suffered harm and injustice from the course of events." Finally he swears an oath; he stakes his integrity as a person on his innocence. Then the Almighty answers as a Voice from the Whirlwind. He answers the oath, the commitment, not the arguments. He begins with a rebuke: "Who is this that darkens counsel by words without wisdom?" and ends with another: "My wrath is kindled against you and your friends, for you have not spoken of Me what is right, as Job has." The Voice from the Whirlwind says that both Job's defense of himself and his friends' defense of the Almighty are foolishness, but offers no explanation, only simple confrontation, omnipotence to contingency. The speech of the Almighty, one of the very greatest poems in all literature, is a parade of power—devoid of moral content, but intolerably charged with the *tremendum*, the awe and judgment of the utterly other.

There could be no greater tribute to the power of the unknown author than that readers in future ages would seldom interpret this great speech as saying that the creative principle of the universe is simply "amoral," that comforting dodge; they would see it rather as positively immoral by any human standard. What is the difference between the game between Jehovah and Satan with their pawn, the soul of Job, and the games the rotted aristocrats play with the innocent in *Les Liasons Dangereuses* or the experiments of Dostoievsky's Stavrogin? This is the final question, and in it the friends of Job tumble, lost in an abyss.

The Voice in the Whirlwind is a person speaking to a person, and so, looking back from the point attained by the wisdom of Job, is the Voice on Sinai. The Torah is transformed from a legal document to speech: "I am the Lord thy God. . . ." It is remarkable that dialogue in the Bible is brief and peremptory and rare—Abraham, Amos, Moses, Isaiah, Jeremiah—less than a hundred verses altogether, of command and submission; and even dialogue between man and man is almost as scarce—until we come to Job. Suddenly dialogue is imported from the wisdom literature of the ancient Orient and placed at the center of Jewish religion.

The acceptance of the incomprehensibility of the justice of God is not a rational act; it is an act of prayer, of communion. Job's final words are a prayer of humble access, a voicing of the breakdown of logic and evaluation in an abiding state of calm ecstasy. *The Book of Job* makes sense only as a vehicle for contemplation, for the deepest kind of prayer, which culminates in the assumption of unlimited liability: what the Byzantines and Russians loved to call the divinization of man.

The Upholder of the Universe takes Job into communion with Himself, with the awefullness of infinite process. Job no longer needs vindication. The word becomes meaningless, a vanished shadow lost in the terrible illumination of a tragic sense of being, beyond the natural and temporal order altogether. Jewish mystics, Kabbalists and Hassidim, seized on three words as telegraphic as Chinese, *Job* vi, 14: "For the fainting—from his friend—loyalty." Rationalist commentators are still arguing over the meaning of this verse. The mystics said it was the secret key to the unsolvable problem.

The best way to read *The Book of Job* is in one of the pocket editions of the King James Version with William Blake's illustrations—if you are lucky enough to find one. I believe there is none now in print. The best way to study it is in the Anchor Bible volume by Marvin Pope.

The Mahabharata

The Mahabharata is the last of the great classics that those who read only English must take on faith, at least as poetry. The translations are all unsatisfactory, and most of them are appalling. Yet few works of the imagination have ever had a more profound and lasting effect on their own culture.

Embedded in The Mahabharata is the Bhagavad Gita, not only one of the world's major religious documents but, like the Bible and the Koran, an epitome of the virtues and vices of the civilization that produced it and even more of the one that followed it. If the world's classics are in any way keys to the understanding of man in history, The Mahabharata is an essential key to an entire subcontinent which now contains over five hundred million people.

So we must perforce struggle and suffer through the inept translations and try to imagine the original. Few indeed will be able to endure the entire book, but most translations are drastic abridgments anyway. The faults are not all in the English. Hindu literature by our standards is decadent from its prime foundations. Overspecialization, proliferation, gigantism—like Hindu sculpture, Indian poetry and prose have a jungle profusion that sparer cultures can never assimilate. Indian art and literature must be pared and boiled down before they can be transmitted—even to the Far East. So Buddhist art came to China simplified and ordered by transmission through the Bactrian Greeks and the peoples of the desert oases.

But The Mahabharata cannot be pared down to a simple substructure. Profusion is inherent in every sentence. Read as a whole, in the unidiomatic English of the translators—a job that will take even the most rapid reader a very long time—it gives an impression of disorder in the overall organization, in the main line of the narrative, and in detail—in the rhetorical proliferation of each sentence. In addition, the psychological and symbolic monotony of the hundreds of episodes and anecdotes (a characteristic *The Mahabharata* shares with *The Ramayana* and *The Ocean of Story*) has the cumulative effect of a narrow but unending dream, a kind of relentless impoverishment of the unconscious, that finally produces a comatose and uncritical acceptance.

Partly these effects are inherent in Indian culture, in the aesthetics implicitly accepted by the society. Partly they are due to the evolution of the epic itself.

The critics of the last century might be right—Homer might be the product of "the folk" rather than of a single poet—but it is easy to demonstrate that *The Iliad* is as tightly organized as a play of Sophocles. The "Cnidian Aphrodite," one of the most erotic of all works of art, is a single statue of a single nude girl in a comparatively modest pose. The great Sun Temple at Konarak is a large building completely covered with small statues of men and women in every erotic posture. The Western mind boggles, attention fails, and monotony destroys stimulus and response. Perhaps, following Coleridge, we have misjudged the mental structure of the creative act. Perhaps the unconscious is fundamentally unimaginative and unoriginating.

The legendary author of *The Mahabharata* is called Vyasa—"the arranger"—simply the personification of an obvious fact. About one eighth of the more than one hundred thousand couplets—in other words, about as many lines as *The Iliad* and *The Odyssey* together—are devoted to the core narrative, a superficially complicated but fundamentally simple story of a feud between two barbaric families of cousins, the Kauravas and the Pandavas, both descended from the king of a town between the rivers Ganges and Jumna, in the vicinity of modern Delhi.

The original epic may well have begun to take shape about 500 B.C.—the time of Buddha, when this entire region, from the plateau that divides the Indus and Ganges basins on around the foothills of the Himalaya, was in a state of intense political and intellectual ferment.

Like *The Iliad*, and most other epic poetry, *The Mahabharata* describes a far earlier period, and unlike Homer, the original compilers seriously altered and updated the original primitive material. Thus, the conflict of the two families of cousins was probably the story of the war over the newly burnt-off land of two small, tribal groups: one, the Kauravas, early barbaric villagers; the other, the Pandavas, a pastoral and forest people like the present Bhils, Todas, Santal, and Oraon. They were not cousins—they were probably not even of the same race. Much has been made of the polyandrous relationship of the heroine, Draupadi, the wife of all the Pandava brothers, as a memory of Stone Age matriarchy. Overlying this original stratum are many others.

Next earliest was a Bronze Age civilization of battling warrior herdsmen and town dwellers who drove chariots like the heroes of the first Irish epic. In the Iron Age the ferment in North India in the sixth century B.C. was due to a revolt of the warrior class against the religion of the priests—the Brahmins—who had come to dominate the society and whose excessive ritualism was uneconomic.

Buddhism, Jainism, and other movements of the time were comparable to the West's Reformation and were led by members of the warrior class, the Kshatriyas, of which Buddha was a member. Buddhist ideas—not only of religion, but of social relations—survive everywhere, interwoven throughout the text of *The Mahabharata*. Centuries later, with the decline of Buddhism, the Brahmins were able to accomplish a Counter Reformation and establish modern Hinduism, a religious syncretism with little continuity with the ancient Vedic past.

This Hindu-izing movement is responsible for the present overall character of *The Mahabharata*, and for the exaggeration and proliferation that make it so difficult for Westerners to accept.

Still later rescensions of *The Mahabharata* turned the entire epic into a celebration of the incarnate god Vishnu: Krishna (the combination of warrior, trickster, and medicine man of a forest tribe), today the most popular of all Indian deities.

Inserted in the epic is the *Bhagavad Gita*, Krishna's religious teaching of the Pandava hero Arjuna on the brink of the monstrous battle that gives the rule of North India to the Pandavas. The *Gita*, however, is a separate "classic," existing in its own right. Millions of troops of highly civilized nations including Greeks and Chinese take part in what originally was a fight between a few hundred barbaric tribesmen and a band of savages. Everything that could be poured into the narrative down the ages has been; no other book has so many subsidiary stories, anecdotes, and subplots. In addition, there are long passages on everything from medicine to domestic economy. Somewhere along the line someone got the idea that the epic could be expanded with technical advice on warfare and politics—so *The Mahabharata* was also reworked as an extensive treatise of advice to princes, with examples.

The reworking of the poem with every cultural change, and the Indian conservatism which cannot bear to throw anything out, result at last in the erosion of personality and human interest in the characters and their relations. The vast mass of contradictory moral ideas cancel each other out and leave only a lowest common denominator of motivation, an undramatic expediency and impassivity in the face of determinism. If all actions are separate but equal, there can be no drama. Homer has the sharp dialectic conflict of Greek logic or Euclid. India has a kind of logic, but it is founded on the denial of the principle of identity. It is neither deductive or inductive but all-enveloping—like *The Mahabharata*.

India had no written history until Muslim times, but *The Mahabharata* is a kind of written archeology, and the reader can dig down, like Schliemann through the ten towns of Troy, encapsulate like a golden onion—down from the latest, nineteenth-century additions to Stone Age India—and find at last, in the entire stratified epic, something very like the Indian present.

For a person with Western standards there is only one way to read *The Mahabharata*: a complete suspension of not just disbelief—but all critical faculties. There are modern prose versions, tremendously abridged, which are easy reading. Chakravarthi V. Narashiman's is the most recent, but it reduces the jungle of the original to a small cultivated field. Perhaps the best idea is to read such an abridgment for "the story" and then sample a complete version at leisure, for *The Mahabharata* is as inexhaustible and as exhausting as India itself.

The Kalevala

Philosophical critics in the nineteenth century decided that a culture is most solidly based on a great epic which incorporates all the prime factors in the national or folk consciousness—or "unconscious." There is a whole nest of very disputable assumptions hidden here. First, that Greek culture was solidly based. It was not. Its glory was in its dynamic equilibrium—which was short-lived. National consciousness does not come from the *Nibelungenlied* or *The Iliad*. It is an intellectual notion, born with the nation-state, which came to fruition with the State as an Armed People in the French Revolutionary Wars and degenerated into the idea of the "folk unconscious" in the long drawn-out struggle of the Germans for a national identity.

All national literatures today seek for epic foundations—the *Shāh-nāma*, *The Knight in the Leopard Skin*, *Digenes Akritas*, the *Ramayana* and *Mahabharata*, the Serbian Ballads; even Dante's *Divine Comedy* has been forced into the service of the national consciousness. (The Italian national epic is in fact the operas of Verdi.) In many cases these constructions are purely synthetic, as manufactured for the purpose as ever was Virgil's *Aeneid* for Augustus, or Kallimachos' Serapis Cult for Ptolemy. Yet astonishingly, this does not necessarily invalidate them.

It would be easy to narrow the definition of a classic to the point where it applied only to literature that fulfilled such a role. Conversely, all literature that deserves the name of classic does, in a sense, define the consciousness of a particular people and yet is in extension a moment in the conscience of mankind. In the narrowest sense again, many synthetic epics, written as myths to shape the life of a people, have been successful and have been classics in the wider sense as well. The *Aeneid*, the *Kojiki* and *Nihongi*, the *Kalevala*, the history plays of Shakespeare, the *Shāh-nāma*, these are all synthetic myths, made by intellectuals, which succeeded. They did provide foundations for the structural relationships through which their peoples saw themselves. There is nothing really strange about this. The *Iliad* and *Odyssey* and even *The Epic of Gilgamesh* are literary products. The notion that they were grunted out by Folk sitting about a fire and munching bones was a hallucination of a few nineteenth-century German scholars.

If effect on his own people is a measure; if intensity, profundity, and duration of impact is a measure, the most successful of all was Elias Lonnrot. "Who on earth was he?" most people will say. He was a country doctor in the most remote country in Europe, a country that had never been a nation and would not become one for another century: the Grand Duchy of Finland. As with so many country doctors, his hobby was philology and folklore. Early in the last century he began collecting the folk songs and narrative ballads of the peasantry, especially in the most remote regions—along the borders of Lapland, and in the forests of Karelia. He became convinced that these songs were fragments of a connected epic narrative that had once been as coherent as the *Iliad*, or the *Nibelungenlied*.

In this assumption he has been proved wrong, but it does not matter. As he worked his folk materials into what he imagined the original must have been, he produced the most successful constructed myth in modern literature, and one of the most successful of all time. The *Kalevala* saturates Finnish life. Its deep, resonant evocation of the natural environment, the rich dark green or snow-white land of forests and lakes and pastures where herdsmen, hunters, and fishers go about their timeless ways; its strong matriarchal bias; its ironic acceptance of the tragic nature of life; its dry humor; its praise of intelligence and hospitality as prime virtues—all these elements go to sustain the unique Finnish character to this very day, and that amongst the most advanced sections of the intelligentsia as well as amongst the common people.

In recent years there have appeared in several magazines little anthologies of modernist Finnish poetry, edited by Anselm Hollo, who himself now writes mostly in English and who is very much a part of the international avant garde community. All this poetry, including his own, may or may not echo Voshneshensky or Gertrude Stein, Allen Ginsberg or Pierre Reverdy, but it is all marked by the influence of that one great book of ballads, collected in fragments from the Finnish countryside, over one hundred years ago by one man.

Gallen-Kallela, Finland's greatest painter, did his finest work as illustrations for the book and is famous for a sort of Pre-Raphaelite, Jugendstijl, Art Nouveau style, invented by himself and known as the Kalevala style. Either through Gallen-Kallela or directly, *The Kalevala* influences the most modern Finnish architecture and textile, ceramic, and silver design. What William Morris tried so hard to do for English art and letters, and failed so badly to do, the Finns do naturally. It is questionable if at any period the *Odyssey* and *Iliad* ever had as deep an influence on Greek life.

Yet most non-Finnish readers find the *Kalevala* puzzling and hard to read. In the first place, the trochaic meter, which is natural to Finnish, sounds artificial and monotonous when imitated by German and English translators. In *Hiawatha*, Longfellow deliberately imitated the *Kalevala* in meter, method, subject, and purpose. He took one of the first comprehensive collections of American Indian legends, itself distorted and Europeanized, and formed them into a connected narrative with many elements of the story borrowed from the *Kalevala.* He cast his American epic in the same eight-syllable trochaic lines and used the same repetitive devices and fixed epithets—none of them natural in English or American speech.

He hoped to write a poem that would connect white Americans with the earth beneath their feet through the Indian past, as the Greeks had been connected with groves and springs and mountains through their nymphs and satyrs and local deities. For two generations *Hiawatha* was taught in school and every American child could recite it, and the poem did play, feebly, something of the role Longfellow had hoped for it. Then it began to fail, and today most Americans, young or old, consider it comic, if they have ever heard of it. Yet the *Kalevala* is still successful amongst Finns who read Paul Éluard and Finns who read nothing. Why?

First, both Elias Lonnrot and his peasant informants were much better poets. Recited in the original language, the *Kalevala* has a gripping sonority and haunting cadences that make it quite unlike any other great poem in any language, and the repetitions and recurring epithets have a chime and echo very different from Longfellow's mechanical use of them. Longfellow's trochaics have the thump of doggerel and, since the meter is so unnatural in English, sound absurd. Lonnrot's meter swings; the rhythms are native to the language, and he continuously varies them; his trochees shift back and forth across the beat—swing, in other words. It is the difference between a heartbeat and a metronome.

The plot of *Hiawatha* is as clear as Longfellow could make it, far clearer than his sources—an incomparably more logical narrative than anything in the *Kalevala*. Modern research has proved that Lonnrot's sources were inchoate indeed, much of them not narrative at all. He reworked them into a most extraordinary pattern—not a story or series of tales, but a long-drawn-out dream sequence. The heroes of the *Kalevala* are not warriors or knights-errant; they are shamans—magicians, smiths, and dreamers—men of mystery and cunning. Their adventures are inconclusive, often seemingly pointless, and cryptically frustrating, and their connections are hidden underground.

The original Hiawatha was such a person too, but Longfellow exorcised him—took away his magic—and assimilated him to nineteenth-century rationalism. Lonnrot did the opposite. He awoke the night side of the nineteenth-century professional and middle-class mind, represented by himself, and connected it with the prehistoric culture of the subarctic medicine men which he found surviving amongst the Finnish peasantry.

No wonder Carl Jung was fascinated by the *Kalevala*. It is a kind of socially negotiable Jungian dream, full of archetypes and animuses and animas, totemic symbols of the soul; Methusaleh figures; sacred, unobtainable maidens; impossible tasks and mystic beasts—all set in the forests, lakes, and waterfalls of primeval Finland. All its tales seem to be moving toward an unknowable end—the ultimate integration of the integral person—just like the dreams of Jungian patients under analysis.

Yet the *Kalevala* is far more than any psychoanalytic text. Its heroes struggle in dreams, but they simultaneously live wide awake in the Finnish land, in conflict with a hard but beautiful environment. They are undivided beings, in a real world. In our modern

destructive world civilization, Finland stands out as enjoying a high
level of ecological success. The Finns cope with their setting of
living nature far better than do the Russians or Americans. This
talent is reflected in and reinforced by the *Kalevala*, certainly the
most ecological of epics. In the poem, as in Finnish life, there
survives that ecological life philosophy without which no subarctic
people could endure. Like the Lapps or Eskimos, they must cooper-
ate with nature or perish. They are still there. So the *Kalevala*
succeeds and endures because it expresses not just a national consciousness, but the consciousness of the kinship of a race of men
with all living creatures about them. Maybe it was put together by a
country doctor five generations ago, but it is the opposite of a
synthetic epic: it is a synthesis of nature, man, time, and place.

The only cheap, easily available English translation is in Everyman's Library (Dutton), two volumes, by W. F. Kirby, in rather
antiquated language and with poor notes. There is a fine, scholarly
edition by F. P. Magoun, Jr., published by Harvard University Press.

Sappho

Poems

Since they began in the early days of the popular-education movement in nineteenth-century Britain, five-foot shelves, world classics,
hundred best books, have hardly ever included poetry as such, and
drama and epic have been distinguished for the trashiness of their
translations, because these collections are all programmatic—"the
great ideas that have influenced the progress of mankind." I doubt if
works of art as such do any such thing; yet no one would dare give
his selections so vulgar and unimproving a label as One Hundred
Books That Have Thrilled the Ages. Down the millennia since the
cave painters the arts have sharpened and refined human sensibili-

ties, yet no one can even be sure that this is a good thing. The screen of history, like the taste of politicians, churchmen and university presidents, has been programmatic. So we have a large collection of Aristotle's lecture notes on politics and ethics, and we have only random fragments of Sappho's poems.

Matthew Arnold said Homer was eminently rapid, plain, direct, in thought and expression, syntax, words, matter, and ideas, and that he was eminently noble. Arnold refused to define the ambiguous word "noble," but he meant by it his own special virtue of his idealized Victorian ruling caste: disinterested responsibility. This final criterion eliminates Sappho, although she shares with Homer and Sophocles their splendor, clarity, and impetuosity. She, above all others, is bright, swift, and sure. She surpasses all other Greek poets in immediacy of utterance and responsiveness of sensibility.

The greatest Greek writers, read in Greek, seem hypersensitive to us and possessed of a higher irritability in the medical sense; amongst us this is considered a morbid condition, because it has been cultivated excessively or pretended to by modern decadents. There is no reason why it should not be thought of as quite the opposite—a symptom of superabundant health. Sappho is as exquisitely sensitive to objective reality as to her own subjectivity, and she organizes the poignancies of these interlocked realities with consummate taste. As Sophocles is a man, so she is a woman, functioning at maximum realization of potential.

Since we have only fragments of Sappho the size of Japanese poems, one short complete poem, and single words or phrases quoted by grammarians to illustrate the Aeolic dialect, is it possible that we delude ourselves with the Sapphic legend? If attention is focused sharply on anything whatever from which we expect aesthetic satisfaction, a process takes place similar to the raptures of nature mysticism. Our own hyperesthesia is exacerbated; we become hypnotized; the object of contemplation, like a crystal ball, acquires a significance with unlimited ramifications. Is this what we do with the shards and ruins we call Sappho?

> . . . about the cool water
> the wind sounds through sprays
> of apple, and from the quivering leaves
> slumber pours down . . . .

is, just as it is, a most impressive poem. Whatever its original context, it is as moving as any similar poem in classic Japanese. How about "more gold than gold," "far whiter than an egg," "neither honey nor the bee"?

The two Edwardian poetesses who wrote under the name of Michael Field expanded many of Sappho's fragments into poems of great poignancy. The best was taken from a scholiast's commentary on a line of Pindar's, where the reference to Sappho is in indirect discourse: "Yea, gold is son of Zeus, no rust/ Its timeless light can stain;/ The worm that brings man's flesh to dust/ Assaults its strength in vain./ More gold than gold the love I sing,/ A hard, inviolable thing." Does the original justify this enraptured response?

It has been difficult to come at Sappho without the Greek. Nineteenth-century England swarmed with mediocre academicians and country clergymen, all in a conspiracy to prove to those without the tongues that Western Civilization had been founded by tenth-rate minds who wrote atrocious doggerel. Translations of Sappho, until recent years, have been fantastically inappropriate. Catullus, with Baudelaire and Tu Fu, in all the world's literature most nearly approaches Sappho's special virtues. His translation of her lessens her intensity.

Today a sufficient number of literal translations by modern poets may enable the reader of English to envelop Sappho and measure her as we do distant stars by triangulation from more mundane objects. It then becomes apparent that we are not deluding ourselves. There has been no other poet like this. Wherever enough words remain to form a coherent context, they give one another a unique luster, an effulgence found nowhere else. Presentational immediacy of the image, overwhelming urgency of personal involvement—in no other poet are these two prime factors of lyric poetry raised to so great a power.

Both the ancient legend of a romantic, tempestuous life and the Victorian one that portrayed her as a schoolmistress of an academy for brides were constructed from her poems. We know nothing surely except the poetry, which, on the face of it, is the passionate utterance of a woman whose life was spent as lover and guide to a small circle of younger girls. There is no evidence that this was an institutional relationship, like the *thiasos*, the dancing school, of her friend Alkaios. He is obviously a doting professional teacher of chorus girls; Sappho's relationships are as obviously openly erotic. The poems certainly mean what they say.

Passionate love is the very substance of Sappho. In ancient Greece as in China, the love between men and women was of a totally different character where it existed at all, and seldom passionate. In most Greek poetry, however noble or erotic, relations between the sexes are institutionalized, whether Alkestis or the prostitutes of Paulos Silentiarios. Romantic love, with its destructive potential, is found only between members of the same sex.

Sappho's poetry is not only intimate, it is secular. Myth hardly exists and is never the cohesive cement of institutions as it is in Pindar's lyric odes, which are hieratic, hierarchic, and impersonal. The idylls of Theokritos are court poetry, like the eighteenth-century French Rococo poets who imitated him. Behind the flirtations of his deodorized shepherds and shepherdesses we always hear time's winged chariot hurrying near, loaded with marriage contracts arranged by treaty between warring dynasties. So Kallimachos was an Alexandrian Voltaire, one of a committee to construct the synthetic religion of Serapis for an atheist court. His one intimate poem is to a man. Erotic love returns in *The Greek Anthology* with late-born Levantines like Meleager and Isaurians with Hittite blood from the Anatolian highlands. Except for them, and a few passages in the choruses of Euripides, what we consider the proper subject for lyric poetry does not exist in Greek verse outside the fragments of Sappho and one tiny bit by the similar Erinna.

Central to the understanding of Sappho as of Plato is her sexuality. Critics down the ages have exerted themselves to deny this, most especially when they shared it. To judge by primitive song, legend, and epic, romantic love has commonly existed between members of the same sex, and seldom in the institutionalized relations between men and women until those institutions pass through formalization to etherealization, as in the court circle of *The Tale of Genji.* Romantic love appears between men and women only when it becomes economically feasible. The problem is neither to explain nor to explain away Sappho's homosexuality. It is to explain the accelerating homosexualization of love between Western men and women since the eleventh century, with its culmination in the movies and the more urbane girlie magazines.

Although women in Lesbos were more free than their sisters in

Athens or Sparta, they were far from free in our sense. Sappho's poetry reveals the intensity of the hidden life of ancient Greek women. The curtain is raised for a moment and we see into purdah. For the rest, history and literature are silent.

Aeschylus
The Oresteia

"Aeschylus, son of Euphorion, an Athenian. This tomb hides his dust, here where he died in Gela amongst the wheatfields. His fame lives in splendor on the battlefield of Marathon, and the long-haired Medes remember him well." Dying in Sicily, far from home, the first and greatest dramatic poet wished to be remembered as a citizen who had acted with his fellows at the moment when glory came to Athens.

Swinburne called The Oresteia the greatest spiritual achievement of man. The majority of critics consider it the noblest of tragedies. Yet, after the soaring climaxes that close the Agamemnon and The Libation Bearers—the murder of Agamemnon and Cassandra by his wife, Clytemnestra, and her lover, Aegisthus, and the killing of them by his children, Orestes and Elektra—the concluding play, The Eumenides, may well seem to the modern mind anticlimactic and empty. For us the State is ruled by venality, covetousness, fraud, vulgarity; an appeal to it for absolution is not a proper and is far from a transcendent denouement. Aristotle considered democracy, worn out by his time, the worst of governments. Yet a little while before, its forms possessed for Aeschylus a new and splendid sacredness.

Modern criticism, influenced by discredited nineteenth-century anthropology, reads in the Oresteian trilogy conflict between ancient matriarchal blood ties and nature religion and the superseding patriarchal abstract law and Olympian gods. This may have been the ideological struggle of Neolithic and Bronze Age cultures, but the Greeks of Aeschylus' time had certainly forgotten its emotional meaning. Why should the vendettas dogging Orestes, Oedipus, and the Theban brothers, as far removed from Aeschylus as he is from us, suddenly have appeared so relevant?

These myths raise the question that haunts and defines the human condition. The long, unwinding *karma* of family curse takes life from spilled blood, but it is worked out in individual wills of men, perpetually reborn in moments of flawed decision. No one is innocent. Fate is the multiplication of the corrupt will by itself, as it raises itself, step by step, to second, third, fourth, and higher powers of entanglement. This is the mystery of original sin—the conflict of destiny and free will, the greater and the lesser good—focused in the Socratic dilemma: the bitter conclusion of experience that reason, that knowledge of good and of the consequence of choice, far from guarantee that man will choose his own good. Dependent on this mystery is the mystery of Job, the unmerited suffering of righteous men. Orestes follows one moral imperative rather than another, either course justifiable and each horrible. He acts obedient to Apollo and is punished by the primitive goddesses of the under-world. He cannot choose a greater good, but is forced to decide on a lesser evil.

The actions of Greek tragedy are not battles between chimeras of the unconscious; they are real and intrinsically dramatic. The tensions in Greek life between what Nietzsche called Apollonian and Dionysiac powers result from constant polarities in the characters of all men. Nor are conflicts of the rights of mother, father, children, ancestors, threat of consequence, peculiarities attending either the Urban Revolution at the opening of the Bronze Age, the birth of the democratic city-state or the dawn of the technological age today.

Again, Aristotle said that what elevates the language of the characters of Aeschylus is not rhetoric but a kind of transcendent politics. The actors are caught up in the shimmering flux—warp and woof and flying shuttles—of a kind of political ecstasy. Athens in the days of Aeschylus, like London in the days of Shakespeare, experienced a true dramatization of life. Whether Aeschylus invented tragedy or not, he is the first Western writer to understand process—the essence of drama. The Athenian community of his day was continually discovering new realms of value in its own interpersonal relationships. Aeschylus gives expression to a civic dynamism more intense than Western man would ever see again. Meaning was being won from Time.

In *The Iliad*, experience always narrows judgment and value. In Aeschylus, the self absorbs irrational divine and reasonable human imperatives and transmutes them into decision. Agamemnon, Clytemnestra, Orestes all confront destiny in specific instances of dilemma and make determining choices. If doom is female continuity, organic process, and choice is the male will to achievement, and the first two plays are their tragic conflict, in "The Eumenides" this conflict is resolved in community—the classical balance of personal form and impersonal law. Apollo, Athena, and the Furies are reconciled under the rule of reason, order, public welfare. This is the gospel of the newborn citizen, participant in a new kind of freedom. It is not Aeschylus' fault but history's that it bears for us an uncomfortable resemblance to the religion of Robespierre.

The meaning of *The Oresteia* is an ever-widening ray that expands to judge history as it penetrates time. Atreus and Thyestes, Leda and Zeus, Artemis and Iphigenia, Paris and Helen, Cassandra and Apollo, Achilles and Agamemnon, lust and power, adulterous and quarreling men and gods—generations of conflict pour into the retort of tragedy and are reduced to one complex molecule. So too symbolism and imagery are characterized by expansion—by scope, vastness, physical grandeur. Elements far widely separated in time or space or differing greatly in scale are juxtaposed with overwhelming sensory effect. Under all runs a counterpoint of simple antitheses—light and dark, eagle and serpent, home and battlefield, glory and nurture, wife and warrior, child and parent, community and ruler—tensions that polarize every sustained passage of verse. A sense of demonic possession builds in the audience, to discharge in a final reconciliation of contraries. The Furies of blood vengeance turn to the Eumenides, "The Gracious Ones," guardians of the reasonable fellowship of Athenian democracy. The audience did not believe this mythic plot as the orthodox Christian believes the Apostles' Creed. It was rapt away with the protagonists in a twisting net of fate and will, act and consequence—an existing experience.

So the exchange of compliments between the deities at the end is not an Aesopian moral. The trilogy is moral existence throughout. "The troubled memories of pain seep through the dreaming heart. Men learn against their will." "Man learns by suffering," said Aeschylus. Does he? At the end, the virtuous and wise pass from the ruin of history to a new family of love and devotion. Do they? Two thousand years later, we may disagree and accept the ignoble fact that burned babies return tirelessly to the fire; yet we sustain ourselves with faith that somewhere is a realm where the ennobling insights of Aeschylus and Job are true and real.

Aeschylus has attracted the most abominable translators in the history of literature and few good ones. The *Agamemnon* of Louis MacNeice is excellent, but cut and altered slightly. Incomparably the best for American readers is Richmond Lattimore's, published by the University of Chicago Press and the Modern Library.

Sophocles
The Theban Plays

Sophocles' life might have been lived by his statue in the Louvre— so wise, so calm, so marmoreal. The same exemplary image could well have written his tragedies. Sophocles sang and danced as a boy in the choir of thanksgiving for Athens' naval victory over the Persians at Salamis. He was the intimate of Pericles and the friend of Phidias and Thucydides. Speakers in Plato's dialogues remembered him as an aged man. He died before the capture of Athens by Sparta. That was all there was: just the long lifetime of one man, from 495 to 406 B.C.

In Renaissance Florence, T'ang China, or Elizabethan England, he would have been too good to be true. His was a time never to occur again, and he was superlatively true to it. The unique artistic experience of Attic tragedy was contemporary with the glory of Athenian power, between the wars with Persia and Sparta. It lasted less than three generations; its perfect expression, only one. Aeschylus speaks at the opening of the greatest generation in the experience of man; Sophocles, for its brief years of mature achievement. To understand the Periclean Age requires an effort like no other. We find about us no standards or experiences that warrant a belief that life was ever like that. If the societies of other times and places are the measure of humanness, the Athenians for a moment were superhuman. The men and women in the tragedies of Sophocles are human as ourselves but purer, simpler, more beautiful—the inhabitants of a kind of Utopia. With all its agonies, this is life as it should be lived.

Sophocles' dramatic world, like Periclean Athens itself, is self-contained. Its ultimate sanctions are immanent, not transcendent. The mythic beings of Aeschylus are supernatural references for a new system of values, otherworldly midwives of a new social order. In Sophocles, this order is operating. The dilemmas of the natural community are not solved by reference to a supernatural one. Aeschylus' sacred democracy is personalized by Sophocles. For him a person is the most concrete thing there is. Tragedy arises out of the flux of fate and oracular doom, but so arises from the acts of free persons. The age-long puzzle of fate and free will is solved by the dialectic of dramatic moral action.

From the style of Aeschylus one could construct a rhetoric of majesty. Sophocles, a few years younger, has already learned to avoid all appurtenances of sublimity. His style is simple, almost plain. Its majesty owes little to symbol, metaphor. His figures of speech arise from the ordinary linkages of direct communication— the opposite of the vast disjunctions and incongruous juxtapositions of Aeschylus. This is the optimum human of Aristotle's ethics speaking. The virtues of his style are grandeur, grace, control, dynamic balance, proportion, dialectic organization, the equipoise of strength and beauty. Nothing is mean; all is golden. His characters may be infatuated, but never ignoble. Their calamities are their own fault, but that fault is never base. Their sins are arrogance, rashness, overconfidence, presumption, contempt, cruelty, anger, lust, carelessness—the family of pride. Not even the soldiers, slaves, and messengers are guilty of gluttony, sloth, cowardice, venality.

The plays themselves form the transcendent community whose natural product is value. They are the etherealizing mirror of contemporary Athens. It is because there was majesty in the audience that the Sophoclean chorus can so directly "bridge the footlights." The chorus is us. As the dialectic of dramatic speech and situation unwinds with that inevitable order which Sophocles learned from the Sophists and which they had learned by an analysis of the talk of Athens, the audience is transported into a purified region of conflicting hypertrophied motives. The audience is not "purged of pity and terror," but those emotions themselves of their dross—fear, of cowardice and pity, of sentimentality. Caught up in the catastrophe of tragedy, the audience learns compassion and dread. Unfortunately, it was not possible for the later Greeks, faced with the dilemmas of their deteriorating secular society, to transfigure their situation by joining a Sophoclean play, as one might join a church or monastery. So the nobility of Sophocles becomes for future ages the private consolation of the mature and never again functions as a social paradigm.

A humanistic religion like Sophocles' demands less and seems more impregnable than transcendentalism. It answers the mystery of evil with the qualities of art and with tone of character. Men suffer unjustly and learn little from suffering except to answer unanswerable questions with a kind of ultimate courtesy, an Occidental Confucianism that never pretends to solution. The ages following Sophocles have learned from him the definition of nobility as an essential aristocratic irony which forms the intellect and sensibility.

Oedipus the King, Oedipus at Colonus, Antigone are not a trilogy. Their chronological order is not that in which they were written. *Antigone* is the play of a mature man; *Oedipus the King* of a middle-aged one; *Oedipus at Colonus* of a very old man; yet they are, in spite of minor anachronisms, interdependent. It is as if Sophocles had held within his mind from the beginning a general structure for the Theban Cycle. The acts of Antigone and Creon in *Antigone* are made plausible by their behavior in *Oedipus at Colonus*, written fifty years later. The central play, *Oedipus the King*, is first in dramatic order. It may be the most perfect play ever written, and since it is the primary subject of Aristotle's *Poetics*, it has been the model for most tragedies since. It is by far the most dialectic of all Greek plays. One situation leads to another with an inexorable necessity. Yet each is created by the interplay of the faulty motives and rash choices of the protagonists.

Oedipus discovers that he has murdered his wife's husband; that he was a foundling; that he has murdered his father and married his mother in a series of dialogues more inevitable in motion than those of the Platonic Socrates evoking the realization of truth amongst his fellows. Realization comes in a succession of blows, and each blow reshapes the character of Oedipus as hammers form a white-hot ingot on the anvil.

In *Oedipus at Colonus*, there is hardly a plot at all—only the contrast of the aged, dying, blinded Oedipus with his daughters; his sons; his successor on the throne of Thebes; Theseus, his Athenian host; and the common people of the chorus. Each character's contrast illuminates him with a growing glory until, as he walks away to die in the sacred grove of Colonus, he has become a sacred being, a *daimon*.

This apotheosis is totally convincing, though Oedipus has lost not one of the faults that led him to disaster in the first place. He is still a rash and angry old, old man. He has learned only wisdom, wisdom that is indefinable, a quality of soul that comprehends suffering and evil, without understanding. Aeschylus justifies the ways of God to man by placing the mystery in God. Sophocles justifies the ways of man to man by placing the mystery in man.

Antigone, although written first, is a fitting conclusion. It is a conflict of people who have learned nothing and forgotten nothing. Creon has forbidden the burial of Polyneices, killed as a traitor attacking Thebes. Antigone defies him, buries her brother, and is condemned to death. Creon's son, Haemon, affianced to Antigone, kills himself; last, his mother, Eurydice, commits suicide. We are back with Aeschylus in the conflict of state and family, male and female. The drama is human, not mythic; the protagonists not wiser; experience has been in vain; the burnt children still love the fire; but the characters are real, each an end in himself, concrete with an absolute concreteness.

Sophocles has found better translators in the past than has Aeschylus—Richard Aldington, Yeats, Browning, Shelley. The best contemporary edition of the Theban Plays is published by the Modern Library and the University of Chicago Press. The translators are David Grene, Robert Fitzgerald, and Elizabeth Wyckoff.

Euripides

When Aristotle said Euripides' plays were "for the most part unethical," he was using *ethos* in his own special sense. He meant that Euripides' plots, his characters, and he himself were unbalanced, exceptional, wavering, tactless. If Sophocles perfectly exemplifies Aristotle's taste, Euripides is tasteless.

In Aeschylus and Sophocles two different concepts of rational order, cosmos, are counterpoised to chaos. Euripides attacks not only rational order in the affairs of men, but reason itself. Aeschylus and Sophocles use myth to reveal reality. Euripides uses myth to mock reality—not, as is usually said, the reverse. No educated Greek "believed in" the factual reality of myth.

The poetic style of Aeschylus is continuous, controlled linguistic adventure, a conscious expansion of meaning. Sophocles is unique in literature for his achievement of a steady, high level of semantic purity. He elevates and illuminates Athenian speech at its most communicative. In Euripides, speech has broken down. Thucydides writing on the effects of war on social and personal relations, and hence upon communication, and the resulting debauchery of meaning, might well have been describing the rhetoric of Euripides. Long after the Peloponnesian War had done its destructive work, Aristotle had to redefine a philosophic vocabulary, to refound the meaning of meaning. He did it so well that his linguistic analysis has lasted to this day in the assumptions of the man in the street. Plato, like Alfred North Whitehead in our time, failed at this task because of the overspecialization of his caste dialect. The evocative, connotative, ambiguous language of Euripides is the opposite of the pure poetry of Sophocles, as it is the opposite of the aristocratic clarity of Plato or the forceful commonplaceness of Aristotle.

Criticism down the centuries has tended to arrange the three tragedians in chronological order. We should not forget that Euripides was 64 when Aeschylus died and that, though fifteen years younger, he died in the same year as Sophocles. In the three tragedians the wheat and tares of the Athenian mind were harvested together in one long season. The differences are spiritual rather than temporal. Each poet speaks for his own kind in Periclean Athens. True, Aeschylean man more or less died out; the Sophoclean became the public mask of the elite, while the people for whom Euripides spoke were the future.

Sophocles has the interests of a civic leader who is a country gentleman, as in his memorable evocation of the suburban village of Colonus. Euripides was an alienated intellectual, an ironic wanderer in Baudelaire's "city lit with prostitutes." Like Baudelaire, he was unsuccessful in his lifetime and the favorite of the megalopolitan culture that came after him. His virtues are the virtues of that culture, as they are vices in the world of Aeschylus and Sophocles. They are thoroughly metropolitan and bourgeois: domestic realism, entrancing rhetoric, ironic philosophizing (like that of the characters in Chekhov), witty intellectualism, literary professionalism, moral eclecticism, subjectivity, and the attitude of tragic alienation.

In Sophocles each drama is a cosmos. The characters fit together like gears to produce dramatic power. The episodic crises of Euripides' plays are a series of judgments on autonomous characters, amongst whom the author takes sides. This is sympathy, a virtue invented by the middle class. Tragedy and this kind of sympathy are incongruous. So too are sympathy and the greatest comedy. Richardson could certainly not have written *Tom Jones*, any more than Beaumont and Fletcher could have written *Volpone*. Plays like Euripides' *Orestes* and *Iphigenia at Tauris* are comedies, and even *Medea* has a mocking comic finale. Phaedra's nurse in *Hippolytus* is the first of many pimping domestics who see through the grandiloquent self-images of heroic life, who give the clysters and empty the chamber pots for the golden people who claim to be more than human.

Not only are Euripides' plays romantic; so, in the pejorative sense, are his heroines. They are all Emma Bovarys, as adept at role-playing as his heroes are at acting-out. Euripides' characters—not the actors, as in Brecht's theory of theatrical alienation—are pretending to be Medea, Orestes, Elektra. Although *Hippolytus* is a highly skilled job of archaizing, Phaedra deliberately plays the part of the ruined queen of the overcivilized, conquered Sea Peoples, the embodiment of their mysterious goddess and her snake priestesses. *The Bacchae*, like *Hippolytus*, is almost a play by an anthropologist.

Offended holiness conditions all the dramas of Sophocles and Aeschylus. In Euripides there is usually nothing there to offend. The *tremendum* is comic and without *mana*. Where Sophocles and Aeschylus thrill to the aweful or the intensely humane, Euripides' intensity is usually only aesthetic. Again, this is professionalism and alienation. Euripides has no operative connection with the holy in being. When he wishes to evoke it as a context to support his own philosophy of life, he must construct it like a doctor of comparative religion. The *tremendum* of *The Bacchae* is not being with the supernatural or transcendent locked into the common order. It is beyond or outside the order of being altogether. *The Bacchae* is Euripides' evaluation of life. This is what being means to him. This is the first psychedelic system of values, a middle-class substitute for mystical vision. Lyrical ecstasy is the only answer to mystery.

Euripides invented comic, as Sophocles invented tragic, irony. The tragedies of Sophocles are conflicts of fate and personality, will and time. The tragicomedies of Euripides are confusions of luck and individuality. Egocentric people are caught in the falsehoods, not the truths, of time—misrepresentations, mistakes, confusions, doubles, incognitos. They play their roles in picturesque, romantic landscapes, quite unlike the classic parks of Sophocles or the immense vistas of Aeschylus. Their morality is a deliberate, ironic imitation of the real Heroic Age *ethos*—pluck, gang loyalty, sexual passion. Suffering never ennobles them, as it does the Greek gentlemen of Sophocles, but only coarsens still more the bourgeois sensibility beneath the heroic mask—to an appalling degree in *Orestes*, *Medea*, *The Trojan Women* or Pasiphaë's speech in a fragment of a lost play.

In each of these cases occurs a deliberate, specific denial of the Socratic fallacy. The typical Euripidean heroine usually finds opportunity to repudiate the idea that if man is reasonably convinced of a good he will choose it. Again and again his frantic women say that reason is morally impotent. The conclusion follows that the cosmos is not a cosmos at all, for to the Greek mind moral order is the necessary reflection of physical order. When the Euripidean hero or heroine looks upon the world of fact, he finds it worthless.

In Aeschylus, far and near fuse to give transcendence to the here and now. In Sophocles, all time is immanent and forms the abiding skeleton of value for here and now. In Euripides, here and now are devalued by the far-away and long-ago, the hopeless wish to escape from a present without value. So the rhetorical intensity of his vertiginous verse, certainly as overpowering as any ever written, couples luster with mockery, radiance without wholeness and harmony, and is for that very reason so much the more intense. In the Hellenistic world of great cities and warring empires, Euripides came into his fame. The Hellenistic world was Euripidean through and through, and so is the one in which we live today.

The most convincing contemporary translations of Euripides are in the University of Chicago Modern Library edition. The nearest approximations to his hypnotic verse are the translations of the choruses of *Iphigenia at Aulis* and *Hippolytus* by H.D.

Herodotus
History

For a century or more, both historians and Greek scholars dismissed Herodotus as a teller of tales and, in comparison with Thucydides' tightly structured history, a garrulous rambler. Most scholarship today has moved to the other side. Actually, debate over the merits of Thucydides and Herodotus as scientific historians is not very illuminating. It is really a question of taste, and there is no reason why a catholic taste should not admit them as equals. However, it is true that Herodotus is what today we would call more scientific. For many centuries he was to stand alone as the only historian of the Western World to think of the affairs of men in anthropological, sociological, economic, and ethnic terms.

A great deal of taste in Greek literature is shaped by the study of Plato, Aristotle's *Poetics*, and the plays of Sophocles. It is a deliberately elitist taste, the core of all those systematic judgments we call Classicist. In human affairs, its emphasis is upon the interrelations of the highly privileged, where privilege means precisely the ability to indulge in such moral luxuries of conscience. So Werner Jaeger in his great study of the Greek *ethos*, *Paideia*, dismisses Herodotus as "quasi-anthropological" and as "an explorer of strange, half-understood new worlds." We now have better information about even the remotest peoples, says Jaeger, and only in heroic political history, as written by Thucydides, "is it possible to achieve the true understanding of the inner nature of a race or epoch, to realize our common fund of mature social and intellectual forms and ideals," regardless of the accidents of occasion. The idealist taste of this requirement is evident, and it effectually eliminates the pluralistic, polyvalent, democratic Herodotus no matter how up to date his information might be. Modern research has, it so happens, revealed Herodotus as an exceptionally accurate informant, even on such subjects as Egypt, Scythia, and the outer barbarians, where skeptical nineteenth-century critics assumed that he was romancing.

The subject of Herodotus' *History* is the successful defense of a democratic, rational, secular society against the onslaughts of what Gibbon in another context altogether was to call barbarism and superstition. However far the narrative may wander, its center is always Marathon, Thermopylae, Salamis, the yeomen and merchant seamen in their little bands defying the perfumed might of the Persian Empire—The King of Kings with half the East at heel; illimitable piles of arms, armor, and armament; gold for bridle ornaments and Greek brides; and silk for tents—and all the mysterious gods and priests and shamans gathered up from four thousand years of a hundred dead and living civilizations and innumerable barbarisms. Herodotus' book is as closely structured as Thucydides'. It is simply not so obviously schematized a tableau of the conflict of personal vices and virtues. It is the story of the triumph of an idea of civilization. Without this initial concept of the good society as a nursery of integrity and freedom, the stage for the conflicts of Thucydides' stylized heroes would never have existed.

Again and again Herodotus drives home his point with crucial anecdotes. Solon confronts Croesus not as an aristocratic lawgiver but as a spokesman, in the court of an oriental despot of incredible wealth and absolute power, of the independent yeomanry of a land so poor that hard work, the cooperation of equals, and ingenuity in outwitting nature were virtues essential to survival. When the Great King crosses the Hellespont, his flying arrows dim the sun like any massive inhuman natural phenomenon, like an act of God, one of Homer's gods, the embodiment of the frivolity of the nonhuman.

Herodotus' tone has misled many critics. It is almost colloquial, folkloristic—another Odysseus spellbinding an audience of prosperous farmers with the tall tales of *The Odyssey*. The narrative is so exciting that it has taken the careful archaeology of this century to overcome our tendency to disbelief. Today we know that the Scythians of the Ukraine or the nomads of the desert and the merchants of the oasis cities of the far northeast inter-Asian frontier of the Persian Empire were really as Herodotus describes them. It is amazing that at the beginning of historical and geographical writing in the Western World one man could so carefully have sifted and judged his evidences.

One man did not. The most significant thing about Herodotus is that he is the literary expression of a whole people, as cunning in their ability to deal with facts as their prototype, Odysseus, was cunning to deal with monsters. Herodotus traveled widely and judged rationally of all he saw, but in the vast scope of his story he perforce relied mostly on hundreds of other Greeks who had gone to all the limits of the world with which he dealt, or who had lived before him and handed down to him information on the past, and who were as questioning and as sane as he.

The epic subject of Herodotus will haunt the philosophy of history from his day to ours. The conflict of the molar, obliterative mass civilization emanating from a single power center versus the dynamism of the manifold-centered city-state—eighteenth-century America versus 1968 U. S. A.—Herodotus' *History* is the first large-scale anti-imperialist indictment. But what is wrong with imperialism? Did not Persian ecumenical egalitarianism, so like the empire of the Incas, ensure a greater good to a greater number than did the anarchic communalism of Greece? Eventually the city-state failed so completely that there was no other solution than the takeover of the Persian Empire itself by Alexander.

This would certainly be the utilitarian judgment; but the "Senatorial party"—Herodotus, Tacitus, Cicero, de Tocqueville, Lord Acton—have always disagreed. The heroic drama of Thucydides, with its Classicist stage and its limited cast, would be impossible in a monolithic society. Thucydides' drama is tragic but, in his eyes, worth it. Tragedy is impossible in the oriental palace, where man's fate depends on the incomprehensible wrangles of incomprehensible forces. Nor are there tragedies of the masses—themselves an incomprehensible force. In the Greek community, man's fate depended on himself, on his follies and his virtues in his relations with his fellows.

Herodotus' *History* is a prologue; the denouement lies ahead of him in the next generation. If he could have seen the breakdown of Greek polity in the hundred years following the Persian Wars, certainly he would not have said it were better had Xerxes prevailed. There have always been those who, though they see tragedy as the outcome of freedom, will nevertheless judge that tragedy is not too high a price to pay.

Thucydides
The Peloponnesian War

At the conclusion of his own introduction to his history of the war between Athens and Sparta, Thucydides announces his intention: "It will be enough for me if these words of mine are judged useful by those who want to understand clearly the events that happened in the past and that will, human nature being what it is, at some time or other and in much the same ways be repeated in the future. My history has been composed to be an everlasting possession and not to win the prize of an hour."

He then observes that the Greek strife between Athens and Sparta wrought far greater physical damage than the Persian Wars, which were decided in two battles by land and two by sea. Implicit is the contrast between the liberation of creativity amidst the Greeks during and following their struggle for freedom and the irreparable moral damage done by the struggle for power amongst themselves. Thucydides goes on to trace the spreading corruption of power from the war between states to its internalization in each state in civil strife, and finally to its corruption of the individual leaders, the conflicts and defeats of conscience, and the monstrous growth and ultimate destruction of individual wills.

In Herodotus, history emerges from epic and anecdote into the beginnings of the science of man. Thucydides is the first to treat history as moral drama. The emphasis in Herodotus is on people. In Thucydides it is on persons. He never deals with the forces that operate in the affairs of men in abstract terms, but only as embodied in characters. Sometimes this comes dangerously near to personification. From Thucydides descend those generalizations so misleading and convenient to demagogues—the French are lewd and frivolous; the Swedes commit suicide because they drink too much coffee.

Thucydides himself avoids such generalities. His Athenian and Spartan generals and statesmen speak in accordance with national character that Thucydides presents empirically, inductively, but he is careful to distribute the components of that character amongst real men, balanced with human contraries and contradictories in each case. It has often been remarked that Thucydides' point of view is medical. His subject is the disorder that threatens the life of Greece. He treats it in terms of symptoms, etiology, diagnosis, implicit therapy, and prognosis. His characterization of his protagonists is remarkably like that of the Elizabethan playwright who had a medical concept of drama, Ben Jonson, with his theory of humours.

Themistocles the wise man; Pericles the urbane and skillful politician; Cleon the demagogue; Nicias the pious, naïve soldier; Archidamus the cautious and wily man; Alcibiades the insolent spoiled adventurer; the envoys of the contending allies who speak with caution and rashness, truculence and prudence, turn and turn about. Behind them, as in Shakespeare, the mob functions at first as the residue of those impersonal forces which do not lend themselves to casting in Thucydides' *dramatis personae.* As time goes on, the moral base of the contending leaders is eaten away in the attrition of war. Each at last operates as the embodiment of the narrowest possible character consistent with his essential humanness—of which Thucydides never quite loses sight. Virtue and vice together fall away into the sump of the inchoate mass—the war of each against all.

The method of Thucydides has obvious faults—"Life is not all that simple." To which the response of the Classicist, or of what we call the inner-directed man, will be, "Ah, yes, but the *lessons* of life are precisely that simple, and the job of the historian is to arrange, without falsifying, his material to show forth the lessons of history in their natural simplicity." At the moment we are in an anticlassical and other-directed period of taste, and Herodotus is preferred to Thucydides.

The difference between the two authors is manifest in their greatly disparate styles. Herodotus is one of the most engaging writers who ever lived. He is always interesting, eventful, and pictur-esque. His prose is always relaxed. We never have any feeling of pressure. Thucydides amongst prose writers might be called the inventor of the antidemocratic style. His sentences are at once hard and complicated, clear and businesslike. The narrative proceeds like an inescapable argument, with the snap of a Jesuit disputation.

Herodotus is the source of our knowledge of those great battles against the Persians which have become precious myths for West-ern Civilization. When we read over sentence by sentence his story of the fighting, it is often difficult to tell what is going on. Herodotus personalized combat like Tolstoy, Stendhal, or Stephen Crane. War to him was a vast disorder intruding like a poisonous storm upon the decency of civil life. Thucydides thought like a tactician and per-sonified the forces of battle. He always knows who is doing what to whom; who advances, who threatens, who overcomes, just as in a game of chess. Battles in fact seem to have been down the ages pretty much as Herodotus or Tolstoy described them. However, it would not pay a general to deploy his men against the enemy with any other guiding principles than those of Thucydides.

The famous speeches scattered throughout the narrative unfold a philosophy of history. History acquires a logic, almost a geometry, which can be learned and applied by the men who come after to create a politics of wisdom. Thucydides conceives of history as depending ultimately upon the interaction of gentlemen like himself. Although he sees the struggle for power as the operative dynamism of history, he sees it in a contrary manner to that of Machiavelli. Those recipes for politics which we call Machiavellian, Thucydides attempts to prove unworkable because they are imprudent. Although he cuts through the cant and propaganda, still he deals with politics as a department of ethics. It is not that in his eyes might makes right—but that might makes the inescapable historic fact and the politician who uses power with prudence, firmness, balance may make right in fact.

This is the political philosophy of Aristotle or Sophocles. Behind its clear Euclidean relationships, Thucydides is always aware of the ungovernable irrational factor of *tyche*: not doom or fate, in his use of the word, but chance. If the will holds firm and the reason preserves its order, the man of power, says Thucydides, can rise above the disasters of chance—if not always, at least often enough to make a significant difference in the history of the people over whom he rules. This may be the moral of the most exemplary of all historians; but as he casts backward glances in the course of his narrative, you feel that Thucydides realized its only truth might be that of operative myth, of necessary fiction.

Plato
The Trial and Death of Socrates

Four dialogues of Plato tell of the last days of Socrates. *Euthyphro* is a conversation with a self-righteous bigot of the New Morality before the judgment hall. The *Apology* is a record of Socrates' trial and his three speeches in his own defense. *Crito* is a conversation with a devoted disciple who visits Socrates in prison the night before his death to persuade him to accept the escape his friends have arranged. *Phaedo* is a conversation with a few disciples during the last hours preceding his death.

It is certain that Plato wrote these dialogues at wide intervals and not in that order. Too, the contrast between what Socrates says about the immortality of the soul in the *Apology*, in which he is agnostic, and the *Phaedo*, in which he devotes his last conversation to dialectic proofs of immortality and a description of the future life, raises most sharply the disputed question as to where in Plato's writings the real Socrates leaves off and Socrates the mouthpiece of Platonism begins. Even the prose style differs. The *Apology* is rough and colloquial. The *Phaedo* may well be the most beautiful, carefully constructed prose ever written in any language. Yet the four dialogues hold together as an artistic unity, a systematically developed tragedy whose impact on the conscience of Western man has been surpassed only by the equally incongruent narratives of the passion of Christ in the four Gospels. We cannot get behind the *Phaedo* to the last hours of a simpler Socrates, as there is no simple story of the Crucifixion. The trial and death of Socrates was not only a tragic moment in the conscience of mankind. It was a pivot in the history of civilization.

Euthyphro is Socrates' own foolish disciple. He proposes to denounce his father for murder because a slave whom he had imprisoned had died, possibly of neglect. He can claim the sanction of Socrates' lifelong analysis of the social morality and motivations of the citizens of Athens for his act, for he seems to himself to speak for the gods of justice, for a city-state governed by abstract law and against the tribal loyalties of the family. In fact he speaks for the moral vulgarity and lack of sensibility of Socrates' accusers. Socrates is amused and shocked. His irony is aroused, and he engages Euthyphro in a discussion of the meaning of piety, its relation to the gods and the community, that causes Euthyphro to run off in confusion. Socrates proceeds to judgment.

Though the *Apology* is self-sufficient, like the Lord's Prayer it can be enriched endlessly by historical and moral exegesis. It was not what Socrates' accusers expected. His defense was an attack. His speeches were judgments of his judges. He insisted on honoring the law. He refused to suggest exile instead of death. The night before his execution, his opponents still hoped he would escape.

The reason for the trial is never stated. Many of Socrates' disciples had been sympathizers and eventual agents of Sparta during the long and disastrous war that had destroyed the morale of the Golden Age of Pericles, Sophocles, and Phidias. Alcibiades had been the most licentious, unprincipled leader of the democracy; Critias, Plato's uncle, the most rapacious and violent of the oligarchy. Both had been traitors, deserters to Sparta. After the destruction of Athens as the maritime and mercantile power of the eastern Mediterranean, Critias had been one of the Spartan puppet rulers, the Thirty Tyrants, who had executed possibly eight per cent of the male citizen population. Those who voted to condemn Socrates represented the restored democratic mercantile interest, but they dared not charge him with being a leader of the friends of Sparta because all political crimes had been amnestied when their party took power. This is the meaning of the ambiguous indictment, that he had corrupted the youth of Athens.

The second charge, that he did not believe in the old gods but had introduced new religious ideas, was pure demagogy. No one was required to believe in the gods as Christians believe in their creeds. Socrates had always been scrupulous in observance of every accepted principle and practice of community life. However, from his questioning he had developed a civic and personal morality founded on reason rather than custom. He envisaged it as subject to continuous criticism and revaluation in terms of the ever-expanding freedom of morally autonomous but co-operating persons, who together made up a community whose characteristic aim was an organically growing depth, breadth, intensity of experience—experience finally of that ultimate reality characterized by Socrates as good, true, and beautiful.

The accusers were right. This is a new religion which bears scant resemblance to the old. Civic piety is founded on the recognition of ignorance and the nurture of the soul until it becomes capable of true knowledge—which is a state of being, a moral condition called freedom. The Greek city-state, not to speak of the tribal community, knew nothing of freedom in this sense, but only the liberty that distinguished the free man from the slave. To this day there is no word for "freedom" in those languages shaped by Classic law—only *liberté*. The sanctions of any static community—tribal, barbaric, or feudal—are not moral principles deduced from the interaction of self-controlled free persons. They are irrational powers embodied in myth and derived from organic relationships of family and loyalty in battle, designed to keep the inrush of disturbing experience of novel scope and intensity to a minimum. From the point of view of ancient, conventional Athens, both the overt and the unmentioned accusations were justified.

The Socrates of these four dialogues finds opportunity to state or imply all those ideas which we think of as essentially Socratic. Virtue is knowledge. Evil is ignorance. No man willingly does wrong. The essential being of each man is his soul, the spiritual form of his moral integrity. Powerful, but not conclusive, arguments can be constructed for its pre-existence and immortality. Things are not what they seem. The waste of value; the power of evil; the triumph of injustice, falsehood, and ugliness are illusory. Behind the apparent world the cosmos is good, true, beautiful, and rational, and so is its own principle of integrity in action—God. Truth can be discovered by thought and conversation modeled on the dynamics of the rational order of the cosmos. This means not just the dialectic analysis of the "Socratic method," but discipline of the abiding will. The knowledge that is virtue in the famous Socratic paradox is the nurtured practice of life that the Medieval scholastics were to call "habitude."

Socrates on trial is the greatest historical exemplar of just this life process of finding out truth—that of a life with four cardinal virtues like points of the compass organizing it as a cosmos: prudence, courage, piety, justice. He had defined in his own person philosophy as the care of the soul—the moral integrity of the individual—and therefore as a perpetual challenge to public apathy, ignorance, lack of integrity or sensibility. "Conscience judges power" is the meaning of philosophy. Had he given in to the compromise offered by his opponents and even by his friends, he would have betrayed the foundations of his being and the community of friends, the interrelationship of the free and self-controlled in which those foundations were laid. He could not subvert the public order that condemned him without subverting the community that he had brought to birth out of it—like his midwife mother, as he said.

The arguments for the immortality of the soul in the *Phaedo* are not very cogent, and the myth of the future life is only an ironic pleasantry. This is not the point. The dialogue is a community prayer like a Quaker Meeting, a group meditation on the ultimate worth and meaning of existence. Watching Socrates and his friends there is another world, always present at each man's elbow and acutely near in those crucial hours. Its purer beings watch us and judge us constantly. We are only the temporarily blinded members of an invisible community. In their company the cardinal virtues are transformed into the transcendental ones—faith, hope, and charity—terms for the substance of the mystical confidence of Socrates in his vision.

Finally, the death of Socrates establishes a special tradition of martyrdom, the just man just unto death, which will give an abiding character of polarity and tension to Western political morality. And last of all, the dialogue ends with the familiar Socratic ironic whimsy: "I owe a cock to Asclepius, Crito. Do not forget to pay it"— the price to the god of health for a good death. The cadence is resolved in joy.

Plato
The Republic

Plato says, in a letter now commonly accepted as genuine, that the shock of the execution of Socrates overturned his life. He left Athens. He visited the Pythagorean Brotherhood in the Greek cities of Southern Italy. He became disillusioned as adviser to the contending despots of Syracuse. He returned to Athens and in middle life founded his school of philosophy, The Academy. *The Republic* was written close to this latter time. We can understand Plato's intention better if we think of it in this context.

First, *The Republic* is not a manual for practical politicians, like the *Politics* of Aristotle or *The Prince* and *The Discourses* of Machiavelli. It was intended as a model in the mathematical sense, a Platonic Form of the Perfect State, which even an actualized state, as perfect as could be conceived, would resemble no more than a plate does the circle in Euclid. Second, *The Republic*, influenced by Greek medicine, attempts to define justice by situating the just man in the theoretically best possible society to enable his justice, his perfect health. Third, discussion of institutions in *The Republic* concentrates on the basic outlines of the education of its Guardians, that tiny minority of spiritual aristocrats who are the state's only fully morally responsible citizens. The earliest critics pointed out that the community of *The Republic* is more school than state. So finally, we should think of the book as a founding manifesto or prospectus for Plato's Academy.

As a working blueprint for the framing of an actual constitution, *The Republic* is everything its enemies have called it—an open conspiracy of gentlemen pederasts; the prime source of pious justifications of totalitarianism; the humorless description of a garrison state of three castes: the commons, permitted only to work and otherwise totally disregarded; the soldiers and policemen, allowed nothing but their duties; and Guardians, who spend their time studying geometry and astronomy. All amenities of life are banished along with the poets, and all play after childhood. Even the play of children is a trick, a method of teaching them to be content with their caste position. Surely Plato knew that such a society would be utterly intolerable and could not endure a week.

Another aspect of the book reflects the tragedy of Plato's life. It is antithetical to the Socrates of the *Apology*. He could not have existed in any society, for instance Sparta, remotely like it. For Socrates, the four classic virtues are nurtured by conflicts and contradictions which arise from the daily encounter of continuous novelty. They are the fruit of the life course of Socrates' just man, who becomes self-controlled and self-motivating by learning to judge the myriad contending values of a metropolitan society. *The*

Republic is antimetropolitan. It seeks to restore the lost security of the static community by etherealizing the sanctions of the pre-civilized tribe.

Like a cubist picture, *The Republic* is a conscious dissociation and recombination of the elements of the *Apology*; like those of a cubist picture, its determinatives are lattices of "dynamic symmetry," mystic Pythagorean harmonics. The classic virtues emerge as functions of abstract structure—Justice Itself, Temperance Itself, Courage Itself, Piety Itself, The Good Itself—like the construction of the regular pentagon and dodecahedron, occult Pythagorean symbols that crown the work of Euclid.

Justice finally may be defined in *The Republic*, as in the *Apology*, as the care of the soul; but the soul of the *Apology* is a self-determining node emergent from dynamic flux, while the Platonic soul is a moral Golden Section radiating beauty into its ambient spiritual universe. The Socratic soul inhabits a metaphysical democracy; the Platonic soul is the pinnacle of a rigid hierarchy of splendid crystals.

For Plato, Socrates' death was the triumph of the unwise and vulgar over the wise in a society organized to ensure that result. *The Republic* erects principles and axioms from which a society can be deduced, where the wise will always be insured against the unwise. Socrates spoke of his life as one long education. He defined education as we would: as training of personality to absorb the greatest possible scope and intensity of meaning and value from experience. Life so lived is dangerous. *The Republic* is an institutional symbol of educative process, of the care of the soul—a charade of *paideia*, from which movement, novelty, development have been eliminated. Plato's Guardians suppress new values, changes of meaning, disturbing intensities and preserve, above all else, an exalted security.

Politics is the one subject of human study that cannot be defined mathematically. Even to consider the state as organism can only produce pernicious delusions. The State, Society, Community—these words mean nothing but individual men, each an end in himself. Social values, even bare comprehension of social forces, can be discovered only as end products; they cannot be found at some beginning before the infinitely varied acts of men. Politics has no first principles which exist prior to experience. Whether the historic

Socrates believed in the Platonic Forms or not, Plato always represents him in the early dialogues as coming at them dialectically, by induction from experience. In *The Republic* a polity is deduced from timeless Forms, as if in a logic textbook. The constitution of this state could be a series of syllogisms, with no checks and balances whatever. The only guarantee that the Guardians will not become evil despots is their education in the art of arranging combinations of nonexperiential first principles, their study of a higher mathematics that reflects the transcendent eternal constitution of the Forms of The Good, The True, and The Beautiful.

At the heart of *The Republic* is the flaw of the Socratic fallacy: if man truly knows the good, he must infallibly choose it. Those who know the good to the fullest human capacity are the Guardians, philosopher-kings in whom wisdom and power coincide and who therefore cannot err. Again Plato surely knew he had reduced the theory of the just state to an impossibility. After long discussion in which he manages to include in the construction of his model society all the key notions of his philosophy, Plato, speaking as "Socrates," sees no mediation, no transition, possible between ideal and reality, and he returns to the apolitical Socrates of the *Apology*. Philosophers are never likely to become kings. When they play with power, as Plato had done at Syracuse, they betray themselves. They can function only as a school of renunciation, a sect apart whose influence is proportionate to its powerlessness. Education can indeed mediate ideal and reality, but in The Academy alone, the optimum environment where virtue is the health of that only truly just state which is within, like the Kingdom of God. At the end Plato psychologizes, internalizes, spiritualizes his *Republic*. He puts it aside as a political model and offers it as the inspiration of a spiritual brotherhood.

Such has been its role in history. Where it has justified practice, it has etherealized and elevated to the ruling principle of the State the very vulgarity that killed Socrates. Where it has been used as a fiction, the most elaborate of Plato's myths, it has reinforced dedication, awakened vocations to leadership, and strengthened the morale of those modest and competent souls who are always in reality the guardians of society. It has inspired theories and practices of education. The nineteenth-century British public servant was taught at Eton an ethic derived from *The Republic*. The Rule of Saint Benedict and the constitution of the Bolshevik Party have both been influenced by it. Where it has been a guide to power—Calvin, Robespierre, Lenin, Mao—it has spawned monsters. Where it has been a metaphor of dedication for those who have sought not power, but responsibility, it has been beneficent.

No English translation has ever conveyed the unsurpassed beauty of the Greek prose of *The Republic*. F. M. Cornford, H. D. P. Lee, and W. H. D. Rouse do transmit the intellectual excitement of the discussions of Socrates and his friends. The best Platonic dialogues are truly dramatic, unique achievements in a never-repeated theater of the intellect. Of the older translations, Vaughan and Davies are clearer and more accurate than Jowett. Paul Shorey, one of the great teachers of Plato, is unreadable. Cornford and Shorey have both written good introductory books. Extremes of the fascinating Plato-Socrates controversy are represented by A. E. Taylor's *Plato* and Hans Popper's *The Open Society and Its Enemies*. All these books are available in cheap editions.

The Greek Anthology

Most people are unaware, and even scholars seldom pause to consider, that the Greek literature on which our civilization is so largely based survives as a very small library indeed. It would be quite possible for a skilled reader to go through it all in a couple of years, and anyone could read all the really important works in a winter. Only a small selection of Aeschylus, Sophocles, and Euripides survives; of other tragedians we know practically nothing but their names. We have considerable Aristophanes, but of the New Comedy from which our own and Roman Comedy derive we have only a few plays of Menander, and those in bad condition. Of the

Greek lyric poets we have even less: of Sappho two poems and miscellaneous fragments. Many of the most important writers of ancient Greece are known only by reputation. Greek literature is a ruin—like the Acropolis. As with the Acropolis, most of what survives is monumental, impersonal, "classic." Intimate poetry seems to have been written rarely, and hardly any survives—except in the *Anthology*.

What we call the *Greek Anthology* is a Byzantine collection and rearrangement of an unknown number of earlier anthologies, the best of which was gathered by the Syrian-Hellenistic poet Meleager, who included a liberal selection of his own verse. Almost all the poems are written in the elegiac distich—the meter used for monuments and gravestones. One of the largest books is made up of sepulchral epigrams. Some are real or imaginary epitaphs; others are actual dedicatory poems or votive offerings—or, again, imitations. There are a large book of inscriptions on statues and monuments; a surprisingly mediocre book of homosexual poems; a collection of rhetorical and declamatory short poems in elegiac meter; collections of quite tedious Christian epigrams, decidedly inferior to either the great Byzantine hymns or medieval Latin poetry; satirical poems, epigrams in our sense; and, most famous of all, a book of love poems which contains the core of Meleager's original collection.

The nature of the meter and its traditional origin dictated the form and substance of all the best of these poems—in any category. An inscription on a gravestone should be simple, succinct, poignant—and a personal expression of either the subject or the mourners. An actual stone at Corinth: "This little stone, dear Sabinos, is all the memorial of our great love. I miss you always; and I hope that you did not drink forgetfulness of me when you drank the waters of the new dead." An imaginary epitaph: "Here is Klito's little shack. Here is his little corn patch. Here is his tiny vineyard. Here Klito spent eighty years." Purest of all, the acknowledged grand master of the epigram, is Simonides, of the classic age. On the Spartans (the Lakadaimonians) fallen holding back the Persian host at Thermopylae: "Stranger, when you come to Lakadaimon, tell them that we lie here, obedient to their will"—which is certainly the greatest poem of its kind ever written.

The epitaph of Meleager to his mistress Heliodora, too long to quote, intensifies and further personalizes this emotion, as special a sensitivity as that which distinguishes Japanese classic poetry, and the transition to the simple love poem is hardly noticeable—the same sensibility is speaking in the same form: "I swear by desire, I would rather hear your voice than the sound of Apollo's lyre." Or the bitter scholar Palladas in decaying Alexandria, mourning the passing of Greek civilization itself: "We Greeks have fallen on evil days and fancy a dream is life. Or is it we who are dead and seem to live, or are we alive after life itself has departed?"

Later, in the classic revival under Justinian, the lawyer Paul the Silentiary would write poems to courtesans that are elegiac in our sense, full of the sorrow of the ruin of all bright things and the wistful momentariness of a girl's body. No other Greek poet is quite like Paul; only the Latin Petronius captures the same sense of man trapped in history. The relics of over a thousand years of Greek verse are gathered in these books, and we can relive the history of the Greek sensibility—from the first unself-conscious clarity and sensual glory of Sappho to the fatigue of the last disciples of paganism in Byzantium and Rome.

What distinguishes this verse? What is the pagan sensibility? What grows fatigued? Confidence. The classic poets are sure; they are certain of their senses, of their bodies in the clear Greek air, of their relations with one another. They know what death and love are—far simpler things than what we, with Romanticism and psychology behind us, mean by those terms. Sex is sex. Infidelity is infidelity; there is nothing complicated about it. Death is death. Heroism is heroism. The response is as direct as that of Simonides' Spartans, and as directly and gently ironic.

This is the "tragic sense of life" reduced to its simplest terms— "Gather ye rosebuds while ye may"; it would sustain and re-invigorate the erotic lyric and elegy for over two thousand years. Ben Jonson and Waller, William Carlos Williams writing of cold plums and white chickens and cautious cats, or Robert Desnos remembering his girl as he lies dying in a Nazi concentration camp: the greatest poetry still speaks Greek—in the simplest tragic language, the plain confrontation of beauty and love with Time, and nothing complex about it.

The simplicity of this acceptance gives life or, rather, living a confidence that modern man usually troubles with the imaginations of his conscience which only confuse and compromise the issue. The pagan sensibility, whether Greek or Chinese or Japanese, has no conscience in our sense. Melancholy saturates the later poets of the *Anthology* and even tinctures Meleager—but it is utterly unlike the melancholy of Proust or even Goethe. It is simply a more somber, more continuously haunting realization of the final term of the good, the true, the beautiful—and of the self and of civilization itself. Paul the Silentiary, courtier of the orientalized Christian emperor, is haunted by the remembrance of things past, but he would have thought Proust a madman. The ghosts that lurk behind the last poems of the *Anthology* are as definite ghosts as the athletes and lovers of Sappho and Simonides are definite. These Greeks never ceased to see clearly. The complicated sensibility can never reveal reality as more complex than its own complications.

Out of the stark simplicity of the finest poems of the *Anthology*, whether erotic or sepulchral, satiric or convivial, flows all the endless complexity of reality itself. "Take off your clothes and lie down; we are not going to last forever." "Pass the sweet earthware jug made of the earth that bore me, the earth I shall some day bear." The simplicity is highly deceptive—as misleading as the complexity of Kierkegaard, or the knotted webs of tergiversation in Henry James, which go not further than the printed page. The modern sensibility attempts to drain the contents of experience; these Greek poets strive to state the fact so poignantly that it becomes an ever-flowing spring—as Sappho says, "More real than real, more gold than gold."

There are many translations of the *Anthology*, in styles to suit every taste. Dudley Fitts in modern verse and Richard Aldington in prose are contemporary in style. Mackail's nineteenth-century prose is still popular. I've done a book of selections myself, from which the translations in this essay are derived. The Loeb Library gives a good Greek text and a rather wooden English one.

Lucretius

On the Nature of Things

There is a special style of nobility that we think of as that of the Roman at his best. Like most myths of social ethic, it was mostly pretense and rhetoric. Only Lucretius of all Roman writers fully exemplifies it. We do not read Lucretius primarily for his cosmology, for the atomic materialism that he inherited from Epicurus, even though it is the only natural philosophy of antiquity that can stand today with little modification or correction. We go to him for a kind of tough-minded grandeur he has taught us to think of as specifically Roman.

It has been said of Lucretius that he concerned himself almost exclusively with the natural philosophy and slighted the ethics and logic of Epicurus. Quite the opposite is true. His careful description of the universe and its functioning has, as he says, one purpose only: he hopes to produce a condition in his reader based entirely on a rational understanding and acceptance of his place in nature.

For Lucretius, courage in the face of life is a constant habitude, based firmly on understanding, and is the distinguishing mark of character, not a posture assumed when life or its benefits are threatened. Freedom from fear, most especially the fear of death, and from terror in the face of overwhelming natural events. Freedom from want, from appetite for inconsequential or unrealizable pleasures and from covetousness for the goods of others. Freedom from worship, from the superstition and priestcraft with which tyranny protects its power; Lucretius, like a later materialist, believed that religion was the opium of the people. Freedom from organized fraud; Lucretius is the only major poet in all literature who dissents relentlessly from the Social Lie.

This is really quite a different ethic from that of his master Epicurus, who was something of a valetudinarian, who sought above all other things security, and who assumed a position of passive neutrality toward state and church. Epicurus is dependent on the status quo of the old Greek city-state, absorbed and made impotent by the new Hellenistic empires. Ultimately, his ethic is parasitic.

Lucretius hoped to produce a character distinguished by true freedom of the individual. His success can be measured by the unparalleled nobility of his verse. The argument against the fear of death is one of the most imperious and solemn musics in all literature. Even when he is discussing minor problems of meteorology he never relinquishes his tone of impetuosity bridled by dignity and intellectual passion.

All Latin poetry is rhetorical, and so most of it is difficult for modern taste to accept at all. Ovid's lengthy soliloquies of lovelorn women make tedious reading today. Lucretius is rhetorical too, but his is a special kind of rhetoric. The incongruous fervor of his quest for impassivity, coupled with his passionate desire for forceful and direct communication, creates its own disinterested rhetoric. That is, the persuasive structure of language is refined not for some ulterior motive but to mean exactly what it says.

Lucretius comes immediately before the new style of Latin poetry, in which the language and the form of verse became completely modeled on Alexandrian Greek theories and practice. The "Classical" Latin of the Empire is as artificial a language as ancient literary Chinese, but Lucretius still retains the immediacy of the old speech and echoes of the rhythms of pre-Hellenic verse. His language is rustic. He complains of the primitive state of Latin for his purposes. Whatever difficulties there are in his style are caused by the fact that he had to shape this rustic language to the uses of a highly civilized philosophy and style. Unusual in Latin verse, his images have a sharp clarity—quite unlike, for instance, the *sfumato* and suggestiveness of Virgil. His argument and his syntax are as direct as he can make them. The pleasure principle in ethics and materialism in philosophy— Lucretius strives always to deal with life in terms of the irreducible facts.

Besides the overmastering impulse to communicate what he felt was an urgently needed truth, Lucretius was also conditioned by the turmoil of a time of most savage civil contention, bloody intestine war, and wholesale betrayal of friend by friend—a time that gave rise to the saying "Man is wolf to man." It is this background that explains the desperate intensity of feeling and the intellectual passion, stronger even than the most passionate erotic poems of Catullus. Lucretius, unique in his time, was impelled by an awareness of moral crisis.

There will not be so intrepid a literature of ideas again in Latin until we come to Abelard, although the rhetoric of Latinity will return to the honesty of Lucretius in the meditations of Saint Augustine and in the hymns of Saint Ambrose to the Light of Lights. Between Lucretius and those bishops on the brink of the Dark Ages will intervene the whole history of the Empire.

The verse of Lucretius twists and knots like powerful muscles under the strain of tremendous work, but fundamentally what he says and the way he says it he keeps as simple as he possibly can make them. He is sparing of metaphors and seems to have believed that he who sees things double sees poorly. The metaphors are often in the verbs: "The house glows with silver"; "Summer sprinkles the fields with flowers"; "It gleams with silver and shimmers with gold"; "Sheep graze on the hill, the legions go through their manual of arms"; "The purple fades as the toga wears out"; "Motes dance in the sunbeam"—and as a very late Latin poet was to paraphrase him, "On the fingers of the mighty the gold of authority is bright with the glitter of attrition."

Epicurus' own definition of pleasure was "the equilibrium of the body restful in its avoidance of pain," and he paraphrases Aeschylus with a meager echo. "The memory of past pleasures seeps through the brain in sleep and compensates for present pain." The asceticism of Lucretius was far more robust and confident, designed to get the greatest joy out of life at the least expense or waste of spirit. Joy seems a concept foreign to Epicurus; but Lucretius glories in the very meteorology of a thunderstorm or the physiology of animals. He was the first and has remained one of the few thinkers whose love of life was so intense that they were able to deny the fear of death with the knowledge of their total extinction. This, I suppose, might be called the ultimate paradox of wisdom.

It is remarkable how successfully Lucretius' atomic materialism fulfills the prime requirement of Greek science—it "accounts for the phenomena." So successfully does it do so that, although it was elaborated without microscopes, telescopes, instruments of precision, or experimental testing of its hypotheses, much of it still stands today.

It has been said of Lucretius, as of modern science, that he confuses description with explanation. He answers the question "how?" but not "why?"—and so his philosophy, like all materialisms, is irrational at its foundation. True—but perhaps there is no answer to the ultimate "why?"

No sounder view of nature was to appear for almost two thousand years. We should understand that the atom of Lucretius is not our atom, much less our molecule, but our ultimate particles—electrons, protons, neutrons, and the rest; limited in kinds but infinite in number, moving at an absolute speed and unaccountably swerving in their orbits. The nineteenth century objected to this swerving, or *clinamen*, as irrational. Today it is the foundation of our physics of ultimate particles. So with his anthropology and pre-history. Archeology and the discovery of pre-civilized peoples have substantiated the general outline of his history of human society.

His personal psychology is singularly modern: his fervid denunciation of romantic love, and the first and still the best succinct description of *accidie* in literature—the sickness that destroyeth in the noonday, the sickness of the self. In the great invocation of Venus, a goddess he did not believe existed, he rises to a kind of natural mysticism, a vision of the universe polarized between the creation and the destruction of novelty—Venus in the arms of Mars, Yin and Yang, Shiva and Shakti. Lucretius felt that his evangel was of the greatest urgency. Only the knowledge of the nature of things could restore the moral tone of civilization.

He failed. He was read little by his successors—mostly, apparently by poets for the abstract virtues of his verse, which they never imitated. Had Lucretius had followers, the story of Roman civilization would have been different, and so therefore would that of our own.

Livy

Early Rome

The average well-informed layman is quite unaware that we know very little indeed about Roman religion. The gods and goddesses of Rome are Greek, and the myths and legends we associate with them are not only Greek in origin but the end product of centuries of literary treatment by agnostic Hellenistic and Latin writers. Before the Great Gods of Greek Olympus were given foreign names and Italian residence by Latins and Etruscans, Roman religion seems to have resembled that of pre-Buddhist Japan. Deities, *noumena*, were something like Japanese *kami*: amorphous, floating clusters of holiness that attached themselves to things and places—sacred stones and springs, holy trees, the hearth—or haunted the crises of individual life and of nature in its seasons, but hardly emerged as persons. Marmar, who became the Greek Ares under the name of Mars, was more the focus of rites of passage and of the year than he was a god. With the beginning of the Empire under Augustus, Roman religion and the Roman past underwent a restatement and reevaluation disguised as a revival—again, much like the pseudo-revival of Shinto, nativist literature, and Emperor worship in seventeenth- and eighteenth-century Japan.

The intellectuals patronized by Augustus created a past which rapidly became history, accepted as true by most people to this day. Along with this fictional archaism went a tremendous reorganization of religion, culminating in vast civic ceremonies provided with imaginary tradition, new temples and rites of the gods of the assimilated Greek Pantheon, all centered around the first deity to be recruited to their ranks since Hercules—the Divine Augustus, once a priggish but prodigious young general called Octavian.

We can't understand Livy unless we realize that the first books of his great history of Rome provided the citizens of the Empire with many of the satisfactions we identify with religion. The Kings, the formation of the Republic, the first conflicts of the classes, the deeds of heroes, function as the Gospels do for us. This certainly is history as operative myth. We have no way of knowing if any of it is true, and we do know that many strands of Livy's story are false—the distortion of Etruscan hegemony, the interpretation of the class struggle, the relations with the other Italian tribes, the early kingship, the Hellenistic religion, and not least, the portrayal of a small, barbarous town in the vesture and with the ideals of the Republic in its last hundred years. More subtly inaccurate is the imaginary spirit, the *geist,* that Livy has taught all succeeding centuries to think of as peculiarly Roman. Vesture and ideals indeed—these were realities at the end of the Republic, but as the pieties of a special group of intellectuals.

For all this, Livy is not false. Myths are not false or true, but less or more effective in gaining the allegiance of men and sustaining them in their achievements. No historian has been more effective in this way than Livy. He did not merely provide generals and leaders and poets and orators of the Empire with a meaning for their own history. His gospel remained effective when Rome had long ceased to be pagan and the Empire stumbled into night. His heroes gave the German Theodoric inspiration as a ruler and were a consolation to Theodoric's Senator, Consul, and finally prisoner, Boethius, on the eve of torture and death. Livy was an inspiration to Gibbon when he came to tell that story.

Livy's heroes were to revive again and again—in eighteenth-century Virginia and in Revolutionary Paris. There are still statues in the public parks of the founders of the American and French Republics and the great politicians and soldiers of England clad in the togas or the armor of Cincinnatus or Horatius. It is only a little while ago that the veriest schoolboy, as Macaulay would say, knew by heart Macaulay's retelling of Livy in his *Lays of Ancient Rome,* probably the only poetry most schoolboys have ever enjoyed memorizing. Macaulay was effective because he himself had modeled himself with the most consummate care on the perfect Roman gentleman as he emerges as a composite from the pages of Livy.

What a gallery of gentlemen they are! Romulus, who might have founded one of the First Families of Virginia; Numa, a shaman with the dignity of Archbishop Laud; Tarquin the Proud; the wily queen, Tanaquil; Coriolanus; Scaevola; Manlius; the sinister Etruscans, like the villains played by Von Stroheim—gentlemen all. Livy is so effective because although what the nineteenth century accepted as facts may well be myths, his myths have the power of living fact.

The anthropological background is probably true. The connection with Troy or the Levant; the first settlement in the marshes by the ford "where Hercules crossed with the oxen"; children ritually suckled by a she-wolf; young men plunging into earthquake fissures; marriage by capture; the ever-burning community hearth fire guarded by virgins; priestly brotherhoods dancing in full armor; the Pontifex, a sort of head witch-doctor; outlandish jujus like Horse-Neptune; the hardly personified sky like the Chinese Tien, speaking to man in birds and lightning bolts; Quirinus; Lares; Penates; a witch who guarded a spring and slept with King Numa and taught him the art of ruling—all this is very un-Greek: at least, unlike historic Greece. Yet Classic Greek civilization was coming to its close before Rome emerges into true history.

Livy, not Virgil, gave Rome her epic. The first books of Livy's history are the epic of the beginnings of Iron Age civilization, as *The Iliad* and *The Odyssey* are really Bronze Age epics and *Gilgamesh* a Neolithic one. The economic picture is fundamentally different, as is the organization of society, however primitive. Livy's heroes no longer fight from chariots but are commanders of heavy-armed infantry and of gentleman cavalry. The knight appears in history and replaces the prince hurling javelins from his chariot. This provincial Early Iron Age culture must have been more squalid than anything in the *Nibelungenlied* or the Sagas and comparable to the societies that produced the earliest Russian epics.

Livy populates this backwoods culture with the aristocrats, as they fancied themselves, of his own day. How convincing they are! So convincing that whenever the type reappears in history, Livy provides the models. However incongruously, both Corneille and Henry Adams look to Livy for their patterns of contemporary noble conduct.

Julius Caesar
The War in Gaul

Practically all teachers of Latin agree that it would be hard to find a less appropriate textbook for second-year students than Caesar's *Gallic War*. His prose is eminently simple and clear—to those who read Latin fluently. Yet his use of the language is not just eccentric; it is entirely peculiar to him. Caesar was one of the most completely competent writers in all literature. It is impossible to doubt his meaning, if we have an ordinary grasp of the Latin language; but his style is nervous, full of surprises, and deliberately odd. His syntax on the page looks like speech; but like Ernest Hemingway's, it is not talk that can be uttered. It is as formal, with its own special formulas, as that of Racine or Pope, who are also supposed to have written simply. Reading Julius Caesar, if you read Latin and have never read him as a child (a most unlikely contingency), is like riding a high-spirited horse who for all his nerves is always completely under control. There is no prose just like his in any language, so it is hardly pablum for schoolchildren or a "Basic Latin" introduction to Roman literature.

All Caesar's attitudes, as they move behind the crystalline surface of his objectivity, are as adult as can be imagined. Masterfully concealed in *The Gallic War* and *The Civil War* is a philosophy of human relationships that only maturity can comprehend or even recognize. The masterful concealment, of course, is an essential part of the maturity. Caesar's style has been called unsophisticated. It is exactly the opposite. In fact, his books could be called manifestoes against the florid writing of Cicero or Livy. His style is so important because here to an exceptional degree the style is the man. What he does with language, so he did with life.

It is essential not to judge Caesar after the fact. He did not know that the Roman Empire, the principate of Augustus, the kingship and palace system of Diocletian and the Byzantines would come after him. As a historical figure he was a brilliant improviser. The prose, the battles, the dictatorship are expressions of an integral personality.

On every page of *The Gallic War* the simple, unambiguous nouns and verbs carom off each other like billiard balls. There are few adjectives, and they serve mostly to fix the nouns in place. The adverbs are all active—they aim the verbs. Prose that exhibits so high a level of irritability, in the physiological sense, usually lacks unity of effect, subordination of parts to the whole; but not Caesar's. The rapid and complex movement of simple elements deploys on the page exactly like the battles it describes.

The strategic contexts of the Gallic and Civil Wars are a reflection of the social context, the transition from Roman Republic to Empire. Caesar's life was lived in a permanent crisis of institutions. Political and social events flashed about him like a deadly kaleidoscope. His writing mirrors his time with an all-enveloping unconscious presupposition deeper far than motivation. It is the appeal of Roman *libertas* (a word that has changed its meaning several times since) to a unitary authority.

The conflicting authorities of Rome as a city-state had outlived their usefulness, but their forms would never completely disappear. Rome never became a pure despotism. Roman history has been called a collection of political pamphlets for the Senatorial caste. The Senate not only defied Diocletian or Constantine; it went down into the Dark Ages defying Theodoric. The inhabitants of Britain thought of themselves as citizens of no mean city as they guarded the Saxon shore. Feudalism arose in Gaul in the forms of, and out of the ruin of, the substance of the polity of Rome.

In all his battles Caesar was driving not toward a *Basileos 'o Soter*,—an oriental, Hellenistic sacred monarchy—but toward a transvaluation and universalization of the same settlement Rome had been making during the past hundred and fifty years in the Peninsula. Caesar's improvisations are the bridge from Republic to Empire. *The Gallic War* and *The Civil War* are the story of the beginnings of the spread of reconstructed Roman institutions from

Britain and the German forest to the limits of Egypt and Asia Minor. Again, the universalization of the city of Rome is a fundamentally different thing from the old, familiar, always-failing leagues of city-states that had brought the Greek world nothing but trouble.

Today in the most fashionable circles subjective, rhetorical writing is at a decided discount. There are few better models of pure narrative than Caesar. He concerns himself almost exclusively with action. Characters and personalities are revealed by the kinds of action his people perform. He rarely discusses his plans beforehand with the reader. The results reveal the plans. The consequences award praise or blame. This is far from being a value-neuter scientific style. It is simply an immensely clever one. The reader is outwitted as Caesar outwitted the Allobroges.

How sharply in fact action does reveal an immense cast of characters: officers who are little more than names and yet who show up with the stark clarity of men under action—Sabinus, deluded and tricked to death by the enemy; Cotta, wounded and unflinching; conscientious officers devoted to the welfare of their men like Marcus Cicero; dozens of little anecdotes of the men in the ranks—the standard-bearer of the Tenth Legion leaping to the British shore to shame his comrades into following him; Piso, rescuing his brother from the German cavalry at the cost of his own life and his brother refusing to survive him; the Centurion Titus Balventius fighting with both thighs pierced by a lance, like the man in "The Ballad of the Battle of Chevy Chase"; all these vivid anecdotes, usually no more than a couple of sentences long, personalize history. Caesar knew them personally.

Most such anecdotes are concerned not with the planned evolutions of war, but with what Caesar constantly called "the fortune of war." Fortune to him is completely secularized and depersonalized—luck or chance in the modern sense, not a capricious goddess or an implacable fate. Caesar's is one of the most *laïque* minds that ever existed; no transfinite powers move in his battles, but men called Labienus, Vercingetorix, or Pompey, men made known by their deeds.

The worst thing about using Caesar as a textbook is that he is the last author in the world to be parsed and construed and read a page a day. He should be read as he wrote, at great speed. *The Gallic War* can be got through in two quiet evenings with port, biscuits, and a thick slice of Caerphilly, and that is the way it should be done. *The Civil War* can easily be read in a night.

If you still remember your Latin, you are due for a surprise. Any English translation must convey Caesar's special qualities, not least that he was a great gentleman—always debonair, concerned with the welfare of his men, and living under the same conditions—who, when he was served asparagus dressed with myrrh instead of olive oil, ate it up and rebuked his officers: "It is not enough to eat what you don't like; to object to bad manners is bad manners." Moses Hadas' translation in the Modern Library is one of the most sympathetic, and it contains almost everything Caesar wrote.

Petronius
The Satyricon

He spent his days in sleep, his nights in attending to his official duties or in amusement; by his dissolute life he had become as famous as other men by a life of energy, and he was regarded as no ordinary profligate, but as an accomplished voluptuary. His reckless freedom of speech, being regarded as frankness, procured him popularity. Yet during his provincial governorships, and later when he held the office of Consul, he had shown vigor and capacity for affairs. Afterward returning to his life of vicious indulgence, he became one of the chosen circle of Nero's intimates and was looked upon as an absolute authority on questions of taste (*arbiter elegantiae*) in connection with the science of luxurious living.

He excited the jealousy of Nero's pathic, Tigellinus; an accusation followed, and Petronius committed suicide in a way that was in keeping with his life and character. He selected the slow process of opening his veins and having them bound up again, whilst he conversed on light and trifling topics with his friends. He then dined luxuriously, slept for some time, and so far from adopting the common practice of flattering Nero or Tigellinus in his will, wrote and sent under seal to Nero a document that professed to give, with the names of his partners, a detailed account of the abominations which that emperor had practiced. Just before his death he destroyed a valuable murrhine vase to prevent its falling into the Imperial hands.

Such is the portrait the Roman historian Tacitus gives of Gaius Petronius—one of the most startling candid miniatures in all history. Tradition has always said that this is the Petronius who wrote *The Satyricon*, the first and still the best picaresque novel. Tradition also has it that we possess only the fifteenth and sixteenth books and a few other fragments of the narrative. In addition, there are a handful of poems that customarily have been attributed to Petronius, although on no better ground than a haunting style unlike anything else in Latin literature. If *The Satyricon* holds its position as the finest tale of roguery in any language on the merits of only two out of a probable twenty-four books, what must the original have been?

Most likely it would have outranked *Don Quixote* as the greatest prose fiction of the Western World. There survive for us a few chaotic adventures in brothels and stews of Mediterranean ports which have changed little from that day to this, and a full-dress circus of vulgarity, a banquet given by the get-rich-quick freed slave Trimalchio.

Like *The Iliad*, *The Aeneid*, and the later *Golden Ass* of Apuleius (which may have been modeled on *The Satyricon*) but especially like *The Odyssey*, *The Satyricon* is an epic of a hero dogged and driven by the vengeful wrath of a god. In this case the god was Priapus, whose statue with its monstrous member stood guard over Greek and Roman gardens, marriage beds, and brothels.

Encolpius is a hero whose every advantage and opportunity is reduced to folly and shame by his impotence. At his moment of achievement the outraged god smites him in the part sacred to himself, as Poseidon smote Odysseus with the fury of the sea.

Encolpius and his friends are all bohemians—unemployable, over-educated, miseducated members of the *lumpen* intelligentsia. They are the first of their kind in literature, but from Petronius' day to this they will be the common characters of all picaresque romance. Kerouac's *On the Road* differs vastly from *The Satyricon* in lack of insight, irony, and literary skill, but its characters are all drawn from the same unchanged class.

What most distinguishes *The Satyricon* is its extraordinary style, a style that is a conglomeration of every Greek and Roman style reduced to mockery and held together by that special quality which has led to the gathering of many minor poems and short fragments under the general attraction of the two surviving books. This quality is a melancholy like no other in literature. The Romans had a catch phrase—*tristia post coitum*: the sadness that follows sexual fulfillment.

As a living body is sustained and nourished by its bloodstream, the style of Petronius is suffused by a sense of indefinable sorrow which haunts and corrupts all possible achievement. The nostalgia of the gutter and the melancholy of grandeur flow together and wash away the very idea of accomplishment. Because *The Satyricon* rises above the classic definition of comedy as an eventful tale of the disasters and disgraces that beset vulgarians and fools, it engages us, the readers, in the same way in which we are personally involved in a tragic narrative. *The Satyricon* is all uproar, guffaws, rumpus, commotion, but behind its noise there is always present a long recurrent note—the ebb and flow of human irrelevance.

Although he was far from being a parvenu himself, Nero was the first Roman emperor to employ those guides to the culturally perplexed whom David Reisman calls ironically "engineers of taste." The mentor of his youth was Seneca, the Stoic rhetorical philosopher, one of history's outstanding hypocrites, whose sterile tragedies have never been equaled for bombast and falsity. Petronius, the adviser of Nero's manhood, is a kind of anti-Seneca. He too is a master of all the flowers of rhetoric, but he knows they are paper flowers and he delights in showing them up by setting fire to them. Against Seneca's pompous Stoic heroes, the perfect embodiment of melodramatic absurdity, the Epicurean Petronius deploys his farcical rogues, so like the Marx Brothers in a tragedy of the absurd.

From Samuel Beckett to Charlie Chaplin, many people have attempted just such a comic answer to the ever-recurrent questions "Who am I?" "What can I believe?" "What can I do?" "What can I hope?" Petronius surpasses them all in the humor of his comedy and the cogency of his irony. Why? Probably because he was far more a man of the world than any such writer who has come after him.

Irony is a gift of experience, and only the most comprehensive experience can provide a truly solid foundation for irony that claims to be a diagnosis of being itself. The Existentialists can talk of ontological irony. *The Satyricon* as we have it, a hundred or so pages torn from the rubbish heap of five Mediterranean civilizations, embodies in action just such a judgment of the meaning and destiny of man. Its author realized his comic vision at its fullest in his own life, and seems to have written with the foreknowledge of his own end as it is told by Tacitus. Petronius, the most worldly-wise courtier of Nero, would of course have written with just such foreknowledge.

Tacitus
Histories

In the popular mind, the history of Imperial Rome consists of the scandalous biographies of Emperors at the center and the battles of military textbooks at the periphery, linked by marching and countermarching iron-shod legions building bridges and roads, and constantly revolting and hoisting one of their number aloft on their shields and onto the Imperial throne—rather without meaning as we understand history. The life and works of Tacitus are themselves a revelation of meaningful history in the first generations of the Empire. He was born in the onset of the collapse of the first

principate, grew to maturity in the dark days of the reign of Domi-
tian, wrote his greatest works under the benign Trajan, and probably
lived on into the reign of Hadrian, the first Roman Emperor to
achieve the omnipotence of the Hellenistic King of Kings, *Basileos
'o Soter*, which the passionately philhellene Nero had so barbarously
failed to even understand.

In Tacitus, Senatorial history reaches its anticlimax, for he is the
propagandist of the caste that in Chinese affairs we call the scholar-
gentry, which would never again, if the plot of the historical drama
is the shifts and conquests and losses of real power, play a major role
on the stage of Western history. After the Punic Wars, Roman
Senators were hardly gentry. They certainly never were scholars. On
the face of it, each book of Tacitus—*The Germania, The Agricola,
The History*, and *The Annals*—is a party pamphlet; yet we believe
them because of their unparalleled trenchancy. Succeeding ages
assumed that his *Histories* suffered only from the commendable
virtue of Republican party enthusiasm and took it for granted that
the perverts and gangsters of Suetonius' *Lives of the Twelve Caesars*
were figures of embittered, comic romance. Tacitus persuades us
that Tiberius and Claudius must have been the sort he says they
were.

Modern historians and the experience of a century more embit-
tering than the first of the Christian era prove us wrong on both
counts. Today we know that clowns and blood-drinking perverts
climb to the summits of power, pushed on by the enthusiastic
applause of the majority; nor is it now unbelievable that a Roman
Emperor enjoyed being sodomized on the public stage. But the
destructive policies of morose Tiberius, the sloth and foolery of
Claudius, the lunacy of Nero are not substantiated by research.

In Tacitus' day the economic, social, and political system against
which his work is a polemic came to its full power. Devoted to
the imaginary frosty virtues of the Republic of Livy, he lived to see
the midsummer of Empire. He first appears as the prosecutor in the
Senate of the crooked Proconsul Marius Priscus for "conduct unbe-
coming a gentleman." In youth he visited Germany and married
the daughter of Agricola, the Governor of Britain. In the first work
attributed to him, he bemoans the decline of oratory and says flatly
that the art of persuasion has passed from the halls of justice to the

study of the historian. His life of his father-in-law is a celebration of an ideal Roman gentleman of the oldest school, a Cincinnatus reborn; his description of the heir-apparent Germanicus, the romance of a new aristocrat, stainless, decorative, and as politically ineffectual as Sir Philip Sydney.

Roman history as Tacitus knew it in his own time began with the last days of the struggle to reorganize the Republic, while preserving its ceremonial forms, into an imperial-palace system of the Mesopotamian-Egyptian-Chinese-Byzantine type. It was necessary to deprive the senators and all other Republican castes of every vestige of real power. Before Tacitus was born they had already lost all power; but he was to establish for posterity their oligarchic mysticism as it expressed itself in impotent resistance two generations after actual total defeat. The social role, the moral qualities, the political competence the Senate imagined it still might reclaim, Tacitus sculptures out of granite into an image for all time.

The real Roman oligarchy—the gentleman-farmers, scholar-statesmen, amateur but indomitable warriors of legend—in Tacitus' day were precisely the new technocrats, proprietors of immense slave-operated estates, court poets, holders of imperial franchises. They were creatures of the court, eunuchs and freedmen, mostly highly cultivated Greeks and Levantines who had never heard of the right and wrong defined in the pages of aristocratic history and were beyond the good and evil of the heroes of oligarchic myth.

It is because Tacitus knew this bitter truth in his heart, although every word he wrote was devoted to countervailing it, that his is perhaps the most mordant style in the history of prose. It was as though he sensed that long legend of martyrdom working out in pitiful reality which lay ahead of him—Boethius defying Theodoric, Arnold of Brescia, Rienzi, Daniele Manin, Matteotti. So his prose gnaws and chews with a grimness unknown to Burke, Gibbon, and their French congeners, for these men believed that a European scholar-gentry, which in reality was to play so fleeting a role, would succeed and all the world would be united under the benevolent sway of enlightened Whigs and Girondins, brave and learned landlords.

In Thucydides, Plutarch, Livy, and, above all, Tacitus, we willfully suspend disbelief and enjoy the ceremonial stateliness of the drama and, in Tacitus' case, the grandeur of his malice, a style like a tray of dental instruments. So deeply is this style embedded in the narrative, in every inflection of perception and judgment, that even the most inept and donnish translators have never been able to erase it. We read it for its relentless bite. Tacitus' images of two great Roman emperors are mirrors of contemporary figures who have created out of aristocratic republics the all-encompassing structures of the oriental palace systems, the imperial bureaucracies, of our own day. Tacitus too speaks against The Palace and for his Founding Fathers, although he certainly never met a contemporary Roman who bore the slightest resemblance to one, just like our own Jeffersonians.

In spite of disaster, Thucydides had the confidence of a man who could see no threat to his own kind on any horizon. Alexander and the constellations of perfumed and jeweled Ptolemys and Antigonids were rising slowly from the nadir of time and some day would dominate the Greek empyrean, but of this Thucydides never dreamed. His heroes, for all their folly and pride and covetousness, are like the self-determining personalities caught in the dooms of Sophoclean tragedy. The figures of Tacitus act out a melodrama in which powerless men are whirled through catastrophe by impersonal force. The mask that garbs such force, the Emperor as the embodiment of a dark, inscrutable Imperial will, can never be more than a figure of gruesome farce, like the Fu Manchus, Mad Scientists, and Master Bolsheviks of our own fictions; his opponents can never rise above the condition of marionettes of pathos. Neither can be fully fleshed as complete men, as heroes of a tragic history like Thucydides', because they can never generate their own motives.

The sharpness of Tacitus' bite makes it easy to forget that melodrama prevents him from being a writer of the first rank, from having a genuine political morality or philosophy. Many a disgusting old fraud in Roman literature managed to convince himself he was a Stoic. Even this was not permitted Tacitus. His personal life attitude must have been like that of one of the gloomier Existentialists of the present day—a clerkly individual who has discovered that his kind is no longer useful and who therefore has lost hope in the future, faith in natural process, and charity toward his fellows. Tacitus, writing in the Empire's most halcyon season, could survey its human relationships and come only to the judgment: no exit.

Plutarch
Parallel Lives

It would be easy to write abusively about Plutarch's *Parallel Lives.*
They could be called "The Myth of the Ruling Class Dramatized,"
"The Social Lie Personified." More perhaps even than Plato, Plutarch is the founding father of the notion of a heroic elite. His great
Greeks and Romans, with few exceptions, do not only seek power,
they assume responsibility. As he compares them, from Romulus
and Theseus to Mark Antony and Demetrius, he judges them
always according to the degree to which they successfully assumed,
as leaders, unlimited liability for the commoner men they led.

Although succeeding ages have believed Plutarch, it is doubtful
indeed if human affairs are put together or if political morality
functions as Plutarch conceived it, or even if nobility can be found
at all amongst generals and politicians—Greek, Roman, Russian,
American, or Chinese, then or now. Yet, like the Bible and Shakespeare, *Parallel Lives* is a desert-island book. Classical literature
contains a good many greater works of art, and many truer pictures
of the ways of men. But Plutarch never palls. He is always engaging,
interesting, and above all else, to use a word that will provoke smiles
today, elevating. Men as they are described in Homer's *Iliad* are like
the quarreling chiefs of a predatory war band. They are like the
neurotics who destroy one another in Euripides. But they are not
like the heroes of Plutarch. Some men may be noble—John Wool-
man or Martin Buber or Albert Einstein or Martin Luther King.
Our common sense tells us that men who came out on top of
political systems far more corrupt than those of Kansas City,
Newark, Memphis, or Chicago in their heydays and at least as
merciless as that of Moscow may have been heroic in a sense, but
they were not noble by either Plutarch's definition or ours. They

were not great and good men as judged by Greek, Jewish or Christian standards. They were not by the standards of Plutarch's Romanized Stoicism.

It has been said that Plutarch was simply a propagandist for the truculent Roman Senatorial caste and for their traditional ancestors, the Athenian partisans of the Spartan despotism. It could be said, too, that out of the legendary materials provided by Plutarch we still construct the legendary idols of our own rulers—Franklin Roosevelt, Winston Churchill, Douglas MacArthur, Dwight Eisenhower.

It doesn't make Plutarch any the less absorbing. Nobody has ever been so foolish as to believe society would ever be ruled by the wise, the philosopher-statesmen of Plato's *Republic*. We hope of the human social structure that somewhere—far away, long ago, or in ages to come—it may rise at its summit into regions of nobility. Society would not be better if its masters were like Plutarch's heroes. It would certainly be more satisfying. This is the great secret. His characters may be bloodthirsty, lustful, treacherous, but they are never trivial. They are always purposive. Plutarch's is a world in which men do not live at random, as we learn in our hearts that, in fact, they do.

The *Parallel Lives* are lives of adults of the kind we all thought we would meet when we grew up, which we never did meet, and which we have ceased ever to expect to encounter. Or have we? Perhaps we always hope that we will meet nobility and responsibility walking together just around the corner. We can accept sin in our fellows and even learn to forgive it, but it is a bitter and endless chore. We never really learn to accept gratuitous meanness, least of all in our masters.

Plutarch compels us to believe of his characters that they are masterful because they are never mean. Although this is diametrically opposed to the facts, it is not a falsehood. It is the kind of truth that, like "The School of Athens," the *Jupiter Symphony*, or the *Saint Matthew Passion*, provides life with meaning which it does not in the least deserve. It is obvious why Plutarch gave Shakespeare some of his greatest characters. They had similar life attitudes. Even Bottom is not mean. Coriolanus was an arrogant traitor. Mark Antony was a bloody demagogue infatuated with an aging nymphomaniac. There is nothing whatever trivial about them.

Plutarch's book is a kind of antonym to Petronius' *Satyricon*. Petronius knew power. His hands were on the levers of decision until they were cuffed away by the fasces of Nero's lictors. His view of human motivation was dim and bawdy. Plutarch did not know power but only honors, and so he believed that the wielders of power were men of honor. I think he really believed it, as certainly many of the Stoic mythographers—Seneca, for instance—of Greek and Roman upper-class morality did not. He is nothing if not persuasive. There are few more convincing narrators in all literature.

We need to be persuaded. If we accept the fiction that society is put together this way, we are likely to find ourselves perpetually duped; but it is good for us to believe that even if we aren't noble we can hope that we ourselves might possibly be so put back together. If we accept the testimony of experience with too much pessimism, we demean ourselves. Alas, that pessimism continually forces itself upon us and we need such reassurance as Plutarch provides. It may lead to role-playing—Roger Casement or his caricature, T. E. Lawrence, or our own tedious adulteries elevated to the barge of Cleopatra—but role-playing is better than nothing. In acting-out there is hope. In the words of Gabriel Marcel, "Without hope, nobility is impossible."

No modern translations of Plutarch's *Lives* compare with North's Elizabethan version from which Shakespeare transcribed almost verbatim great sections of his Roman Plays. If North's English is too strange for your taste, Dryden's, in the plain but elevated style of the late seventeenth century, seems today much more like our own speech as well as more like Plutarch's Greek. This is complete in the Modern Library Giant and is to be preferred to any of the many paperbacks of selections. Get the complete *Parallel Lives*. They are endlessly satisfying. Sooner or later you will read them all—and besides, you never know when you might find yourself on a desert island.

Marcus Aurelius
The Meditations

If a college student's mother died, his girl got pregnant, he acquired a loathsome disease, or he decided to become a conscientious objector, would he go to his philosophy professor for advice? What we call philosophy today is a complicated method of avoiding all the important problems of life. This was not always so. From Thales to Kant, philosophers justified their art as the foundation of the understanding of human conduct. Cosmology, ontology, metaphysics issued finally in ethics, politics, morals—the principles of the relationships between men, in their understanding and in their action upon them, which is called wisdom or virtue.

Even with the current fashion of Existentialism, no one would now dare write a book like Marcus Aurelius' *To Himself*, or, as we call it in English, *The Meditations*, and present it to the world as philosophy. He didn't either. But once published, these, his most intimate thoughts, were considered among the most precious of philosophical utterances by his contemporaries, by all Western Civilization after they returned to favor at the Renaissance, and most especially by the Victorian English, amongst whom *The Meditations* was a household book.

By and large, most Roman exponents of Stoicism are suspect. Seneca and Cicero were patent rascals and hypocrites. Roman Stoicism was a systematic apology of the ruling class to its own conscience. Of all the systems of late antiquity, Stoicism had the most coherent philosophy of nature, all elements of which were in immediately demonstrable necessary relationship with its ethics. Virtue and physics were interdependent and deducible one from the other, in either direction. Yet it all made so little difference! The style of Seneca gives him away: a spellbinder of the Social Lie. We might deduce from his prose that he was the mentor of Nero, the man who butchered Britons to collect a bad debt. Marcus Aurelius has been condemned in similar terms. Is this just? I think not. The style reveals the man. Where Seneca is nothing but shameless rhetoric, Marcus Aurelius is utterly unrhetorical. His crabbed Greek is as honest and as uncouth as the writing of Theodore Dreiser at his most sincere. Contrary to all the critics, this is a great style of a great man.

Those with an apocalyptic view of history—Augustine, Gibbon, Spengler, Toynbee—date the decline and fall of Rome from the reign of the noblest of her emperors. His rule extended from the Carpathians to the Sahara and from Scotland to Persia. Never again has life been so secure and affluent all over Western Europe. Only this once, in the years from Hadrian to Marcus, did Europe achieve the ecumenical peace and civilization of the Chinese Empire at its greatest periods. Under Marcus it began to disintegrate.

There have been other philosopher-kings—Alfred, Federigo Due, Saint Louis, Friedrich der Grosse—but their powers have been feeble, or their nations barbarous, or their philosophies pernicious. Marcus ruled over an entire and achieved civilization, and he was a saint as well as a philosopher. Gibbon's description of Antonine Rome is simply the generalized Utopian myth of his own eighteenth century at its narrow best. This is the world Gibbon would have liked to live in. Once it had actually existed, and it has never come back.

In twenty years under a wise ruler who was also a skillful and intrepid general, the ripe midsummer of Empire tumbled into stormy autumn, beset with foreign invasion and domestic strife that would persist relentlessly until the end of Western Civilization— until, in fact, today.

Literary masterpieces should be independent of their authors. The background of nemesis against which we project the devotions of Marcus shapes our judgment. Would his book be a great classic if we knew nothing of its circumstances? It is impossible to say, because the two factors are inextricably confused. What is great about *The Meditations* is not philosophy. It is autobiography.

If we want Stoic ethics pure, we can always turn to the dry, sharp paragraphs of Epictetus, whose works are commonly bound up with those of Marcus. He philosophizes; Marcus prays. So *The Meditations* have a certain monotony—the monotony of the first phase of prayer, examination of conscience. "Have I kept my temper?" "Have I given way to despair?" "Have I accepted Reality's orders of the day?" "Have I forgiven insult and injury?" "Do I fear death or disaster?" Epictetus preaches Stoic ataraxy, apathy, the unruffledness of the Buddhists, the acceptance without resentment of whatever may befall. Marcus struggles to obtain it in act. So Epictetus is arrogant. He knows. Marcus is humble. He tries and admits his failures.

Behind the cocksureness of the Stoic system, to which Marcus gives credal assent and whose argot he uses constantly, hides another, more profound life attitude, similar to what today we call Existentialism, especially as we find it in its most anguished exponents—for instance, Scheler. There is only "This"—beginning and ending in oblivion. Its meaning is mystery. Only one thing is sometimes under my control: my response. I can accept or reject. If I accept whatever happens, I am at peace. Once I disagree with fact, I am doomed to agony and frustration.

Marcus circles around and around the puzzle of being, through the labyrinth of life, like Proust without the narrative. "Nothing can happen to a man that nature has not equipped him to endure." Marcus says this over and over, trying to convince himself of something so evidently false. The final referent is the integrity of the person. The moral issues with which Marcus struggles would be, as he points out, unchanged whether the universe were mechanical and devoid of meaning or value or ruled by deity or Providence; whether the will were in fact free or determined; whether there were or were not a future life, or any even fugitive rewards and punishments at all.

So finally, it is the autobiography that is important as philosophy. Marcus Aurelius is not only the first author of antiquity to give us a spiritual autobiography; he is the first philosopher to found wisdom not on system but on existence at its inescapable minimum. He died in the marshes of Hungary holding the collapsing frontier. He could not control a promiscuous wife, a brutal son, or the growing disorder of the Empire. Who can? But he could leave to posterity the searchings of the heart of a man at the summit of meaningless power in a time of the onset of catastrophe. Since this is always the situation of all of us, his book remains what it has so often been called, one of the sweetest fruits of antiquity. "A little flesh, a little breath, and a Reason to rule all—that is myself. Forget your books; no more hankering for them; they were not part of your equipment." "Among the Quadi, on the River Gran."

Incomparably the best translation of *The Meditations* is the new one by Maxwell Staniforth in the Penguin Classics. It is eminently readable, never rhetorical, and the introduction is both judicious and sympathetic.

Apuleius
The Golden Ass

The accidents of the centuries have left us only two great prose fictions from classical antiquity. They are both in Latin. The much larger body of Greek Romance is definitely inferior, prolix and formularized. We have only fragments of *The Satyricon* of Petronius, but we have all of *The Golden Ass* of Apuleius. The complete *Satyricon* must have been one of the greatest novels ever written. *The Golden Ass* is a lesser production, but still a major work.

Apuleius has been called serene and genial, and rightly so. Pythagorean, Platonist, initiate mystic of Isis—he has none of Petronius secret agony, his melancholy of the rich and corrupt, and none of the Greek Lucian's astringent and atrabilious cynicism. It was from Lucian that he took the story of a well-bred but too curious and randy scholar turned into an ass while meddling with witchcraft.

Lucius, the hero of Apuleius' novel, certainly has an abundance of comic and bawdy adventures before he regains his human shape.

Ridiculous, horrible, lewd, gruesome—the episodes succeed one another at a dizzying pace; but they are all told with the most innocent humor, the most apparent desire to please. *The Golden Ass* is a remarkably good-tempered book, far removed from the solemn or bitter comedy of most great comic writers. Neither *Tristram Shandy* nor *Pickwick* is so easily, so unself-consciously narrated. If Apuleius is a typical representative, the paganism of the period following the collapse of belief in the official religion turns out not to suffer from the "Failure of nerve" and "schism in the soul" attributed to it by modern philosophers of history. Quite the contrary. Apuleius is a confident inhabitant of a homogeneous world. There is even less sense of spiritual disunity in his view of life than in a Chinese adventure-romance like the *Water Margin* or *All Men Are Brothers*. It is the Christian Saint Augustine, his fellow North African and contemporary, who is torn and distracted and frightened by the crisis of classical civilization. He writes of Apuleius with admiration and even something close to poorly concealed envy.

The plotting of the many adventures of Lucius the Ass may be simple. The prose is not. Petronius, like Ernest Hemingway in our time, made a rhetoric out of anti-rhetoric. Apuleius blows up rhetoric until it explodes. His is one of the most extraordinary styles in all literature, comparable to the fantastic obscurities of medieval Irish, or the invented language of the Japanese erotic novelist Saikaku, or James Joyce's *Ulysses* or even sometimes *Finnegans Wake*.

The Classicist taste of even the recent past found the prose of *The Golden Ass* barbarous, "full of affectation and meretricious ornament and that effort to say everything which prevents anything from being said well." Only Walter Pater knew better, and the fifth and sixth chapters of *Marius the Epicurean*, which include a superlative if somewhat dreamy translation of the Cupid and Psyche episode, is the best appreciation of Apuleius' style until recent times. Today, we who read Latin return far more often to the exuberance of Apuleius than to the carefully molded platitudes of Cicero. Apuleius ends his preface to the reader with the words "Read on, and enjoy yourself." His book was written both to amuse the author in writing and to delight the reader.

Although the Greek romances which he imitated are devoid of characterization, and the plots are strings of the stock situations of

serial melodrama, Apuleius, like Petronius, is a psychologist, a quick and accurate portrait painter gifted with that Roman sense of the uniqueness of the individual person which gives Roman portrait sculpture its unforgettable impact. There is actually very little description in *The Golden Ass*; yet in the straight narration of events, nights under the stars, robbers roistering in caves, slaves toiling at the millwheel, any number of witches and warlocks and monstrous mysteries all come to life and carry a conviction of reality. Apuleius gives the impression of a photographic fantasy. When we go back and read him over, we discover that this impression is due to the incisiveness of the narrative and not to a descriptive imagism.

The Golden Ass is not just literature of entertainment. Lucius lives in the body of a donkey from June to June, from roses to roses. Inserted early in his story, apparently gratuitously, as a tale told by an old woman to a captive beauty in a robbers' cave, is the story of Cupid and Psyche, an ideal allegory of the soul redeemed by love. Many critics have been unable to account for its presence in the novel. It is not a gracious idyll intruded into a series of coarse and bawdy adventures. It is the distilled concentration of the meaning of the trials and redemption of Lucius, the man who spent a year as an ass. It is the idyllic microcosm of a comic macrocosm, like a pearl in an oyster, a crystalline lattice from which the roughhewn real world of Lucius' metamorphosis is constructed.

The Magic Flute and *The Tempest* are stories of similar import and have been called thinly disguised occult rituals. Critics have denied that *The Golden Ass* is an allegory. What story of this kind is not? To the anagogic eye, any tale of man in the grip of vicissitude is a re-enactment of the Great Mystery. Certainly Lucius the Ass goes through the Zodiacal houses of the Perils of the Soul and is about to play the role of the sacrificed king in an obscene and comic *hierosgamos*, a parody mystic marriage, when he is saved from all his trials in animal form, transformed into a better man, and devoted to Isis, the queen of heaven.

Even though his hero is saved, Apuleius cannot quite stop his good-humored mockery. There is the subtlest irony in his description of the way the priests mulct Lucius of all his money in one expensive initiation after another: with the result that after he has become an impoverished devotee of Isis of the third degree, he then forms such profitable connections that he ends up richer than before—not at all unlike a modern businessman or lawyer member of a fraternal organization. Irony or no, the final chapters of the book are the purest expression of Late Classical ritual mysticism— more moving, more illuminated than Plutarch's essay on the cult of Isis. Over the page of Apuleius lies the radiance of his own deep, unbreakable happiness, and his metamorphosed donkey on his comic pilgrimage shares with Christian of *The Pilgrim's Progress* the abiding sense of joy of the saved.

The most famous English translation is by William Adlington, one of the finest examples of Elizabethan prose. This is the version, with many mistakes corrected, in the Loeb Classical Library. Robert Graves did a translation for Penguin Books which abandons the aureate Latinity of Apuleius for a dry, sharp, plain style, which is, however, itself a small masterpiece of twentieth-century prose.

Medieval Latin Lyrics

One of the most significant but seldom-remarked changes of taste in the past hundred and fifty years has been the decline in popularity of Roman Latin poetry and the rise in the appreciation of that of the Middle Ages—amongst, that is, the small number of people who read Latin for pleasure outside of the academic world. Virgil may have been what Tennyson called him, "the wielder of the mightiest measure ever moulded by the mind of man"; but after school years the *Aeneid* is seldom taken off the shelf, though the *Georgics* and *Eclogues* may continue to be read to while away a winter evening by the old-fashioned and learned.

On the other hand, especially since Carl Orff's music, the *Carmina Burana* is known by thousands who could not construe a line of Caesar. And now that the Roman Catholic Church is turning to the vernacular, a new appreciation for the great hymns and sequences is awakening amongst people who never paid much attention to them when they were part of the services. In the last century John Addington Symonds' *Wine, Women and Song* was a most popular collection of translations of Medieval songs, and today Helen Waddell's *Medieval Latin Lyrics*, with English and Latin *face en face*, has never ceased to sell and is now a Penguin.

More pertinent to the question of what is in fact the modern sensibility is the remarkable fondness for Medieval Latin poetry amongst the founders of that sensibility. The list of persons who have recorded such preference is rather startling. Coleridge, Poe (who may have been faking), Stendhal, Baudelaire, Nerval, Flaubert, Verlaine, Nouveau, Rimbaud, Mallarmé, Remy de Gourmont, O. V. L. Milosz, Apollinaire, Breton—this is close to being the apostolic succession of the modern temper. Similar lists could be made in other languages. Strindberg, for instance, should be included, and Machado and Rubén Darío, and Liopardi. Furthermore, not one of these writers had much interest in the Classical Latin poets except Catullus, Petronius, and the almost Medieval Boethius. Why? What went wrong with Virgil and Horace? Greek poetry may be read little in the original tongue, but its critical reputation is higher than ever. What is distinctive about Medieval Latin poetry?

The common answer is that Roman poetry is rhetorical and Medieval is not. But Theokritos and Euripides are rhetorical. Much Medieval religious and, following it, secular lyric is heavily influenced by one of the most rhetorical Latin writers who ever lived— Saint Augustine. Certainly lines like Saint Thomas Aquinas' *"Genitori, genitoque"* or the *Carmina Burana's "Fas et nefas ambulant, peni passu parti,"* or *"O comes amoris dolor, cuius mala male solor,"* are pure Augustinian word jewelry. Yet we do not think of them as decadent, nor do we doubt their sincerity. We believe and respond spontaneously, in a way we must specially train ourselves to do to Horace.

It is not an answer to say that Saint Thomas and the unknown writers of love lyrics sound as if they meant what they were saying. Horace sounded that way for almost two thousand years—to Ben

Jonson, to Tennyson, to the very Medieval Latin poets themselves. Nor is it true that the Medieval poets are personal and the Classic ones are not. Who ever gave a more revealing and ironic picture of himself than Horace, or a more shameless one than Ovid? But behind the mask of their hymns, supposedly so unselfing, Saint Thomas and Abelard are intensely personal in a different way from the Romans. They reveal something the older poets seem not to have had and never to have missed: a secret, ultimate self. What we hear in the newly emerged accentual rhythms, which had survived underground in folk song from prehistoric times, is the newly emerging individuality of modern man. Horace is a public personality, not unlike a very engaging politician carefully "personalized" by a public relations firm. We sense that we are being made intimate with a construct, and we suspect Horace, like the politician, of being nothing else. No cry ever comes from a hidden place. Only Sappho, and, to a much lesser degree, Catullus have what we most prize in poetry: the poet's revelation of himself as mystery.

But why should we think we find it in Medieval Latin? The subjects are conventional, and the responses standardized: the events of the Church's calendar, or the lover in spring, summer, and winter. Christ is born, dies on the Cross, and rises again. The Virgin nurses her baby or weeps at the foot of the Cross. Saints live their lives and die their martyrdoms. Lovers drink in taverns, swoon in bowers, or wander lonely amongst the flowers where the nightingale sings. It all seems stereotyped enough. Why should it so move cynical debauchees and atheist bachelors? Why should Baudelaire, Gourmont, and Apollinaire prefer the *Carmina Burana* to *The Aeneid*?

Partly because of the rhythm. The meters of Medieval Latin are accentual like our own, and the rhythmic patterns are those of the vernacular poetry which began to appear just at the height of the development of Medieval lyric. They sing to us in our own fashion in a hundred different ways—dancing, cavorting, staggering, or marching in solemn procession. As tunes they are emotionally meaningful to us, while we have lost the tune to Horace, and never knew the dance steps that were Sappho's and unknown to Horace too.

Far more, the difference is a matter of intention. Who ever wept over Ovid's "Tristia"? We are intended to marvel at his skill in depicting sorrow. But when Abelard, writing a plaint for Heloise and her nuns to sing at evensong, says, speaking in the disguise of David weeping over Jonathan, *"Vel confossus pariter, morerer feliciter, cum quid amor faciat . . ."*—or, as Helen Waddell translates it in the language of Ernest Dowson, "Low in thy grave with thee, happy to lie . . ."—we share directly in the terrible desolation of that one, single man, different from all the world and marked with his own unique sorrow.

One source of what was later to be called Romanticism lies in the very nature of the religious lyrics which preceded the finest secular ones. The Latin hymn writer wanted his listeners and singers to feel directly, to participate in the joy of the birth and the agony of the death of Christ. The Christian story is not a drama played before spectators; it is an actual drama in which the communicant is an important member of the cast. The Homeric "Hymn of Demeter and Persephone" is splendid in gold and ivory, but it moves us remotely, like sculpture or a painted ceiling. In the "Stabat Mater" we are asked to become Mary herself.

Direct attack on the sensibility by the full force of another personality was looked on as barbarous by the poets of the Roman Augustan Age. Many men then and since have considered Catullus' immodesty in the worst possible taste. A small amount of overtly pornographic poetry, as distinguished from scatological satire, survives from Roman times. Pornographic it may be; erotic it never is. Such poems are all rather bleak jokes, in which nobody is involved—not reader nor writer nor subject. Yet chastely worded Medieval poems like *"Ab estatis foribus, amor nos salutat"*—"Love stands in the gates of summer . . ."—or *"Dum Diane vitrea"*— "While Diana lights her crystal lamp . . ."—are profoundly erotic. They certainly never say anything as overtly sexual as hundreds of lines of Horace, but they do what they were intended to do—they hypnotize the listener with a subtle erotic melody until he partakes directly of the passion of the singer.

It is this immediacy of utterance that has fascinated five generations of critics and poets of the modern sensibility. Medieval Latin verse begins that process which finally becomes self-conscious and deliberate in our own age—the use of the word as magic, to subvert experience and alter the nature of the world.

The thirteenth-century secular lyrics are songs; not only that, they are tavern songs. The tradition of the *café chantant* goes back and vanishes in the dawn of Western Civilization. The *Carmina Burana* manuscript comes from the thirteenth century, but *"Phoebe claro,"* the first alba, or dawn song, with its haunting Provençal refrain, one of the first appearances of the vernacular, and *"Iam dolci amica venito"*—"Come live with me and be my love"—may be as old as Charlemagne. Both have strongly the character of songs for entertainment, to be sung in court or parlor or tavern to audiences, and to move them directly and personally. All is not love and wine and laughter; a large percentage are satirical, protest songs not greatly dissimilar in intention to those sung today. It would be a mistake to think of them as literature—as poetry for solitary reading. They were meant to involve singer and listener. Person-to-person utterance was as essential to Medieval lyric in the wine cellar at night as at Mass in the morning.

In addition to Helen Waddell's *Medieval Latin Lyrics*, available as a Penguin classic, there is *The Goliard Poets*, a collection, *face en face*, published by New Directions in paperback.

Tu Fu
Poems

"Tu Fu is, in my opinion, and in the opinion of a majority of those qualified to speak, the greatest non-epic, non-dramatic poet who has survived in any language."

This is certainly true, but it dodges the issue—what kind of poet is

Tu Fu? Not epic, not dramatic, but not in any accepted sense lyric either. Although many of his poems, along with others of the T'ang Dynasty, have been sung from that day to this, and although the insistent rhythms, rhymes, and tonal patterns of Chinese verse are lost in free-verse translation so that we do not realize how musical even the most irregular Chinese verse is (the most irregular, curiously enough, owes its very irregularity to the fact that it was written to pre-existing melodies), almost none of Tu Fu's verse is lyric in the sense in which the songs of Shakespeare, Thomas Campion, Goethe, or Sappho are lyric.

Rather, his is a poetry of reverie, comparable to Leopardi's "L'Infinito," which might well be a translation from the Chinese, or the better sonnets of Wordsworth. This kind of elegiac reverie has become the principal form of modern poetry, as poetry has ceased to be a public art and has become, as Whitehead said of religion, "What man does with his aloneness."

It is this convergence of sensibilities across the barriers of time, space, and culture that accounts for the great popularity of Chinese poetry in translation today, and for its profound influence on all major modern American poets. In addition, Tu Fu, although he was by no means "alienated" and at war with society like Baudelaire, was in fact cut off from it and spent his life, after a brief career as a high official of Ming Huang, The Bright Emperor, as a wandering exile. His poetry is saturated with the exile's nostalgia and the abiding sense of the pathos of glory and power. In addition, he shares with Baudelaire and Sappho, his only competitors in the West, an exceptionally exacerbated sensibility, acute past belief. You feel that Tu Fu brings to each poetic situation, each experienced complex of sensations and values, a completely open nervous system. Out of this comes the choice of imagery—so poignant, so startling, and yet seemingly so ordinary. Later generations of Chinese poets would turn these piercing, uncanny commonplaces into formulas, but in Tu Fu they are entirely fresh, newborn equations of the conscience, and they survive all but the most vulgar translations.

Tu Fu is not faultless. As Court Censor, a kind of Tribune of the Patricians, under Su Tsung, the son of Ming Huang, he seems to have been a cantankerous courtier. He took his sinecure job seriously and, an unregenerate believer in the Confucian classics, proceeded to admonish the Emperor on his morals and foreign policy. He was dismissed and spent the rest of his life wandering over China. He stayed longest in his famous grass hut in the suburbs of Ch'eng Tu in Szechuan. As the dynasty disintegrated and China entered on an interregnum, a time of troubles, he started wandering again, slowly, down the great river, always longing for the capital. His last years were spent on a houseboat, and on it, at 59, he died, possibly from overexposure during a flood and storm.

This is a troubled enough life, but Tu Fu writes of it with a melancholy that often verges on self-pity. He is a valetudinarian. By the time he was thirty, he was calling himself a white-haired old man. He always speaks of his home as a grass hut and presents himself as being very poor. Actually, though they were thatched, his various houses were probably quite palatial, and he seems never to have relinquished ownership of any of them and always to have drawn revenue from the farms attached to them. He had the mildest literary affection for his wife, whom he did not see for many years. He wrote no love poems to women; as with most of his caste, his passionate relationships were with men. Much of this is just convention, the accepted tone of Chinese poetry of the scholar gentry. Tu Fu's faults are microscopic in comparison with the blemishes that cover Baudelaire like blankets. Behind Baudelaire's carapace is a sensibility always struggling for transcendence. In Tu Fu the vision of spiritual reality is immanent and suffuses every item presented to the senses. Behind the conventions, behind the faults which make him human and kin to all of us, are a wisdom and a humanness as profound as Homer's.

No other great poet is as completely secular as Tu Fu. He comes from a more mature, saner culture than Homer, and it is not even necessary for him to say that the gods, the abstractions from the forces of nature and the passions of men, are frivolous, lewd, vicious, quarrelsome, and cruel and that only the steadfastness of human loyalty, magnanimity, compassion redeem the nightbound world. For Tu Fu, the realm of being and value is not bifurcated. The Good, the True, and the Beautiful are not an Absolute, set over against an inchoate reality that always struggles, unsuccessfully, to approximate the pure value of the absolute. Reality is dense, all one being. Values are the way we see things. This is the essence of the Chinese world view, and it overrides even the most ethereal Buddhist philosophizing and distinguishes it from its Indian sources. There is nothing that is absolutely omnipotent, but there is nothing that is purely contingent either.

Tu Fu is far from being a philosophical poet in the ordinary sense, yet no Chinese poetry embodies more fully the Chinese sense of the unbreakable wholeness of reality. The quality is the quantity; the value is the fact. The metaphor, the symbols are not conclusions drawn from the images; they are the images themselves in concrete relationship. It is this immediacy of utterance that has made Chinese poetry in translation so popular with modern Western poets. The complicated historical and literary references and echoes disappear; the vocal effects cannot be transmitted. What comes through, stripped of all accessories, is the simple glory of the facts—the naked, transfigured poetic situation.

The concept of the poetic situation is itself a major factor in almost all Chinese poems of any period. Chinese poets are not rhetorical; they do not talk about the material of poetry or philosophize abstractly about life—they present a scene and an action. "The north wind tears the banana leaves." It is South China in the autumn. "A lonely goose flies south across the setting sun." Autumn again, and evening. "Smoke rises from the rose jade animal to the painted rafters." A palace. "She toys idly with the strings of an inlaid lute." A concubine. "Suddenly one snaps beneath her jeweled fingers." She is tense and tired of waiting for her master. This is not the subject matter, but it is certainly the method, of almost all the poets of the modern, international idiom, whether Pierre Reverdy or Francis Jammes, Edwin Muir or William Carlos Williams, Quasimodo or the early, and to my taste best, poems of Rilke.

If Isaiah is the greatest of all religious poets, then Tu Fu is irreligious. But to me his is the only religion likely to survive the Time of Troubles that is closing out the twentieth century. It can be understood and appreciated only by the application of what Albert Schweitzer called "reverence for life." What is, is what is holy. I have translated a considerable amount of his poetry, and I have saturated myself with him for forty years. He has made me a better man, a more sensitive perceiving organism, as well as, I hope, a better poet. His poetry answers out of hand the question that worries aestheticians and critics, "What is poetry for?" What his poetry does superlatively is what is the purpose of all art.

Classic Japanese Poetry

Possibly the greatest single influence on the poetry of the West since Baudelaire has come from outside: from Chinese and Japanese poetry in translation. Machado, Pound, Rilke, Ungaretti, Apollinaire, Jammes, Lawrence, Pasternak—all over the world, poets who were young before the First War discovered the poetry of the Far East. They allowed it to shape their own styles to a greater or lesser degree. After the superficial imitative elements had been abandoned, basic formative elements remained and link the styles of the most diverse poets. It would in fact be hard to think of more diverse ones than these in my list. The next generation had been prepared by their elders and accepted Far Eastern poetry as the very matter of fact of their art; a whole section of Western European verse after the First War occupies the same universe of discourse as that of Tu Fu or Hitomara.

It is not an accident that the first widely popular book of translation was Judith Gautier's *Le Livre du Jade*. She was the most talented woman in Mallarmé's circle, and no Western poet has ever more deliberately sought the same effects for the same ends as the Japanese and Chinese than Mallarmé.

Japanese poetry is obviously different from Western or even Chinese. It is much shorter. In the Classical period most Japanese poems have only thirty-one syllables, arranged 5-7-5-7-7—the *tanka*. In the seventeenth and eighteenth centuries this was replaced in popularity by the *haiku* of only seventeen syllables.

Greatly as Japanese poetry may differ from all other verse, it does what poetry does everywhere. It intensifies and exalts experience. It differs in concentrating exclusively on that function, and it largely avoids not only all nonpoetic considerations, but most poetic ones as well. Experience is intensified and exalted, but the sole instrument of that exaltation is an exquisitely refined sensibility.

Homer, Dante, Sophocles refine and exalt experience too, but there is no epic poetry in Japanese, and no elegiac either after the *naga-uta*, long poems, of the earliest period. Some of these are by Hitomara, Japan's greatest poet, and they are profoundly moving— but they are far from long: fifty lines of seven and five syllables at the most. Furthermore, their length is misleading. They never lose the character of expanded *tanka*, and they tend to fall into paragraphs of about thirty-one syllables which can be separated out—and they end in a thirty-one-syllable envoi or coda which sums up the whole poem.

Many *tanka*, though few *haiku*, are filled with literary, folklore, and religious references: puns; fixed epithets, called "pillow words," like Homer's "rosy-fingered dawn"; and double or even triple or quadruple meanings. A poem may be carefully constructed to have two contradictory or incongruous meanings. This all sounds decadent and Alexandrine, but in fact the poem stands on its own as a presentation of acute sensibility encountering immediate experience. "Though the purity / of the moonlight has silenced / both nightingale and / cricket, the cuckoo alone / sings all the white night." This can be interpreted: "The peace of Amida has absorbed the monk and the householder; only the prostitute worships all through the night." But it doesn't need to mean that; it is quite sufficient as it is—a statement of presentational immediacy so powerful that it reverberates, by its very simplicity, through all kinds of symbolic realms.

Again—"Guardian of the gate / of Suma, how many nights / have you awakened / at the crying of the shore birds / of the isle of Awaji." The guardians of the gates of life grow weary with the cries of souls migrating from life to life and some passing to Hell, to the Bliss of Amida's Paradise, or to Nirvana. "Shore birds," or plovers, is written with the character "thousands of birds"; the meaning "never finding" is implicit in *awaji*, and *awa* also means spindrift or bubbles. Genji was banished to Suma, and the poet Yukihira, and there the Taira clan, fleeing from the capital with the infant Emperor, camped and were surprised and almost annihilated by the Minamoto in a battle that ended the finest period of Japanese civilization. Not a bit of this information is essential to full appreciation of what the poem is "about," and it was my favorite Japanese poem years before I knew any of it.

Certainly we need know no mythology to understand "In the spring garden / where peach blossoms / light the path beneath / a girl is walking," nor be Buddhists to grasp "The flowers whirl away / in the wind like snow. / The thing that falls away is myself"—as we do not have to be widowers to comprehend "I sit at home / in our room / by our bed / and stare at your pillow."

Whatever the complexities of reverberation in the background, the immediate impact of Japanese poetry is direct participation in objective experience. We are asked not to understand but to participate. So stripped is this objectivism that it sets up the widest possible ranges of reverberation—like life itself, but incomparably more intensely than all but the most crucial experiences.

There may be indefinite ranges of symbolic references behind the simplest Japanese poem—but these have a curious character. The terms may be fortuitous—the battle at Suma—but the symbolic range has a kind of essential necessity. If one did not know the mythology he could, from participation in the poem, invent an equivalent one. This is an objective-subjective, fact-and-symbol relationship which is perhaps the defining characteristic of all great poetry. In Japanese verse it stands alone: not an aspect or factor of the poem, but the poem itself.

Such an aesthetic is the result of a pervasive attitude toward life that finds explicit expression in various schools of Japanese philosophy and religion, an empirical concentration on the religious experience itself as unqualified, a secular mysticism which sees experience as its own transcendence. Again, it is easy to sort out Japanese poetry as expressing different varieties of such an approach to life: Japan's own blend of etherealized animism, the old folk religion; Zen and Esoteric Buddhism from China; the Chinese Sung Dynasty interpretations of "mind only" and "Philosophy of the Void." But these life attitudes are communicated directly: not as interpretations or even attitudes, but as inherent qualities of life itself.

It is the lack of this quality of direct communication of fundamentals which makes so much *haiku* seem decadent. The evocations are there, but they are superficial and sentimental. A great *haiku* by one of the early masters is simple, direct, and lends itself to infinite development. In Basho's "Autumn evening / a crow on a bare branch" or Boncho's "The long, long river / a single line on the snowy plain," the symbolic range is unlimited, in contrast to Kikaku's "A blind child / guided by his mother / admires the cherry blossoms," which might and in fact often does decorate calendars.

In recent years *haiku* of the latter type have spread over the western world, with unfortunate results; they are very popular with amateurs and housewifely poetry clubs. Japanese poetry at its most profound levels has been assimilated, too—but not so obviously. Confucianism shows its influence in Japanese life in the universally held belief that style is of the essence of meaning and being—it is a style of handling all experiences which Japanese poetry at its best has given the Western poet, and this can be communicated as poet to poet only on the deepest level—in other words, only from great poet to great poet; on the other hand, from poet to audience it is, by definition, universally communicable. It is this universality and total communicability which is the aim of all Japanese poetic theory and practice.

There is an extensive annotated bibliography in my own *100 Japanese Poems*, New Directions.

Lady Murasaki
The Tale of Genji

Murasaki Shikibu, the authoress of *The Tale of Genji* and lady-in-waiting to the Empress Akiko, was born about A.D. 978 and died about 1031. Japanese civilization as far as the general populace was concerned was at a lower level than the contemporary Polynesian.

Almost all Japanese lived lives of squalid, laborious poverty. Set apart from the brutalized mass was a tiny aristocracy, a few thousand people at most, whose culture had been transmuted into a way of life of a peculiar refinement so intense, subtle, and delicate as to constitute a utopia of exquisite sensibility and hyperaesthesia.

Nothing like it has ever existed before or since. The records that have survived from other remotely similar ruling castes—of the Egyptian Old Kingdom, Persia, or India, for instance—are crude, impersonal, stereotyped by comparison. From the eleventh-century Heian court of Japan we have a number of imaginative and complex records of the most intimate interpersonal relations, diaries and novels and poems, many of them written by women. Not only does *The Tale of Genji* far surpass all of these, but most people who have read it agree that it is probably the world's greatest novel.

There is a huge and extraordinarily contradictory literature on *Genji* in modern Japanese. Some liberal critics consider it a suffragist denunciation of male promiscuity. Marxists have called it a satire on the evil ruling class. Mystical Buddhists see Prince Genji as a Bodhisattva. Westernized literary taste compares Lady Murasaki to Marcel Proust. The overt plot of the novel is simple enough in principle and infinitely complicated in detail. It is the story of the erotic relationships of Prince Genji, called *Hikaru*, The Shining One; of his friend and brother-in-law To no Chujo; and of their descendants, to the second and even third generation, with an illimitable number of women—wives, mistresses, and wives of others. The story is told entirely from the woman's point of view. The men have titles of generals, administrators, but nothing is ever said of any work they might do beyond writing love notes, playing musical instruments, and climbing over balconies. The Japanese court had already become non-functional and parasitic, but even its symbolic activities are reduced by Lady Murasaki to the basic complexities of sexual refinement.

This is only the superficial plot. Underneath it runs a profound concealed drama: the working-out, reduction, and final redemption of an evil *karma*—the consequence of a moment of irresponsible jealous anger. Early in the book and offstage, as it were, the elaborately decorated bullock cart of Lady Rokujo, Genji's mistress, is scratched by the cart of his wife. She gives way to a spasm of wrath, and a being, an incarnation of her anger, "takes foot," as the Japanese say, and struggles throughout the book with the grace that emanates from Genji gratuitously.

Lady Murasaki in her descriptions of Genji gives many clues to his character. "The Shining One" is a Bodhisattva epithet, and his body has the unearthly perfume that distinguishes such a savior, but she presents him as an unconscious as well as an indifferent Bodhisattva—a profoundly original religious notion. A Bodhisattva is a being who turns away from the bliss of Nirvana with the vow that he shall not enter ultimate peace until he can bring all other beings with him. He does this, says mystical Buddhism, indifferently, because he knows there is neither being nor non-being, peace nor illusion, saved nor savior, truth nor consequence. To this Lady Murasaki adds the qualification that he does it without knowing it—an idea derived from Chinese neo-Taoism, Shingon Buddhism, and rationalization of primitive Shintoist animism and from the philosopher Wang Ch'ung, from whom also comes the clearest statement of the personalized, subsisting embodiment of evil emotion, act, or thought.

Lady Murasaki grew into her novel. The most profound and subtle writing occurs in the later half, after Genji is dead. As the generations go by, the *karma*, the moral residues, of the lifetimes of Genji and his beloved friend To no Chujo cross and recross in their descendants and are at last resolved when a young girl, beloved by descendants of both, struggles with the demon and destroys it forever in a series of gratuitous acts as indifferent and unconscious as the original grace of which she is the re-embodiment.

The story that seems on superficial reading to be only an endless kyriale of philandering turns out to be an unbelievably complicated web of moral tensions and resolutions. Modern Japanese, even more than Western readers, find this outlandish and incomprehensible. The *hannya*, the devil that speaks through the mediums called in when the girls it is killing are dying, is almost always accepted by the critics as the ghost of Lady Rokujo, although at the beginning of its career she not only is still alive but has forgotten the incarnating episode and left the court to become a priestess of the national shrine of Ise, where she eventually dies in what we would call a state of grace. Although the *hannya* speaks in her name, it is only the personalized subsistent moment of hate which grows by feeding on the souls it destroys.

A similar situation surrounds Genji's birth, the death of his mother, and his first love affair. The plot is stated in a kind of overture at the beginning of the novel, as it is resolved in a recapitulation of all the principal motives at its end. Strung on the skein of this subtle plot are any number of subplots of like nature. The episodes, with an ever-receding profundity, are encapsulated one within another like Chinese boxes, or they are reflected one within another like a universe of mirrors and diamonds—the universe of universes of the *Kegonkyo*, the *Avatamsara Sutra*, the most visionary of all Buddhist documents.

When in the Sutra the complex of universes is revealed to the historic Buddha Sakyamuni, he bursts into laughter. I have never known anyone to read *The Tale of Genji* who was not thrown into a state of aesthetic joy, a kind of euphoria of response which very few other works of art can produce—the state of being that Marcel Proust sought in the paintings of Vermeer or the *Jupiter Symphony* and that he tried to reproduce in his readers at the most crucial episodes in his novel. *The Tale of Genji* communicates this ecstatic revery and joy, like Genji's perfume, with unconscious, effortless indifference.

For almost two generations Arthur Waley's beautiful translation has been the standard version. It, rather than the original, has been translated into many languages, including the modern Japanese. Waley has brought out the subtlety, exquisite refinement, psychological complexity, and moral profundity to a degree that could easily be missed by the most learned and astute reader of the Medieval Japanese text. Lady Murasaki's novel is a great but inaccessible classic in Japanese. The Waley translation is both a major English and a major international classic, accessible to all the world.

The Tale of Genji has recently been issued in one volume as a Modern Library Giant. This is the cheapest and most convenient edition now on the market. There is a brief introduction by Waley which provides all the information you need to follow the story. *The World of The Shining Prince: Court Life in Ancient Japan*, by Ivan

Morris (Knopf, 336 pp., 1964), is fascinating background reading *after* you've finished the novel. Following a bout with Lady Murasaki, most people become avid Japanophiles for a while and read everything they can lay hands on about classic Japanese culture.

Chaucer
Canterbury Tales

Chaucer was the first European writer after the Classical period to enter upon the new world of the novel, centuries before anybody else penetrated as deeply into that complicated territory. Medieval romance was exactly that: romance—static, like the art of heraldry. Dante's *Divine Comedy* takes place in moral regions where decisions are over. The inhabitants of Purgatory can grow toward Paradise—but only along predetermined lines, independent of one another and of their own wills. The *Divine Comedy* as Dante's interior panorama, a completely metaphorical *Remembrance of Things Past,* has dramatic development, but not in the novelistic or theatrical sense. Serial and linear collections like Boccaccio's *Decameron* have no necessary connection between the stories and their narrators. The settings are conveniences; the language is rhetorical.

Chaucer's *Canterbury Tales* and *Troilus and Criseyde* are dynamic structures of evolving interpersonal relations. On each type of character, like sculpture on an armature, a unique individual is erected with a minimum of rhetoric and a maximum of effective characterization. At the end of the "Prologue" a crowd of people have come to life. The tensions and affections that exist between them have been defined. From then on the Canterbury Pilgrims jostle, argue, push and pull, and twist in the fields of force set up by their manifold personalities, each one a center of power. However interesting in themselves, the Tales are each a metaphor of the personality of the teller; each Tale affects the listeners. In the "links" between Tales the narrators are represented and redefined in special relationships, much as the characters in a play are intensified in each new scene.

Chaucer's pilgrims can be sorted into categories—the Seven Deadly Sins: pride, sloth, anger, lust, avarice, gluttony, envy; the Seven Cardinal Virtues: faith, hope, charity, prudence, temperance, justice, fortitude; the four humours: blood, bile, black bile, phlegm; the influence of the known planets and the Houses of the Zodiac— but this is far from reducing his psychology or philosophy of the personality to schematization. These thirty-five factors, their com- mutations and permutations, can be figured out arithmetically and are a tidy sum. Besides, each traveler is defined in the first instance by occupation and most of them by native province; each person is strongly characterized by individually developed sexuality; each is a special, complex aspect of maleness or femaleness. This is a larger apparatus for a theory of character than that employed by modern novelists raised on the simple Old Testament schemata of psycho- analysis.

Turn and turn about, the characters of the pilgrimage and the characters of their Tales develop not only a drama of great complex- ity but also a number of theses which Chaucer exposes with artistic discretion and subtle modulation. For instance, a philosophy of marriage is developed by the dialectic conflict of the Wife of Bath, the Clerk, the Merchant, and the Franklin, with asides and assists from the Host, the fictional Chaucer, and various others. Paralleling this dialectic is another on love itself, of which the Knight's Tale and the Miller's Tale as ironic mirror-images of each other are the most obvious. By the time the pilgrimage is over, Chaucer has defined sexual love in terms of a philosophy of the sacrament of marriage centuries in advance of those of most Catholic theolo- gians—a middle-class marriage of free and equal personalities— and contrasted it with feudal chivalry.

There are dozens of subtle touches that show uncanny social and historical insight. In the "Prologue," in fifteen lines given to the Merchant, Chaucer defines mercantile capitalism with the skill and the understanding of a Marx, and with considerably fewer words. The Merchant is dressed at the height of middle-class rather than aristocratic fashion. A master of the new science of double-entry bookkeeping, he is a passionate defender of the freedom of the seas and an expert at taking advantage of *valuta*—the differences in national currencies. He has his own well-developed theology to outwit the feudal Church's prohibition of usury. Most important, his fortune is founded on the skillful, covert manipulation of debt. Most academic critics, themselves still living by feudal standards, miss the irony of this last item. The Merchant is not hoodwinking his creditors; the entire economy that he represents is founded on debt, called credit in the new theology. As Chaucer says, "Forsooth he was a worthy man withall / But sooth to seyn, I know not how men him call"—which doesn't mean the fictional Chaucer didn't know his name.

Hardly a characterization in the Tales or in the "Prologue" and "links" does not lend itself to similar careful exegesis. However, we can approach Chaucer's meanings only through several levels of irony—the irony of the pilgrimage with its incongruous constituents; the irony of the narrators, especially as they use their Tales to attack or flatter one another; the irony of the fictional Chaucer, the overall narrator, represented as an innocent, good-natured buffle-head; and the irony of the real Chaucer. Each of these levels distorts, reshapes, and finally increases the definition of the characters in their interrelations. The last level, the poet and master of the show, can sometimes be slyly bitter indeed. Few people even now realize that his Lady Prioress is portrayed as a profoundly evil woman and her Tale is a piece of bigotry that leaves even the audience of fourteenth-century pilgrims for once speechless. Like a dream told to a psychoanalyst, each Tale reveals the deepest complexities of character. The Tales judge the narrators.

Chaucer was a man of the world in a sense in which no other major English poet has ever been—a man of affairs, like Bagehot, Defoe, Fielding, or Clarendon. This gives his style an operative force found commonly only in China, where great statesmen were great poets. He uses language as a man uses it to get results. His knowledge of human beings is derived from a vast variety of practical situations in a busy life in county courts and in the courts of Italian princes and the French King. His sly knowledge of human duplicity, so like Bertolt Brecht's, he had learned as a Comptroller of Petty Customs and a hearer of provincial lawsuits, an environment not unlike the inner life of the German Communist Party. No English poet is a greater master of words that count. Even his parodies of Early Renaissance rhetoric mock their originals with Chaucer's irrepressible clarity. Each situation, each character, and the overall milieu are defined like the "poetic situation" in Classic Chinese poetry. Hour, season, weather, topography, dramatic context, mood are indicated with just words enough—with controlled modesty.

One of the most remarkable things about Chaucer is that he has almost no vices. Great poets like Shakespeare and Baudelaire are destructive models for poetic practice; Milton and Virgil have so many vices that modern taste can scarcely stomach them at all. In *Troilus and Criseyde* and *The Canterbury Tales* Chaucer is close to being a perfect model. If you want to learn to write, this is the way to do it. If you want to be a writer, this is the way to live—out in the world amongst men who think of language as an effective instrument of action.

A generation ago Chaucer was still being taught to high school seniors in the original language. No translation into modern English can transmit all Chaucer's many virtues. Both wit and music are missed. There are good modern versions in cheap Penguin, Mentor, and Modern Library editions to read along with the original. After a little practice, Chaucer's language turns out to be not all that strange.

Rabelais

The Adventures of Gargantua and Pantagruel

Standards of decorum in literature change with the greatest rapidity. The Regency buck gives way to the Victorian maiden in a matter of months. It is a curious experience to read the apologetic prefaces to the various nineteenth- and early-twentieth-century editions of Rabelais. Even Jacques Le Clerc and Samuel Putnam feel it necessary to apologize for his bawdry and scatology. Today, when prurience so gluts the literary market that the customers are beginning to revolt, the humor of Rabelais seems not just remarkably wholesome but a most aggressive insistence on wholesomeness.

In fact, *The Adventures of Gargantua and Pantagruel* strikes our age—as it must have struck its own—as a manifesto of sanity, health, and general moral salubriousness. Few books in history are more well, no characters in all literature less sick than those genial giants and their companions. This is the secret of the book. Rabelais used the broadest farce, the coarsest slapstick, to portray that primary ideal of the Renaissance, man at his optimum. Although it needed to be explained to several troubled and alienated periods that have intervened between his time and ours, Rabelais' choice of the vehicle of the simplest, least contaminated folk humor was wise indeed.

What does man do at his optimum? He creates. He uses his mind and body to their fullest capacities. His curiosity is always busy. He works with joy. Joy; one thing man certainly does when living at his fullest potential is laugh, and for very simple reasons.

The legend is that Rabelais' last words were, "The farce is finished. I go to seek a vast perhaps." This is one of the most apposite of the tales about Rabelais, but only if we realize what a different meaning the words have for us. There is no bitterness like ours in the choice of the word "farce," no hint of Hamlet's instruction to the players. There is no hint of Hamlet's soliloquy in the choice of the word "perhaps." Rabelais meant a farce like those he had seen a thousand times on a stage of planks in a town square full of sound and fury, uproarious with laughter about copulation and defecation—or as Aristotle would say, coming to be and passing away. The skepticism of the perhaps is an untroubled skepticism, as far from Pascal's agonized wager or Kierkegaard's leap into the dark as could be imagined.

It is untroubled acceptance of all possibilities that gives the work of Rabelais its special character, a character neurotic critics of the modern age are so unused to that they have called it neurotic. *The Adventures of Gargantua and Pantagruel* is an extraordinarily passionless book in every sense of the word. Rabelais feels strongly about the squalor and spiritual poverty of much of the monasticism of his time. He expresses these feelings in guffaws, an expression we do not usually call passion.

Although the latter part of the story is concerned with Pantagruel's quest of a wife, women appear rarely in the book, and the lust for them never. Legend may be right, that Rabelais had a mistress and a bastard son, Theodule; but on the evidence, he might just as well have been a perfectly content celibate. Every sentence is lusty, but no sort of lust ever appears. Greed, pride, the itch for power are comic masks in a Medieval charade. They are hilariously funny because Rabelais cannot believe in his guts in their existence. People eat and drink wildly exaggerated quantities, even for giants, but this is not gluttony. It is farce.

Today our point of view is so remote from that of Rabelais that it requires a special effort of will to even know what he is talking about. Our science of the mind is founded on the study of the behavior of the mentally ill; our Public Health on epidemiology; our practical sociology on a kind of social worker's criminology; our economics on Marx. It has been said of America that its philosophy of life, like that of the ancient Greeks, is medically oriented. The ethics or the politics or the psychology of Aristotle or Plato is founded on a clear concept of the fully healthy man. Our parallel disciplines begin with pathology. Psychiatrists say we are all neurotics. Rabelais would not have known what they are talking about.

Rabelais' giants live in an optimum moral environment in which they are free to develop the utmost of every potential, and it is this, not the mere description of their size, that gives them their tremendous scale. Rabelais thought of the ethics he preached as enabling an explosion of human energy. "Do what you will," says the inscription over the gate of his abbey of Thélème—his answer to the monasticism of his day.

We should never forget that Rabelais was himself a monk. However he may have wandered about the world and may in a measure have been excused from his vows, he never left the ranks of the clerical elite. The rule of Saint Benedict is, after all, a "mandarin ethic" for an elite that was otherworldly because this world was not subject to its control. What Rabelais is preaching is a mandarin ethic of the elite of the onrushing secular civilization. With him and with his colleagues Erasmus and Dolet, the first generation of humanists of the northern Renaissance, this ethic worked. As portrayed by them it has remained attractive and satisfying.

As we look back over history, we realize that it has actually attracted only a small minority, and even fewer have made a success of it. Perhaps they are the tiny minority of the sane. François I, Henry VIII—were they contemporary successful embodiments of Rabelais' optimum man? Was Saint Thomas More? And what happens when this gospel is given to men not at their optimum, too ignorant to understand it and too malformed to act upon it? The secular religion of the Renaissance, like all the historic religions, demands the capacity for nobility in those who come to it for salvation.

The favorite translation of Rabelais is the Urquhart-Le Motteux, done in the seventeenth century. It is in itself a great work of literature—or at least, Urquhart's share is—but it is seriously misleading. Urquhart was a dotty Scotch eccentric, more like a character of Rabelais than like Rabelais himself. His translation is in a spectacularly eccentric prose that readers of English have come to think of as specifically Rabelaisian. There are a number of modern translations in plainer English, which, though none of them are works of art, do show more of the character of Rabelais—the magnanimous humanist, the very opposite of an eccentric.

Marco Polo
The Travels of Marco Polo

The Travels of Marco Polo and *The Pilgrim's Progress* of John Bunyan must make one of the most obvious comparative doublets in all literature. One is an allegory which is a story of a journey through real life, and the other is the real-life narrative of a journey to the ends of the earth which is an archetype of all adventures of man into the unknown. Like Bunyan, Marco Polo wrote, or rather dictated, his odyssey in prison. Unlike Bunyan's, it is a great literary achievement by a man who, if not forced into leisure and isolation, would probably not have written at all. Both were activists, and they wrote the prose of men who act. Great poetry may or may not be emotion recollected in tranquillity, but most of the world's great prose is certainly action recollected in tranquillity.

Before the first dawn of the Renaissance, Marco Polo is already a man of the new age that was approaching its climax in the wars and revolutions of Bunyan's day. Marco Polo's youth overlapped the middle age of Saint Thomas Aquinas for twenty years. Yet he writes of a strange and often culturally antagonistic civilization with a scientific, dispassionate objectivity that would be rare enough six or seven hundred years later. It is the matter-of-factness of a business letter, utterly unlike other Medieval prose.

Marco Polo was certainly a bourgeois, but he comes before the days when the middle class were revolutionaries. In his time they were merchant-adventurers. What is most impressive about Marco

Polo is not that he finds men in distant lands strange and their ways outlandish, but that he does not. Today the world teeters on the brink of extermination over differences that would have been hardly perceptible to Marco Polo, that would have seemed to him as trivial as they do now to an Eskimo or an African. To him the court of the Great Khan was understandable as an activity like that of the Doge and Councils of Venice. He had what we have lost—an ecumenical mind, an international sensibility. As Medieval merchants, he and his father and uncle had the tolerance that comes from thinking of one world linked together by caravan journeys and sea voyages, three years or more long; the tremendous civilizing force of business as business in the face of the most anomalous customs—the opposite of the ruthless destructiveness of trade, flag, and Bible in Victorian days. Few things shock him—only cannibalism, temple prostitution, the hospitable sharing of wives and daughters with guests—and his outrage seems perfunctory. One suspects that he cheerfully took advantage of the latter two barbarities.

Although the Polos are the most famous of the tiny handful of travelers between China and Europe who have left records, they are the only ones who were simply merchants and nothing else. Had Marco Polo not been in prison, we might know of him only through casual mention in a few tattered Venetian documents or not at all. Yet the Polos must have been three out of many more. The chance existence of Marco Polo's book makes us realize how much of the most important history happens and then is silent forever.

We are especially lucky that it was Marco Polo, a citizen of no mean city, who, out of all the travelers of the Middle Ages, left us the most complete record. He was a merchant of Venice, a republic which did not need a bourgeois revolution but which, alone in the Western world, where feudalism would continue to hold sway in some places for another half-millennium, kept alive the ancient Mediterranean city-state, the oligarchic commune of trader aristocrats—a form of society older than ancient Crete, old before ever there was a Greece or an Odysseus wandering the sea.

Thirteenth-century Venice was the only city in Western Europe that produced people capable of adjusting to the high culture of Yuan Dynasty China. This was a period at least as civilized as our own. The Mongols were the inheritors of the previous Sung and

T'ang Dynasties, times when civilization rose, as it did in Periclean Athens, to heights it is doubtful we will ever reach again. China was included in an empire that stretched eastward from Poland to the Yellow Sea and from Siberia to Mesopotamia, Persia, Burma, and Indo-China. The Mongol Empire was contemporary with the momentary achievement of an all-encompassing Medieval synthesis in the West—the only time Europe would ever approach an international Christian civilization. Marco Polo has been described as a human individual linking these two universalisms. He was something more and something less. His was a kind of mind to which abstract concepts like synthesis, internationalism, eclecticism would have been meaningless because they were taken totally for granted—the mind of the practical man. He did not become an exotic favorite of the Great Khan. He became a trusted political and business administrator.

Practical or no, what tremendous exultation there is in Marco Polo's book! It is the first thrilling story of what even in our day is still the land of wonder. The oasis cities along the silk routes of inner Asia, each a complex little melting pot; the great provincial capitals of China with their life of all-encompassing self-sufficiency—as though they contained the only humans on the planet; all the glamour of the South Seas—pearls, spices, naked brown-skinned women who love to love, cannibals; and fabulously rich pirate kings. Not only was Marco Polo the first to record his travels into this world of adventure, opening doors of commerce that swung shut again for centuries, but his book is still for the reader a door that opens into an immense literature, the finest of all travel tales.

Sven Hedin; Aurel Stein; Paul Pelliot; Mrs. Bullock-Workman; Owen Lattimore; Henry Yule; Koslov; Rockhill; Sykes; Shipton; Irene Vongher Vincent; William of Rubruck; Huc and Gabet; Desideri; all the Chinese travelers; and that great favorite of the Chinese theater, movies, and all Chinese children that Arthur Waley translated as *Monkey*—these are a few books on Tibet and the inner-Asian frontiers of China that I happen to remember, a few out of what is one of the most absorbing of all forms of reading matter. Still one of the most wonderful, and most accurate, is Marco Polo's little book, dictated in enforced idleness for the benefit of an unbelieving world over six centuries ago.

The best edition with which I am familiar, for editorial and translating reasons explained at length in the Introduction, is Manuel Komroff's *The Travels of Marco Polo* in the Modern Library. The best expansion and exegesis of Polo's account is the books by Henry Yule, his final edition, with the third volume by Henri Cordier of the book itself and, supplementing it, *Cathay and the Way Thither.* There are many books on the Mongol Empire and a translation of *The Secret History of the Mongols.* The best modern historical and geographical work is Owen Lattimore's *Inner Asian Frontiers of China.* From the Chinese side, *On Yuan Chwang* by Thomas Watters; Arthur Waley's *The Real Tripitaka.* Beyond lies an almost limitless plenitude of vicarious adventure.

Thomas More
Utopia

The past century, and especially the last thirty years, has seen an ever-accelerating interest in Thomas More. He is one of the most popular saints not only with well-educated Roman Catholics, but with Anglicans as well, and at least as popular with nonreligious people familiar with his time. To contemporary taste, Thomas More is not only a saint but the most likable human being of the Renaissance and Reformation. It is this genial personality which overrides obliterating centuries and conflicting points of view. It is integral to the understanding of Thomas More as a thinker.

Baron von Hügel was fond of observing that a prevailing sweetness of temper was one of the essential qualifications in the Vatican process of beatification and sanctification, the so-called "trial" of a saint. Geniality is a quality we think of as primary in hardly any other major writer. The thought of More is an expression of a way of life, and his tragedy resulted from the betrayal of that way of life.

For this reason the *Life of Sir Thomas More* by his son-in-law, Roper, and More's own meditations on the eve of execution, *A Dialogue of Comfort Against Tribulation*, are essential to the understanding of the *Utopia*.

The *Utopia* is the only ideal commonwealth that accepts the obvious fact of what More called original sin. He did not believe that men were either naturally good or naturally bad, but that they desired the good with defective or corrupt wills. Utopia is a society structured to enable the conscience. More's martyrdom, as he was careful to point out in his final struggle with the king and his judges, was an appeal not to external authority, but to conscience. British church authority, except for his fellow martyr Bishop Fisher, was all on the other side.

More was not at all what later ages would call an ultramontane. Quite to the contrary, there was something specially and anciently English about his witty piety, his organization of his family into a kind of lay monasticism, and the quality of his prayer. Just as his English humanism finds its ancestry in the great Oxford Franciscan Bishop Grosseteste and in John of Salisbury, so his religious life was anticipated by Saint Gilbert of Sempringham, who founded an order, which endured until More's day, of monks, nuns, and married couples living in separate buildings but in community.

Beyond More, this religious temper would find expression in the tolerant and balanced humanity of Richard Hooker's *Laws of Ecclesiastical Polity*, in the poetry of George Herbert, and in the High Church lay monasticism of Nicholas Ferrer's community at Little Gidding. More's concept of the religious life was also close to the pietist movements within or without the church in the Rhineland—which survived in the Quakers, the Mennonites, the Brethren, and communal Christian sects like the Hutterites.

The secret of this man whose life and whose ideal commonwealth have caused so much controversy is a tone of personality that is the expression of a specific life of prayer. Like all the Christian humanists between Tyndal, Hus, and the Council of Trent, More was—as his spokesman in the *Utopia*, Hythlodaeus, says, and as his friends Erasmus and Bude say of More—attempting to return to a Christian philosophy of man, an "anthropology" that would be, as scholasticism was not, incorrigibly Christian. Like modern Russian Orthodox philosophers, like the Apostles, the Fathers of the Church, and the Byzantine theologians, More thought of Christianity as the process of the divinization of man. Christian humanism was ultimately a quest for a complete way of life that was a way of prayer, a life of active contemplation that was an assumption of unlimited liability for the realization of the destiny of Christendom and an individual penitence for the failure of that realization.

More, as a secular thinker, like Machiavelli or Fortescue, was a social inductionist, a political naturalist whose methods were the opposite of those of the Medieval authors of "mirrors for princes" with their rationalist deductions from axioms and first principles. The communism of the *Utopia* is not a principle but a conclusion from the evidences. Over half the book is the best of all exposures of the social sicknesses that accompanied the death of the Medieval polity. It is a masterful indictment of a society based on covetousness where *homo homine lupus* is the Iron Rule. The *Utopia* sets itself the problem, How can we reconstruct a pagan "natural" society so that it is prepared to take the next step and become a school of divinity in the literal sense? How can we create and nurture a humane fellowship that will pass into Christian brotherhood?

Enclosures, vagabondage, corrupt courts, depraved courtiers, the boom-and-panic cycle already established in the cloth industry, speculation in and cornering of the necessities of life, the general debauchery of a society that no longer respected its own supernatural sanctions—this indictment is not peculiar to More. It is voiced by all the Christian humanists. His contribution was a diagnosis of the root of the sickness and a program of prognosis, therapy, and cure. What he wished to do was make possible to all men individual lives lived as vocation, "calling." What stood in the way were the predatory sins: pride, covetousness, greed, all the forms of injustice; if they could be inhibited by established social consent, it would be possible to democratize the most elite form of prayer—action as contemplation, life lived in devotion. This he believed was the only force that could prevail against what he called original sin and others saw as the Socratic dilemma.

Can social and individual life be reconstructed so that man will be enabled to choose the ultimate greater good over the immediate lesser good? Human relationships would then be prepared to receive divine grace, as, to use a metaphor that would have occurred to More, the body of the Virgin Mary was prepared for the Incarnation. More's *Utopia* is a kind of perfected and purified Old Testament.

If men do, as the result of a life habitude enforced by an all-enveloping social fabric, learn always to choose the rationally presented good, they will be made ready to pass into a transcendental society, that community of love that was the Absolute for the strange modern British philosopher McTaggart.

More realized none of his hopes; saw not even the tiniest modicum of his reforms come true. Instead, in mid-career Saint Thomas More collided with Pantagruel grown middle-aged, sour, and paranoid. This is the tragedy of a great saint: that he was felled by that most commonplace evil, the delusion of participation. "If I don't take the job, somebody worse will, and think of the good I can do with the power." Confronted the first time with choice, he chose the lesser good—the chancellorship. The second time he chose the greater—his conscience and death.

All of More's life and writing is lit with his martyrdom and distorted by it. In the knowledge of what happened to him, all of his works seem to be wrestling with this problem: "What are the things that are God's and the things that are Caesar's, and what is the meaning of the word 'render'?" So his own life and all his work, although he did not intend it that way, is a dramatic meditation, a prayer on a stage, like *Antigone*. His end is one of the few genuine tragedies in political history, and his writings are its Sophoclean chorus.

More's friend Erasmus has always been held up as the great Renaissance master of Latin style. I find his style the expression of what he was, the archetype of the Dutch Uncle. More, on the other hand, wrote an extraordinarily vigorous, natural, colloquial Latin, a rhetoric capable of reaching behind the emotions to touch the deepest core of the heart. This style survives all but the worst translations, and the English of the current Yale edition of the complete works is full of sparkle and muscle. More's own English is available in A *Dialogue of Comfort Against Tribulation*, edited by

Leland Miles and published by Indiana University Press. The best introduction to the *Utopia* is by J. H. Hexter, one of the editors of the Yale *Utopia: More's Utopia, the Biography of an Idea*, published by Harper. All are available in hardcover and in paperback.

Machiavelli
The Prince

To reread Machiavelli's *The Prince* in middle age in the afternoon of a century of political horror is to experience a wistful incongruity: What were the four hundred years of scandal all about? As objective analyst of successful despotism, Machiavelli seems today too confident of the good sense of those clever and forceful enough to rise to positions of tyranny. He assumes the fundamental good will of his prince toward his subjects, or at least his intelligent rapacity and his accessibility to advice. Our twentieth-century dictators all claim to have learned from Machiavelli. Mussolini even wrote a preface to *The Prince*. Since the fall of Bismarck, they have violated every item of his advice.

Machiavelli's defenders have said he studied politics with the value-neuter eye of a scientist. Yet in spite of his doubts of the natural goodness of man, he like Socrates hoped that rulers of the State, one or many, might be more open to reason than not and if presented with a demonstrable good would probably choose it. We do not think of Machiavelli as tainted with the Socratic fallacy, but so it is. He is the most astute philosopher of history after Thucydides, but both believed history might be taught to behave itself—a belief for which their narratives give little warrant.

Most people read only *The Prince*, and they read that as advocating, from general principles, a set of rules. *The Prince* and *The Discourses on the First Ten Books of Livy* should be read together.

Machiavelli's realism brings to its end a long tradition of manuals of advice to princes and descriptions of ideal states. However much he tried for objectivity, Aristotle's *Politics* is half-prescriptive, and its Medieval successors are nothing else. Machiavelli realized that the student of politics must concern himself with what is, not with what should be; that if there was any meaning in historical process, it could be found only by inductive analysis of what men have actually done; and that the greatest of fallacies is to start by seeking first principles, transcendental sanctions, and final causes. He knew that the hortatory philosophers of history and politics have only provided makers of history—finders, keepers, and losers of power—with a rhetoric of noble fraud. He was the first to understand that history is not going anywhere, it is just what happens, and the only values operating in it are those of general welfare, the simple goods of actual men. Neither history nor politics is logical. They are the first empiricisms, and the only first principles of politics are the individuals who live it. *The Prince* studies a practicable despotism—Cesare Borgia's; *The Discourses,* a successful republic—Rome, from the fall of the kings to the rise of the demagogues. Although the analysis is couched in imperative form, the source of this imperative is mundane and secular: the well-being of each citizen—not Freedom, or The Good, or Kingship, or Democracy.

If we think of Machiavelli as writing speculatively in leisured retirement, we miss his urgency. Venice, Milan, Florence, Naples, the Papacy were being emasculated, reduced to pawns, and impoverished by the imperialism of France and Spain. In Dante's *De Monarchia* the union of Italy is an ideal. Machiavelli knew that it would have to be achieved within a generation or the Italian cities would never recover. Union or decay—this is the concern that motivates *The Discourses, The Prince, The Art of War, The History of Florence, The Life of Castruccio.* The plays, *Mandragola* and *Clezia,* satirize a sick, parasitic society.

Where even favorable critics have found Machiavelli's attitude toward human nature "crude, unsympathetic, and cynical," I see the exasperation of desperation. When he says that, tempted, even enlightened politicians probably will behave like fools or rascals, he was hardly provided with contrary evidence by the words of Livy or the experience of a lifetime. So he assumes that historical action will take place at the lowest moral level necessary to ensure continuity. When the State or the individual actor falls below that level, it goes out of existence. When it rises above it, history gains an unexpected bonus. With a minimal faith in human motives, a tough-minded optimist may shape a politics of possible goods. The alternative is withdrawal into a tightly organized subculture where men live not by accident but for values, a garrison of ideals—Plato's *Republic.* Machiavelli is generally ironic, but his most overt irony is reserved for the subculture he saw all about him that made such claims—the Church and its territorial expression, the Papal state.

He believed that although men do not infallibly choose a demonstrable good, society might be organized to ensure that they do so more often than not and that where they do not, their choices of evil may cancel one another out. How? Machiavelli is seldom put forward as an advocate of freedom, least of all freedom of speech. Yet at the beginning of *The Discourses* he says, "Under the emperors from Nerva to Marcus Aurelius, everyone could hold and defend any opinion he pleased, and enjoyed the greatest freedom of action compatible with social order," and this resulted in maximum happiness and security and redounded to the glory of the rulers.

The opening paragraphs of *The Discourses* reveal Machiavelli's difference from previous writers on politics. He is a dynamist. "To have removed the cause of social conflict from Rome would have been to deprive her of her power of growth." He stresses that the Roman constitution both generated tension and discharged it, and "no faction, no private citizen ever attempted to call in the aid of a foreign power. Having the remedy at home, there was no need to look abroad for it."

For Machiavelli the end of politics is man, not the State; nor did he believe that "war is the health of the State," although in Renaissance Italy that was its permanent condition. For him the end of war is peace, even behind the lines while war is going on. Nor did he believe that ends justify means. He considers in detail what means must be employed to create what ends—a quite different concept. He knows that social good is only the good of multitudes of individual men and flourishes in a dynamic, never a static context. The ideal norm, the paradigm structured by logical law, has no relevance. Laws should be framed to enable the creative interaction of contradictories. Perhaps better than Marx he understood that the forces behind contradictions of policy are class struggles, but he believed that the good constitution should use rather than repress class conflict, that it can be the fuel that runs the motor of society or the wildfire that destroys it.

Like More's, the virtues of Machiavelli's prose survive all but the worst translations. He was a man of affairs writing for nonliterary purposes and out of years of experience in using language in matters of life and death. Italian as he wrote it was a medium of direct communication, an instrument to achieve concrete ends—a practice in which he had few followers until recent years. As a diversion he wrote the best Italian comedy—as black humor quite the equal of Jonson's *Volpone*—*Mandragola*, a work of a most unliterary toughness and maturity of mind.

There are many good, cheap editions of *The Prince*; the one in the Modern Library includes *The Discourses*. *Mandragola* is in Eric Bentley's *The Classic Theater*, Volume I.

Malory
Le Morte d'Arthur

There is a kind of ecology of the epic. The necessary social conditions that produce the heroic literature of any culture are of short duration. Although the period of epic creation has always been singularly brief, once written the books have proved the most timeless of all. Thomas Malory's *Le Morte d'Arthur* today is almost five hundred years old, yet it still seems to us—judged on our own terms—not only one of the greatest achievements of English prose style but one of the most absorbing narratives.

If heroic literature is disorder recollected in tranquillity, the tranquillity enjoyed by Sir Thomas Malory seems to have been forced. He wrote the book in prison in a troubled time, the last years of the Wars of the Roses—a time almost as bad as the days of the withdrawal of the Roman Imperium from Britain, of the Saxon invasion and the slow, bloody retreat of the Britons, marked by a succession of tragic last stands, across the island and into the fastnesses of Wales.

Homer's tranquillity, according to legend, was equally enforced—by his blindness—and he too looked back five hundred years from a time of troubles to a period of mass invasion. May be the epic arises out of primitive disorder recollected in a time of sophisticated disorder.

We think of the rhythms of Malory's narrative as being of the very texture of noble chivalric utterance. His style has spawned innumerable absurd imitations of knightly speech. We think of the attitudes of his characters as embodying the very essence of the Age of Chivalry. It's not true. When Malory wrote, in the chaotic beginnings of the English Renaissance, the Age of Chivalry was long over. Its ethic survived only as courtly ceremonial etiquette, in a very few years to be replaced by the deliberate teaching of the *courtoisie* of the Renaissance gentleman. And of course Malory did not write about a historical Age of Chivalry at all but about one laid in the barbaric times immediately after the collapse of Roman civilization.

The world of *Le Morte d'Arthur* is almost completely shaped by the demands men usually fulfill in dream. Into the narrative of the adventures of Arthur and his court and the originally distinct story of the Quest of the Holy Grail, Malory, working in his prison with his French books about him, poured all the shadow life of bygone Medieval Europe. Those who have found in the Grail story the cryptic revelation of a pagan mystery religion or the obscure gospel or the occult ritual of the Albigensian heretics or the ancestors of the Freemasons and Rosicrucians are not correct in fact, but their interpretations are true to the mood that haunts the narrative.

The mysteries that hide behind these tales of knight-errantry, dueling, warfare, adultery, ruined owl-haunted chapels lost in the forest, and wandering maidens lost in enchantment are the mysteries of the human personality itself. It is not just the Unconscious with its universal symbols and archetypes that sets the stage and garbs and manipulates the characters; it is also the essential doom and pathos of the human condition. We all fight a losing battle. Arthur, Tristram, Launcelot, Gawain—even in the beginning, in the days of feasts and tournaments—are losing. We can hear the pulse of their fate in the rhythms of Malory's prose, like the chant of a ritual march.

The story of Galahad and the Grail Quest may well have been included by Malory as a metaphor of the transcendence of the epic's war and adultery, hate and lust. It serves that function in any theoretical analysis of the book. But in the act of reading and appreciation it does not. It separates itself out as a different story. However carefully Malory strives to connect the main story of Launcelot, Arthur, and Gawain with their failure in the Grail Quest, and however symbolical the relation of Launcelot and his bastard son, Galahad, may be, the two plots are really incongruous. The story of the Grail stands best alone.

In spite of tedious detail and naïve style, the Medieval French Grail romances transmit more of the mystery that has attracted generations of cranky interpreters and spinners of learned fantasy, as well as the whole tribe of occultists, to the Grail legends. However, Malory's version is all most modern readers are likely to read, and it is sufficiently awe-inspiring. In *Le Morte d'Arthur* the major actors in the drama of King Arthur's court will find their transcendence not in supernatural vision, but in the common human illumination that comes with the acceptance of tragedy.

Epic in a sense *Le Morte d'Arthur* may be, but above all else it is the last summation of Medieval romance and the first of all modern romances. If the epic heroes of Greece or Iceland are brought down by the monstrous regimen of women, by the malevolence of wives and mistresses, the epic narrator reserves his sympathy for his falling heroes. His villainesses he treats with fear and contempt; his heroines are adoring lovers, dutiful daughters, and loyal housewives.

Tristram and Iseult, Launcelot and Guinevere are equally possessed, equally enraptured, and equally guilty. By no stretch of the imagination was the motive of the Trojans "All for love and the world well lost"; but it is the first and only commandment of all romantic lovers—whether the queens of an imaginary Britain or the emancipated misses of late-nineteenth-century Scandinavia. Launcelot and Guinevere will be reborn many thousands of times in the pages of pulp magazines or in Thomas Hardy's *Two on a Tower* or Lawrence's *Lady Chatterley's Lover.* Their morality will be the dangerous code by which five hundred years of naïve servant girls and oversophisticated and idle millionairesses will live out their destructive lives. Yet we weep for their follies. When they come together in the gloom-enshrouded last days, when all has been spent for love and all the world has been lost indeed, the pathos of their speech is almost more than can be borne, and Malory's prose rises to create one of the greatest passages of literature.

Possibly what gives Malory's narrative structure is its steady progress toward the final judgments of its leading actors upon themselves. Like Lear, at the end they understand their own folly, and so their tragic and romantic lives acquire at last their own significant form. It is ultimately an aesthetic question. D. H. Lawrence's novel is a truncated structure; it lacks a sequel which might have been called *Lady Chatterley's Second Husband.*

The best text of *Le Morte d'Arthur* is the complete and unexpurgated one edited by Eugène Vinaver, based on the manuscript discovered in 1934, which is more authentic than Caxton's edition—one of the first books printed in England. It is published in the Oxford Standard Authors.

Montaigne

Essays

Que scais-je? What can I know? So said the medal Montaigne had struck as the symbol of himself. He was the inventor of the empiric ego. He was the inventor of the word *essai* applied to a literary form. The title of his collection *Essais* did not mean then what we mean. In fact it still doesn't in French—but rather "assay" or the noun of our verb "to essay." For Montaigne existence was an experiment.

The subject was experience; the instrument was the self defined in terms of the experiment. *Expérience* in French also means experiment.

Since Montaigne there has always existed and sometimes flourished one type of characteristically Gallic personality that makes a principle of the equivocation experience-experiment and in literature presents all its products as essays in Montaigne's sense. Raymond Queneau's "Nicolas chien d'expérience"—"Nicholas, the Experimental Dog"—one of the most comic modern poems, not only depends on this equivocation but might well stand as a parable of the Montaignian spirit in France and of Montaigne himself. So Gertrude Stein on her deathbed: "What is the answer?" and after a few minutes, "What is the question?"—a very French death.

There is no answer, no *Quod erat demonstrandum* at the end of a logical operation, but an attitude at the end of a lifelong, inconclusive experiment:

> I have suffered rheumes, gowty defluxions, pantings of the heart, megreimes and other suchlike accidents, to grow old in me, and die their naturall death; all which have left me, when I halfe enured and framed my selfe to foster them. They are better conjured by curtesie, then by bragging or threats. *We must gently obey and endure the lawes of our condition.*

In the final essay, significantly titled "On Experience," epistemology becomes not the reduction of psychology to logic but the basic concern of a kind of psychosomatic medicine, a matter of mind-body "tone." This is the Stoic law of obedience to nature so reiterated by Marcus Aurelius—but the slight difference in mood results in a fundamental difference in meaning.

Because he was afflicted with one of the most painful, in his day incurable but seldom fatal, diseases, kidney stone, the latter part of Montaigne's life was a long medical experiment, and the *Essays* throughout are haunted by the spirit of Hippocrates and Aesculapius. Today such a description would mean that Montaigne would be a hypochondriac, fascinated by his own morbidity. He was quite the opposite. Paragraph after paragraph in "On Experience" are the first French prose poems, written in wry humor to the stone, in thankfulness that the touch of death, so sharp, yet so fleeting and easily sustained, has taught him wisdom. The rhythms of Montaigne at his most lyric survive in the prose poems of Léon-Paul Fargue, the greatest prose poet of the twentieth century and a very Montaigne reborn in the cafés of the Faubourg Saint-Germain between the wars.

Marcus Aurelius struggling on his throne and in his purple tent to achieve the unruffled acceptance of life was a moral hypochondriac tortured by scruple; the resulting virtue, a kind of anguished amiability. Montaigne, writing of the most gruesome subjects, radiates an active joy. His scruples are those of the chemical laboratory, never of the couch or confessional. The dilemmas that create the tensions in Marcus Aurelius are met by Montaigne with the simplest possible solutions of ethical activism, the commonplace relations of a country gentleman with common people, with Henri IV or the woodcutter on the estate.

Of course, it was the historical situation that made Montaigne possible. The viciousness of all parties in the Wars of Religion had canceled out all ideologies. Montaigne is a kind of passive Henri IV. "Paris is worth a Mass"—by this, the French have always known, their greatest king meant not the crown, but a great city "in which there are more than a hundred and twenty thousand persons who do not know their right hand from their left and also much cattle."

We think of Montaigne as the begetter of the English secular sensibility at its most acute, and we trace his influence on Shakespeare and Bacon and Locke; but we must not forget that his great popularity in seventeenth-century England also helped to form the peculiarly English tradition of sweet-tempered spirituality. Hooker, Browne, Jeremy Taylor, even William Law and the Quaker Barclay learned from Montaigne to respond with an amiability new to the Christian Church to the old questions that burned men alive—the older, and newer, answer that turns away wrath. When Barclay says when questioned about the sacrament of Holy Communion, "I do not think that I ever broke bread or drank wine without being conscious of Christ's body broken and his blood shed for me," he is returning an answer Montaignian in temper. It is this temper, forged in the most troubled period in European history before the twentieth century, that is Montaigne's specific contribution to civilization, and it is the essence of civilization itself. In its own day it seemed utterly without influence, yet it made its way. Weariness stopped the Wars of Religion, but skeptical magnanimity healed their wounds. Who can be sure that it is, as it seems to be, ultimately failing in our own time?

Retiring to his sun-gilded tower on his country estate, unguarded, his gates open to all factions, and surviving amidst the pillagings and burnings of religious war, it might seem that Montaigne the skeptic renounced all effectiveness and responsibility. The man who questioned the very existence of the Stoic ordered cosmos without and constantly questioned the evidences of a moral cosmos within to discover if they were delusions—such a man might be said to represent in history the final resignation of Plato's Guardian, the philosopher-aristocrat.

On the contrary, Montaigne was more like the indifferent Bodhisattva or Taoist sage devoted to government by inaction—*wu'wei*; the scholar-statesman who left high office for a thatched cabin amongst mountains and waterfalls and whose meditations were the most powerful force in Chinese civilization. "A wistful tolerance so rare in that age," said Walter Pater, "was the outstanding trait of Montaigne's character." So rare in any age.

One of the great classics of English prose is the John Florio translation read by Shakespeare, available in a Modern Library Giant and many other editions. The best accurate modern translation is by Donald M. Frame, Stanford University Press. There is an excellent selection translated by J. M. Cohen in Penguin Classics.

Cervantes
Don Quixote

Many people, not all of them Spanish, are on record as believing that *Don Quixote* is the greatest prose fiction ever produced in the Western world. Certainly it is one of the few books a genuinely international critic would dare to group with *The Dream of the Red Chamber* or the *Tale of Genji* or *The Mahabharata*. It epitomizes the spiritual world of European man at mid-career as *The Odyssey* and *The Iliad* do at his beginnings and as *The Brothers Karamazov* does in his decline. It is so vast, so ecumenical, that it serves only inadequately as the epic of Spain—a role better played by the more national *Poem of the Cid*. *Don Quixote* represents only a part of Spain, but a part that is far greater than the whole.

Much is made in schoolbooks of Cervantes' intention to satirize and destroy the popular romances of chivalry. What he did in fact was to transubstantiate them. *Don Quixote* is the Quest romance of the Middle Ages raised in power and elevated to an entirely new plane of being. The Mediterranean countries never took kindly to the legend of the Grail, a myth spiritually closer to northern paganism than to Christianity. For all its pseudosacramentalism, the Grail legend is also far more Protestant than Catholic. The doctrine of the body and blood of Christ shared by all the Grail romances has nothing to do whatever with the Catholic dogmas of the Blessed Sacrament. The Quest of northern romance was a Quest of the Utterly Other—true from the *Mabinogion* to Franz Kafka.

Don Quixote starts on his quest with his head full of phantasm. What he finds is his own identity, but he finds it in communion with others. He discovers what Don Quixote is really like by discovering that other people are like himself and that he is like them. The mystery that is slowly unveiled in the course of his complicated adventures is the mystery of the facts of life. His encounters are the opposite of the Gnostic trials and questions of the soul.

In the Egyptian *Book of the Dead*, the ghost of the dead man must answer the riddles of The Mystery with formulas of The Incomprehensible. In *Don Quixote* the living man advances, stage by stage, toward reality through the puzzles of fact. Sancho Panza and the facts themselves share the skepticism and ingenuity of Ulysses. These Sirens and Cyclopes are the subjective corruptions in Don Quixote's head. In both epics the same Mediterranean man of many devices and a thousand journeys seeks the same redemption. What is that redemption? It is merely life lived.

The comic delusions of *Don Quixote*—the sheep and the windmills—fall away as the narrative progresses, but they are far from mere foolishness. As we read we learn that they are not delusions at all, or if so, merely delusions of reference. They are misreadings of intent, misunderstandings of the powerful *mana*, the secret force, with which windmills and sheep and the commonplace life of the country inns and farmhouses of the Spanish highlands are surcharged. Sancho Panza always undercuts this mystery, as Don Quixote overshoots it. For Sancho the common is only commonplace; for Don Quixote it is continually revealed as being its own transcendence.

Possibly all great fictions deal with self-realization, with the integration of the personality. This is, in a special way, the subject of *Don Quixote*. Even more than in the wise reveries of Montaigne, Cervantes in this golden book gives us the purest expression of humanism—not just its message, but its special wisdom that can be found only in adventure in the manifold, inexhaustibly eventful ways of men.

Such humane wisdom is hardly the Spanish temper we associate with San Juan de la Cruz, El Greco, Unamuno, or García Lorca. Black Spain—the Spain of blood and sand, the dark night of the soul, the equation of love and death—is often attributed to the heritage of Islam. Nothing could be less true. The notion of life itself as a kind of *auto da fé* arose in specific reaction against the sensuous humanism of the Caliphate of Córdoba.

Fully as much as *The Song of Roland*, *The Poem of the Cid*, or the Byzantine romance of *Digenes Akrites*, *Don Quixote* is a Border Epic, an artistic resolution of the culture clash of Islam and Christianity. Cervantes spent most of his life in fighting or in captivity with the Muslims who had so recently been his countrymen. Here, if ever captivity took captivity captive, *Don Quixote* is just such a romance as might have been written in Córdoba in its splendor, in Fatimid Cairo, or in the Baghdad of Haroun al Raschid—for the immemorially civilized audience of *The Arabian Nights*.

There is a most important difference of tone. It is an evangelical difference. Don Quixote and Sancho Panza go their way through the windy barrens of La Mancha as Christ and his Apostles wandered through a very similar landscape, snapping the heads of wheat and chewing the green grain on a Sabbath morning, the Don learning, as they say, "the hard way" that the Sabbath was made for man, not man for the Sabbath. This is a moral that half of Spanish culture has consistently and bloodily refused to accept—most surely a vision of real splendors surpassing any imagined ones and, says Cervantes, accessible only to the nobility of a Fool, the most noble fool in literature.

How urbane it all is, although Don Quixote's adventures are set amongst peasants and castles, squalor and brocade. The intelligence operating on this material is the intelligence of a citizen of no mean city—that universal Mediterranean republic that goes back to Stone Age Jericho with its sand-swept streets, its efficient sewers, its adobe houses closed around their garden courts, its forums where men came to hear and talk about every new thing, its life of decency and order. Iberia answers the Visigoths.

Nothing shows better the all-encompassing humanity of *Don Quixote* than the immense literature to which it has given birth. There are as many interpretations of Cervantes' hero as there are of man himself. Theosophists, Christian Scientists, Baptists, Roman Catholics, and the apostles of Service-with-a-Smile—all find themselves in the Bible, and so too can they in *Don Quixote.* There are as many interpretations as interpreters, and most interpretations are very antagonistic indeed to my own.

It is this universality that makes the problem of the translator close to insoluble. The standard classic translations in English of Motteux and Shelton were done in the English Renaissance and to contemporary readers overflavor the narrative with grotesquerie. Modern translations, on the other hand, seem too commonplace. The best writing, grotesque or no, is still Motteux's, and with it I guess we must be content.

There are any number of editions of *Don Quixote* in paperback and hardcover. If the newcomer to the novel only had time and patience enough, he would be well advised to read and compare more than one translation, classic and modern.

There are, incidentally, a number of anthologies of the critical literature on *Don Quixote* that make fascinating reading, not least for their amazing disparity of interpretation. Were it not that my interpretation would then seem unduly flattering to myself, I would say that every man finds himself in *Don Quixote,* as Don Quixote finds himself in his adventures and as Sancho Panza is never lost.

Shakespeare
Macbeth

Of all the major plays of Shakespeare, *Macbeth* is the simplest, most concentrated, and shortest. It was one of the early revivals of a form that was to remain popular for tragedy throughout the reigns of James I and Charles I: the tragedy of blood, like Thomas Kyd's *Spanish Tragedy*, which had been so popular at the beginning of Elizabethan drama. Such plays were considered by their authors to be revivals of the Classic theater of ancient times. Only a few scholars knew anything about the great Greek dramatists. Classic tragedy meant to them Seneca's rhetorical melodramas.

Shakespeare's *Macbeth* is the greatest of the Senecan tragedies and re-established a type that would be continued by Webster's *The Duchess of Malfi* and *The White Devil* and the plays of Cyril Tourneur, John Ford, and James Shirley. *Macbeth* even revives in a new and greatly more efficient form the technical devices of the early euphuistic tragic rhetoric. As *Macbeth* is structurally one of the simplest of Shakespeare's plays, so too is it the least complex in the interaction of persons and motives and in the moral and psychological problem embodied in its central characters.

Although the scene moves around Scotland and briefly to the English court and the time lapse is at least several years, the illusory time and space never violate the dramatic unities attributed to Aristotle. *Macbeth* seems to take place in little more than its playing time, and always in the same desolated place and troubled night. The subsidiary characters are more functions of a dramatic construct than clearly defined personalities, quite unlike the minor roles of even Shakespeare's history plays. Macbeth and his lady are stripped to the moral and psychological essential bone. The play is about impenitence, habituation to sin, remorse, and despair. Shakespeare allows nothing to obscure his point.

The legendary Macbeth of Shakespeare's source, Holinshed's *Chronicle,* is a good king who, with his comrade Banquo, murders a ruler from whom the mandate of heaven had passed and then rules justly—a kind of primitive Robert Bruce. To a man of Shakespeare's time, murder was a historically sanctioned way to a throne, if it was successful. After he did penance for it, Robert Bruce seems never to have given the murder of his predecessor another thought.

Shakespeare altered history to personalize it and, as we would say, psychologize it. Who is tortured like Macbeth? Only the imaginative, who will to murder but never commit it and so cannot repent of it. With the murder of the king, Macbeth goes through a door; but it is the gratuitous murder of Banquo out of guilt and fear that is the more heinous sin and locks the door behind him. This door from one world to another is the pivotal device in the play. When it is properly staged and directed, we are always conscious of doubled universes of good and evil. Macbeth steps from moral order into a world of reversed values and sets loose pandemonium. Reality tips over and Hell is on top, present and visible.

Behind the stage set we sense the movement of a cast of hidden actors who are not just psychic projections but real beings of positive evil. They are of course made visible briefly in their emissaries, the witches. Time, person, place, and thing go continually out of focus. There is constant reiteration of hallucinatory themes: darkness, blood, reversal of values, the unreality of the present, the naked babe, ill-fitting clothes, unknown riders and horses, and toward the end, symbolic references to the Lord of Misrule, brought down at last by resurgent nature. "They have tied me to a stake. I cannot fly, but bear-like I must fight the course," an echo of a fertility ritual that goes back to the Paleolithic caves. "Why this is hell, nor am I out of it." The concreteness and concentration of imagery is astonishing. Here, in contrast to the luxuriance of *Hamlet,* not a line is wasted.

Macbeth is the evil ruler who breaks the shell of nature and lets in anti-nature. It is most important to realize that he does this deliberately. After the witches have hailed him king, he says, "If chance will have me King, why chance may crown me, without my stir." Had he not acted, the ambiguous prophecies of the witches could have fulfilled themselves in some other way. At the end he realizes he has been victimized by the terrible frivolity of Hell. "And be these juggling fiends no more believed, that palter with us in a double sense, that keep the word of promise to our ear, and break it to our hope!"

Macbeth gives himself into the possession of something far more irrational and malevolent than a hidden self—an Id, Animus, or Unconscious. What Shakespeare is saying is that in the deepest pit of being there exists a force not bestial, amoral, but consciously and deliberately immoral, rational indeed in the sense of logical, but frivolous in essence. In the world Macbeth enters, where minus has turned to plus, the equations of life become not nonsense, but anti-sense—hideous jokes. The concept of the devil as trickster is essential to the understanding not only of Shakespeare's fundamentally Medieval morality but of the comedy of Machiavelli, Marlowe, Stendhal, or Samuel Beckett. The tragedy of Macbeth is in the deepest sense a triumph of the absurd.

Lady Macbeth has been called noble, even sublime. The nineteenth-century critics who looked on Shakespeare's plays as a collection of snippets of biography have made much of her. What was she like in girlhood? How many children did she have? Did she really faint when the murdered king was discovered? She functions in the play primarily as a defining factor in the equation that is the moral character and catastrophe of Macbeth. She is the embodiment of greed and vulgar matter-of-factness. She always interprets the omens of the Other-world in commonplace terms. The knocking at Hell Gate—it is "at the south entry"; Macbeth's horrors—"'Tis the eye of childhood that fears a painted devil." Even walking in her sleep, she is remarkably literal and never indulges in remote symbolism. She is a pagan, and *laïque* at that, and kills herself for the same reasons as a cornered Roman usurper.

Macbeth is damned, and that is not a *laïque* condition. His fear is metaphysical. There is no contrition in Lady Macbeth, because she does not believe in penitence. Macbeth believes, and defies the consequences. Yet to the last moment he equivocates with the consequences. Shakespeare, capitalizing on the popularity of the word, which had recently been used by a defendant in the Gunpowder Plot trial, equivocates with the very word "equivocation" throughout the play.

But it is not irony that unites and underscores the equivocations of Macbeth but iron, the deadly weapon itself. So great is the intensity of Shakespeare's dramatic language that the audience becomes hallucinated and, if truly enrapt by the performers, sees messages and equivocations everywhere, until the play becomes an apocalypse of temptation and fall. "Pity, like a naked newborn babe, striding the blast, or heaven's cherubin, hors'd upon the sightless couriers of the air." There is plenty of Aristotle's pity and terror, but not for Macbeth. If at the end of a perfect Classic tragedy we must feel pity for the hero, *Macbeth* is hardly a tragedy, for the hero is damned, and we cannot pity one who Shakespeare believed had exhausted infinite pity. Plenty of modern critics, for this very reason, have called the play disagreeable; and disagreeable it is to those who believe in an easy metaphysical optimism.

Shakespeare
The Tempest

"Those who wonder shall reign and those who reign shall wonder." This is one of the few profound statements attributed to Jesus in the Gnostic Apocryphal Gospels. It conceals the secret of Shakespeare's *The Tempest*. The occultists who have found in *The Tempest* the ritual of a mystery religion or the dramatized rites of an esoteric Masonic order are not wrong. In all dramatic literature the work that most resembles it is *The Magic Flute*, which is in fact a thinly disguised dramatic ritual of occult Freemasonry. This does not mean that Shakespeare was an occultist or that Bacon and a committee of hidden masters wrote the play.

Anthropological, mythic, ritual interpreters of Shakespeare have proved most illuminating to our generation so concerned with the symbolic adumbrations of Jungian or Freudian psychoanalysis in literature. But though the other plays may be made more meaningful by mythic interpretation, *The Tempest* is itself a myth, a source of power. In *Macbeth* a malevolent Underworld lurks behind substance, seeking form. In *The Tempest* the Otherworld seems immanent and benign, as amoral as Paradise beyond the fiery sword and the tree of good and evil. The innocence of nature judges good and evil as the wills of men are brought to bear upon it. In the end, nature is indifferent. But we have been made to realize that this, our own, world is actually the Otherworld.

Man plays out a simulacrum of history in the realm of the amoral angels, who exercised free will once only and then were eternally quiet. Human action is projected against impassive natural processes, is magnified and judged and reduced again to the small and inconsequential. *The Tempest* is a play of judgment, the judging of history and its partisans by the end of history. Again from the same Apocryphal Gospel: "Those who are near to me are near to the fire; those who are far from me are far from the judgment." It is as if the island were a test tube in which men slowly became animal, vegetable, mineral and emerged again into the world men, but altered in secret substance.

The Tempest takes place in a storm of water, in a hidden place. Men go under the storm and are born again as in a Gnostic baptism. The storm is a revenge for evil raised by the personification of energy—Ariel—under compulsion. The music by which the transformation is wrought is a free-will donation of the same spirit.

The mysticism of *The Tempest* is hard for us to understand because it is the forgotten mysticism of the Age of Reason, the taming of magic to the rule of reason. Harvey, Galileo, Copernicus do not seem occult to us, but so they did to their contemporaries, hierophants of the mysteries of Natural Law, revealers of the secrets of a New Order of the Ages. After all, the movement eventually came to be called the Age of Enlightenment.

Macbeth is full of equivocations, but *The Tempest* is entirely composed of elements that are themselves equivocal. Ambivalent, its imagery has been felt and interpreted in opposing ways by critics of different temperament, just as the interests of the characters lead them to evaluate the same circumstances as maleficent or benign.

To me the play has always seemed bathed in the jeweled mist of the warm, surf-rocked Bermoothes, the countryside of Stratford with the long water meadow rimed and glowing in moonlit dew or frost, where every beast, and plant, and man has become unearthly. Others have felt the setting to be exactly the opposite: a world of dry trouble and commotion, the still-vexed Bermoothes.

For the bad characters the island is far from being Fairyland. It is a mad corral troubled by goblins and invisible tormentors. For Miranda and Ferdinand it is Paradise, a garden beyond time. For Miranda even history as it suddenly appears in the persons of covetous and scheming rascals is a brave new world. The setting is one of perfect exile, real alienation. All the characters except Prospero are cut loose from life with no likelihood of ever returning. This is human morality as it judges itself in the abstraction of the cloister.

Like *The Magic Flute, The Tempest* is a rite—it embodies exactly the same range and quality of symbolic psychic patterns and behavior as do the mystery rites of religion. But it is not an exposition of somebody else's; it is its own mystery religion, self-contained within its dramatic form. It is this self-sufficiency that gives it its enormous power. As Mark Van Doren once said, "Any set of symbols moved close to this play lights up as in an electric field."

It should not be forgotten that *The Tempest* was originally a celebration of a major rite of passage. Like A *Midsummer Night's Dream*, it was almost certainly written for a particular court wedding. There is a total difference in the interpretation of the sacrament of matrimony in the two plays. The new definition of the kind of supernatural grace conferred is the product of wisdom gained by a life lived and reflected in the great bitter tragedies.

The circumstances of the production explain the Masque and the hints of an anti-Masque. The Masque has puzzled most critics and is often omitted. Many think it was written by someone else. Its stilted language is comic, a parody of Gonsalez' utopia and a satire on the plot, which is itself a parody of history. It ends with a glorious passage shattered by the eruption of misused nature, the discovery of the plot of the clowns and Caliban.

History does not only repeat itself in the play, "the first time as tragedy, the second time as farce," but becomes a series of multiple mirrors of ever-receding images of the initial usurpation, each more absurd than the last—Prospero by his brother, Ariel by Sycorax, and the attempts by Sebastian and the clowns, a series of overturns culminating in the absurdity of a *coup d'état* amongst castaways on a nightmare island, the seizure of power in a dream. As in the mystery rituals, men act out their good and evil but without effect, in psychodramas.

In the first shipwreck scene, reality becomes a dream and all human status is overturned. So converted, the characters enter an unreality more real than fact and play out their charades of history in the field of the purely natural order, of which Ariel and Caliban are the polarities. In the end the angels are left in possession and the humans depart, back to history. Caliban is cured forever by his brief contact with the farce of history—cured of the humanity given him by Prospero's education. Miranda and Ferdinand transcend history. Their drama takes place among the timeless unities of love, and at their chess game in the inner stage they talk of the unreality of the world.

The final resolution of all the plots drives home the point. Neither history nor nature is moral or even capable of positive value. The Renaissance dream of the moral control of nature cannot be realized. Matter rebels and energy escapes. The dreams of utopia are interrupted by clowns who have used matter as an engine of destruction; and when they are overcome, only love and the forgiveness of evil rise above the passing farce of the lives of men.

Webster
The Duchess of Malfi

The drama of Shakespeare is distinguished, even in the plays in which he is still learning his craft, by an extraordinary coherence of all the artistic processes—of creation, of structure of the work itself, of response in audience or reader. Subjective-objective, classical-

romantic, expressionistic-architectural, realism-symbolism: such antitheses are subsumed in a synthesis of completely integrated communication. It is this massive integrity that has led innumerable
critics to postulate a man Shakespeare far better organized than
most humans, let alone most writers or people of the theater. Even
the plays that seem to reflect a period of personal tragedy and
disillusion, like *Hamlet* or *Troilus and Cressida*, show few signs of
any fragmentation of personality in their author—whatever may be
the case with their heroes and heroines.

Few contemporary artists in any medium could be found to show
forth better the schism in the most fundamental nature, the very
sources, of creativity that has become so characteristic of all the arts
since the early years of the nineteenth century than Ben Jonson and
John Webster, writing three centuries ago. The difference is so great
that we seem to be dealing with two distinct operations of the mind.

The plays of Jonson are classic in structure and objective in their
delineation of motives and behavior, but also, they are conceived of
as taking place "out there." The aesthetic process, from creator to
spectator, occurs in material that is independent of either of them
once it has been formed: the imitation of human action on the
stage, a simulacrum of the real world which is effective to the degree
to which it can take the place of that world for two hours and a half.

Webster is not in the least interested in what happens "out there."
He uses poetry, drama, acting, stage effects solely to work inside the
spectator. The material of Webster is the collective nervous system
of his audience. This is beyond romanticism and its subjectivity.
Nothing quite like it would appear until, three hundred years later,
following Poe, Mallarmé, who would make the method explicit. Yet
how explicit? We have no name for it, and that in a field ever fertile
with jargon—criticism and aesthetics. And few critics watching *The
Duchess of Malfi* or reading "L'Après-midi d'un Faune" are at all
aware of what is happening to them.

The Duchess of Malfi is a fashionable play, a revival of the
tragedy of blood so popular at the beginning of Elizabethan drama.
So are *Macbeth* and *Hamlet*. Webster is a conscious, deliberate
disciple of Shakespeare. So are Beaumont and Fletcher. The *Duchess* is one of the first tragedies that can be called decadent, both in its
verse structure and in its somewhat phosphorescent dramaturgy—

the greatest of a class that includes Tourneur, Ford, and Shirley and would be imitated, carefully but with only limited success, by Shelley in *The Cenci*.

Yet it really isn't like any of these plays. In the very first scene of the *Duchess*, Webster starts out, wasting no time, to do something quite different from Shakespeare in *Macbeth* or Shelley in *The Cenci*. Shakespeare is building a character, setting a scene, creating a psychological environment, establishing certain leitmotivs, image clusters that will recur throughout the play and define the character and the tragedy of Macbeth himself—out there—in a concrete work of art, as tangible as a piece of sculpture. Shakespeare speaks to the audience through the integral object—the little world of the play. Shelley does that too, but he is more interested in himself, in expressing himself, perhaps in scaring himself a little. We call it romantic subjectivism.

In the opening scene of the *Duchess*, Antonio and Delio carry on a dialogue that seems objective enough. They describe as they appear all the important characters and their interrelations and hint at the potentialities for tragedy these relationships embody. But in what an extraordinary fashion! Webster uses a standard device, the opening dialogue, "Hello, old friend, what's been going on while I've been gone?" to string together a series of carefully concealed assaults on the nerves of his audience. "If it chance some cursed example poison it near the head, death and diseases through the whole land spread." "I do haunt you still." "Blackbirds fatten best in hard weather, why not I in these dog days?" "They are like plum trees that grow crooked over standing pools. They are rich and over laden with fruit but none but crows, pies and caterpillars feed on them." "Places in court are like beds in hospital, where this man's head lies at that man's foot, and so lower and lower." "The spring in his face is but the engendering of toads." "The law to him is like a foul black cobweb to a spider." Even compliments assume the form, "So sweet a look would raise one to a galliard that lay in a dead palsy."

"These rogues have cut his throat in a dream." "Their livers are more spotted than Laban's sheep." "There is a kind of honey dew that's deadly, 't will poison your fame." "Witches ere they arrive at twenty years and give the devil suck." "A visor and a mask are whispering rooms." "As warily as those that trade in poison keep poison from their children." "Girt with the wild noise of prattling visitants which makes it lunatic past all cure."

Corruption—the idea echoes with the word throughout the first act in what purports to be the ordinary conversation of a court. It is a court where the head sickens and the members rot, but over and above the careful setting of a situation, Webster is striving to affect the audience directly. This play is going to take place inside the heads—in each individual brain—of the audience.

Is this melodrama? The play is certainly a melodrama by conventional definition, but this is more like hypnotism. As the play goes on, horror seeps into the most commonplace statements until language loses its informative role and becomes a kind of argot whose aim always is not communication between the characters, but manipulation of the minds of the audience. Meanwhile the action goes on; bodies move in space with uncanny haste and glow with foxfire. The stage is lit with decay.

As an actor would say, every part is terrific. Lines like the cardinal's "When I look into the fishponds in my garden, methinks I see a thing armed with a rake, that seems to strike at me" can provide a lifetime's career on the stage with its most satisfying moment. And they are all lines that demand action.

Bosola's final scene with the Duchess is unparalleled even in Shakespeare. Their words are a scenario for an intensely inhibited ballet—twisting, wiry motion, subtly braided together in agony. Yet the intention is not to kill the Duchess in a particularly horrible manner and to further the moral catastrophe of tragedy—it is to horrify the spectator. This is melodrama: overtly on the stage, but— far more violently—an interior melodrama.

Melodrama is supposed to be bad art. Is *The Duchess of Malfi* great art? It certainly is great melodrama, probably the greatest ever written; and in addition, and more importantly, it adds an entirely new dimension to drama, or even to art as a whole. If great art makes us confront the profoundest meanings of life, the *Duchess* is hardly art at all, because it literally doesn't mean much. It has never made a member of its audience, or a reader, a better man or a wiser one. Has it made him a more sensitive one? A more responsive feeling organism? I doubt it.

When we leave the play, our nerves have been rubbed raw and tortured. Does this make them more acute receptors? It may just as well dull our sensitivity as sharpen it. We are left nervously exhausted by a novel like *Les Liaisons Dangereuses*, but we are also left prostrate by a long look into the abysms of deliberate evil, and our valuations of human conduct and our responses to those valuations have been subtly reorganized. The good and evil that struggle in *The Duchess of Malfi*, once the play is over, vanish. The Duchess changes her costume and is just an actress, impatient to be gone to a late supper.

In recent years, the aestheticians and critics who try to establish a moral ground of justification for the arts have shifted their position to a kind of physiological aesthetic. "The arts work upon us through abstract, purely artistic qualities. They do not teach or even communicate. The experience of the subtle architectonics of a great work of art makes us more refined, more efficient organisms, and the cumulative effects of such experiences through life makes us better men."

There is not an iota of empirical evidence for this notion. On the contrary, society has always been suspicious of "aesthetes" as secret rascals given to shocking depravities. This is not true either; Oscar Wilde's Dorian Gray and the heroes of Huysmans' novels are excessively rare types.

Although it follows the conventions of tragedy and deals with great psychological penetration with the slow corruption of consciously chosen evil, *The Duchess of Malfi* is not a nerve tonic or a moral stimulant. It is simply very great entertainment and its own excuse for being.

Ben Jonson
Volpone

Poets and playwrights are seldom intellectuals in the English-speaking world, at least in the sense of being men of general ideas—a vocation that in America has always been left to the professors, as it was in England to the clergy. Only Shaw in modern times is an exception, and his general ideas were both limited in range and eccentric.

Ben Jonson was very much part of the European intellectual community of his time, as was Milton shortly after him. We forget that the great movement of re-evaluation of all values that made both the Renaissance and the Reformation was led by what today we would call literary critics. Whether the reference is to Erasmus or Ficino or Scaliger, whether to the Bible or Plato or Horace or Aristotle, the questions "What is the authentic text?" and "What does it really mean?"—followed by the answers and translation into the vernacular—these were the intellectual germinators of revolution, as, in our time, economics is, or physics, or psychology—Marx, Einstein, or Freud. Only if we keep this in mind can we appreciate Jonson as a source of power to his colleagues.

He was not just a roisterer or prince of poets in the Mermaid and the other bohemian taverns of his day. He was a systematic literary critic, a grammarian, an aesthetician devoted to the re-establishment of poetry and drama as formally controlled, socially normative arts—this is what revival of classicism meant. *Volpone* is purposive in a way in which no Shakespearean comedies are before A *Winter's Tale* and *Twelfth Night,* and it is far more deliberately purposive than any of Shakespeare's tragedies, except possibly *Julius Caesar* and *Coriolanus.* Only Machiavelli's *Mandragola* can be compared with *Volpone* as equal to equal. Machiavelli was a revolutionary intellectual, a man of wider general experience than all but a few writers in history. Jonson was no Machiavelli; he never had his hands on the levers of power; but he seems to have had a much greater range of experience than other Elizabethan dramatists. He knew all kinds and conditions of men and evidently sought deliberately to live as full a life as he could.

Most writers about Jonson begin by apologizing for him. He was scholarly in a way in which no literary scholars are today. Literary scholarship mattered at the beginning of the seventeenth century; it was harder work. Jonson knew much more about erudite matters than scholars know today. And then, of course, he was not an academician but a creative artist, a bohemian intellectual, and a man who was largely self-educated. These are all great virtues, but not to modern critics. Besides, he was patently a man of the world—his plays are intensely worldly, in a positive sense. They baffle the cloistered literary mind and antagonize the schoolmaster. A play by Jonson is often presented as "hard to read" or as "seldom-performed closet drama." Nothing could be less true.

Volpone, The Alchemist, and *Bartholomew Fair* are among the most theatrical and most entertaining plays ever written. They are immense fun to see, to act in, to design for. They are as far removed from closet drama as can be, for above all other English playwrights, Jonson, in his three great comedies, uses words as springs of action; there is business lurking in every line—funny business.

One thing they are not is topical satire. They deal, like the plays of Plautus, Terence, and Menander, with generalized follies and vices, with enduring sin rather than the passing crimes of politics and history. They could take place anywhere. The topical jokes and allusions that abound are not only inessential; today they go unnoticed unless explained in a footnote. Shaw wrote lengthy prefaces as notes to his plays. In a hundred years they will have to have even lengthier notes, and even then will be difficult to grasp emotionally. In a hundred years, Jonson's plays will still be emotionally comprehensible with no notes at all.

Taste in drama has changed; once again the playwright is the scourge of folly—not of capitalism, industrialism, or the double standard. Artaud, Genet, Ionesco, and Beckett are moral rather than political or "social" playwrights. We have come to realize that greed and covetousness, power-hunger and hypocrisy are more important than the temporary social arrangements that facilitate them. So Jonson has been revived with great success all over the world, on both sides of the tattered Iron Curtain. *Volpone*, a situation comedy, based on a purely Roman situation as unreal to a seventeenth- as to a twentieth-century audience, is nevertheless completely germane to the *human* situation—in New York or San Francisco or Berlin or Moscow or Tokyo.

Luxury, greed, avarice, covetousness, fraud—all the evils of which money is the root—are analyzed and parsed out, but in action, in a kind of savage hilarity. Is this the business ethic? Critics have said the play was a sociological criticism of the new mercantile bourgeoisie. If this were all, it would never go on the modern stage. The lust for gold is not a peculiarity of a class or an epoch.

Although every moment of *Volpone* is funny, the cumulative effect is grim indeed—so grim that it ceases to be a comedy, even a black comedy, and becomes a tragedy of human folly.

It generates a growing horror, and rightly so, for it is a feast of death—a double death, for the feast is fraudulent. The characters are named after creatures that feed on carrion; thus Jonson drives home Dante's point—the worship of money is life-denying, a love of corpses, and a feeding on filth. What saves the play from melodrama is Jonson's remorseless logic. It is put together like a fine precision instrument. Every speech, every action counts. All move together like the gears of a watch. We don't see the wheels go round unless we are deliberately focusing on them, but Jonson's dramatic wheels grind like the mills of the gods.

It is this perfection of structure and function that ennobles the play. The purity of form redeems the evil—not in the plot, but in us. And this, says Jonson, is the only way we cope with analogous experiences in life. Rational control transcends the chaos of the world.

Izaak Walton
The Compleat Angler

"Sweetness and light" may be a catch phrase used in our time only sarcastically, but it applies with the greatest accuracy to Izaak Walton's *The Compleat Angler*. Aestheticians have quarreled for years over the question "Can a thoroughly bad man write thoroughly good books?" The reason, of course, is that most writers are not very nice and the number who owe their artistic pre-eminence to their personal morality is very small indeed. Izaak Walton above all other writers in English owes his enormous popularity to his virtues as a man, and these virtues are what condition his style and give his work its fundamental meaning.

Millions have read Walton with joy who have never caught a fish since childhood, if at all. Indeed, he is not a terribly good guide to the art of fishing, and in America at least, most of the kinds of fish he talks about are left to small boys. The second half of *The Compleat Angler* was added in late editions and written by Charles Cotton as a guide to trout fishing in rough water. Those who want to know how to catch fish can learn most from Cotton's additions. In fact, many people on first acquaintance skim through the main body of the book in considerable puzzlement and much prefer the later part. Then, as they keep the book about, and idle through it in the winter months, Izaak Walton overtakes them and captivates them for life.

We do not read *The Compleat Angler* for the fish, or for instruction in how to catch them. There are hundreds of more efficient books for such purposes, whether manuals or ichthyologies. We read Izaak Walton for a special quality of soul. Other books, mostly religious or mystical treatises, may describe such a quality and may even provide the reader with onerous instructions on how to obtain it. Walton simply embodies it unaware, and his example is possibly the most convincing argument that this is the only way it can be embodied.

It would be easy to claim that Izaak Walton is the most Chinese of all Western writers—he and his companions wandering by flowing waters and reciting poems to each other. We know nothing of Lao Tse, or even if he existed. The book that goes by his name is certainly a compilation made over a long period of time; but it has a recurrent symbolism which, although extremely simple, is a revelation of a definite personality. Whoever wrote the little psalms of the *Tao Te Ching* believed that the long calm regard of moving water was one of the highest forms of prayer.

Westerners miss the point of the later Taoist saint who fished with a straight pin and a single filament of silk. It's not that he did not catch fish, but that he caught them with ease, because he was so perfectly attuned to the rhythms of water and of life. We read Izaak Walton for his tone, for his perfect attunement to the quiet streams and flowered meadows and bosky hills of the Thames valley long ago.

Ben Jonson, Shakespeare, in fact all the writers of Elizabethan and Jacobean comedy except Thomas Dekker, portray life in the English countryside as robust and comic enough but also as harsh, brutal, and unclean, for so they saw it. Not Walton. His landscapes are enameled like the meadows about the feet of Medieval saints. His innkeepers are both gentle and jovial. His barmaids are as wholesome as the ale they serve.

What a luminous world it is—delicious fish, twenty inches long, caught in clear, sweet streams that now are gone or flow underground, laden with filth. England was unspoiled and unpolluted then, but the landscape of *The Compleat Angler* is so clean and bright because it is bathed in a light that comes from a lucid heart.

So he saw life, and he would have pictured it thus whatever he had written about. Had his subject been the most squalid modern slums of London and his judgments of the life there an arraignment and denunciation of their evils, his conclusion surely would have been "There springs the dearest freshness deep down things."

Many sports are actually forms of contemplative activity. Fishing in quiet waters is especially so. Countless men who would burst out laughing if presented with a popular vulgarization of Zen Buddhism, and who would certainly find it utterly incomprehensible, practice the contemplative life by flowing water, rod in hand, at least for a few days each year. As the great mystics have said, they too know it is the illumination of these few days that gives meaning to the rest of their lives.

The Compleat Angler has often been compared to the *Idylls* of Theocritus. The ancient Greek may have written great poetry, but his pastorals are not meant to convince. Nobody has ever supposed that Sicilian shepherds and shepherdesses talked like that, however golden the age in which they lived. The *Idylls* are written literature; the diction is a courtly literary convention. *The Compleat Angler* is a country idyll made of talk. The rhythms of speech and turns of thought, however quaint to us three hundred and more years away, are completely convincing. We believe that this is the way gentlemen talked on an outing in those days—learned, peaceable gentlemen in a time of troubles, whose speech had been formed by the gentler passages of the *Book of Common Prayer*: "Hear what comfortable words . . ."

It has been said of Izaak Walton that he was scarcely a literary man and that his style is a perfect example of complete naïveté. Maybe, although there is manuscript evidence to the contrary. But it is this quality that the greatest literary men have sought in pain and conflict and countless revisions in sleepless nights. Like the transparent narratives of those Chinese novels which do not seem to be written at all, Izaak Walton's style is completely lucid. Everything is there that should be there. Nothing is obscure or troubled. Once we have accepted the archaic diction, nothing stands between us and the subject—except the personality of Izaak Walton, and that is as transparent as crystal, with an innate clarity achieved without effort. This may be called naïveté, but a better word is innocence.

It may sound outrageous to say that Izaak Walton wrote one of the Great Books—and that about catching fish—because he was a saint, because of an abiding sweetness of temper, but so it is. It is important to realize that he is not alone in English literature. He is in fact an unusual embodiment of a quietly powerful tradition, that of the contemplative layman—Saint Thomas More, Nicholas Ferrer, William Law, Gilbert White. After the eighteenth century, this type is more commonly found in the sciences than in religion. And like Gilbert White's *The Natural History of Selbourne, The Compleat Angler* is in a sense a scientific work, an outstanding example of the piety of science.

Kant, following Ptolemy, contemplated the starry heavens above and the moral law within. Izaak Walton contemplated fish and flowing water, the streams and banks of the beautiful landscape that is now deep in the slums of greater London. He was more the contemplative because he was the more unaware and the more modest in his methods.

John Bunyan
The Pilgrim's Progress

The Pilgrim's Progress was one of the precious possessions of my middle childhood. When but in skirts, I wrote an imitation of it. Perhaps even that early it was confused in my mind with the Oz books, the I. W. W. Manifesto, the life of a family friend named Debs, and H. G. Wells's *Research Magnificent*. As for so many millions before me, it was a character-building book. I read it to my daughters when they each attained the age of eight or nine—and had not opened it since.

When I picked up my gold-stamped, gold-edged, embossed, Victorian copy with the gracious illustrations by Thomas Dalziel, I was amazed—as the Pilgrim, Christian, was so often by the wonders he encountered—at the limpid beauty of Bunyan's style. Few things in the language compare with its modestly exerted power. In the nineteenth century, this quality passes from the art of literature to the literature of science and reaches its culmination in the crystal-line, utterly unself-conscious prose of the physicist Clerk Maxwell. It is the reflection of greatness of soul.

Of a book like Apuleius' *The Golden Ass* we debate, "Is this story of a life of adventure an allegory?" Bunyan wrote an allegory which is a true story of the adventures of life. His characters, personifica-tions of virtues and vice, are living beings because he himself never thought of himself as living anywhere else but in a vast moral allegory. All men to him were named names like PraiseGod Bare-bones and Madefree Bytruth Odhner—and so in fact they are.

Life may not be as simple as Ben Jonson's Theater of Humours with characters like the Sanguine Man, the Choleric Man, the Melancholic Man, and so on. Life is infinitely more complex. Nonetheless, we live and move and have our being in an ever-shifting dynamic field of moral forces. We are all Christian stagger-ing under the burden of our own consequences; freed, if we are freed, by sacrifice; marching steadfastly through the Valley of the Shadow of Death, the Dark Night of the Soul, if we do get through it, looking back upon life from the Delectable Mountain, which overlooks, in the other direction, the river in which all consequence is washed away.

Bunyan had an extraordinary gift, like second sight, to see ab-stractions as beings moving. After all, that is what abstractions were in the first place. He saw the situations of the soul as landscapes, palaces, dungeons, and cities, all perfectly concrete, rising about him on his own path through life. The descriptive passages in *The Pilgrim's Progress* have often been referred to the English country-side or even to the environs of his native Bedfordshire. Read with care, they turn out to be almost without exception Biblical. Like so many entranced soldiers of Cromwell, Bunyan did not live in England's green and pleasant land but marched a lifetime through the deserts of Sinai, and the Holy Land of Israel, to Jerusalem.

Bunyan's vision of life was seen from the diametrically opposite point of view from William Blake's outlook, but it was the same vision and the same life. It is the same too as Saint Augustine's. Bunyan was, as it were, the Bishop of Hippo reincarnated in an English village, shorn of cope and miter, pomp and circumstance, and the splendors of the rhetoric of the Latin decadence. I was moved to reread some of Augustine: not *The City of God* and *The Confessions* but the sermons on the Psalms, the commentary on Job and the controversies with the men in his day who believed that grace could be merited and man could be saved by good works. It is difficult to believe that Bunyan did not write *The Pilgrim's Progress* with the works of Augustine at his elbow. Of course he had scarcely so much as heard of him.

Here lies the fault of Bunyan's great book. All these sharply realized characters whom Christian meets in the way of life are devoid of any outgoing ethical activism and of the love of man that finds expression in dedication to simple good. Amongst hundreds of personifications, more real in seeming than most persons of realistic fiction, no girl named Charity plays a significant role. Bunyan, like Augustine, says only few out of many, even of those who are called, are saved, and never by the merit of acts of love.

This is certainly one view of life. Shorn of theology and supernatural sanction, it is still arguable, but it is remote indeed to our age, which, if it believes in salvation of any sort, believes that it comes through the assumption of unlimited liability, person for person. When Christian has won through, he spends his time in the land of spiritual peace—The Delectable Mountains, the Enchanted Ground, the Country of Beulah—arguing theology with his companion Hopeful; an indication of what Bunyan thought was the best way to spend your time when salvation was in sight. This unfortunate pre-climax spoils the book for many modern people. It seems a cold, hard view of life, which has produced many great generals and despots but few saints. It makes so little allowance for the frailty of humankind that it is itself more frail than the philosophy of the average man.

The final passages—the passing of the River of Death, the entrance into the Celestial City—have a simple grandeur, a kind of proletarian glory of a sort not to be found elsewhere. Then too, the progress of Christian is only one story. The second book is concerned with the spiritual journey of the wife and children he had deserted for Heaven. It lacks the dramatic immediacy and impetuous delivery of Christian's story; it is not as great a work of art; but it is altogether more gentle and humane and somewhat more wise.

Christian's constant companion is Mercy, the one attribute of

God in the theology of Saint Augustine that is not unlimited. So too in Bunyan's book she accompanies, observes, and weeps, but she seldom acts, and only once decisively—when she rejects Brisk's offer of marriage. Charity plays no effective role in the story as a personification, but charity is an effective virtue in the soul of Christiana. As she goes through the Valley of the Shadow of Death accompanied by her children and a strong protector, Mercy, she says, "Poor Christian, he went this way alone and at night." And she says it of a husband who had deserted her at the call of Scripture. Christian was unhappy in the Valley of Humiliation. For Christiana it was beautiful with lilies.

For a world that mostly believes none of the doctrines on which Christian staked his soul, his little book is still a vision of life. It isn't all of life, but it is a great deal of it, and they are lucky who can see even that much. For all of its exteriority it is the plot of the interior life—a dramatic incarnation, into what seems like a bustling realism, of the hidden story of the way of perfection, the dark night of the soul, the cloud of unknowing of the great mystics.

Tsao Hsueh Chin
The Dream of the Red Chamber

The Chinese *The Dream of the Red Chamber* may well be as great a book as the Japanese *The Tale of Genji*. Its virtues are not as obvious. In fact, they are not obvious at all. They are the virtues that distinguish Chinese civilization from Japanese—the virtues of a vaster humanity. Both novels have a lucidity and immediacy of narrative seldom encounted in Western fiction of a serious character, but amongst us confined to cowboys, detectives, and the funny papers. Alex Comfort once compared Chinese fiction to Pepys's *Diary*, "a perfectly translucent medium through which we see the characters in all their moral nudity." The contemporary author most like a Chinese novelist is Georges Simenon. You are too busy with the story to notice psychological insight or dramatic command until a week after you have finished the book.

The plot is the familiar, recurrent one of so much great fiction, as it is a specialty of both Chinese fiction and philosophy of history— "When women rule, the house decays"—but also its contrary, a celebration of the matriarchy that underlies and sustains Chinese society. Like all great fiction, it is also the story of the immensely difficult achievement of personal integrity. The narrative works toward a transcendental meaning of life through that life itself, which so conspicuously hides all such meaning. The characters are all "fallen beings." The hero is an unprepossessing, idle scholar-gentleman, timid, oversexed, unstable. The two young heroines are both hysterics, the villainess a stock ruthless sister-in-law. The action is confined almost entirely to the women's quarters and consists mostly of vapors, tantrums, fugues, and quarrels. Time goes by. As in life, the characters run down, coarsen, sicken, and die. At the end everybody is worn out.

Yet Pao Yu's meaningless life unconsciously evolves slowly toward illumination. He is a Taoist saint who doesn't know he is one and doesn't want to be one. Like Prince Genji, he is indifferent to and ignorant of his cosmic role. He struggles, unaware, against an embodied principle of hate. When salvation comes, it is scarcely distinguishable from its opposite. Behind commonplace life and death lurks another world which intrudes at all crucial moments, a mirror-image more real than this life, where destiny is achieved and manifest; like the dream time of the Australian aborigines where everybody is his own ancestor that lies dormant below the dust of the desert and is awakened by penances of blood and feathers.

Genji is a mystical Buddhist work. *The Dream of the Red Chamber* is Taoist; its principle of salvation is inaction—*wu'wei*: the strength of the still keystone in the arch; the water wandering amongst mountains, seeking its own level, eventually wearing away the highest peaks. The talisman of Pao Yu's integrity is the uncut stone of precious jade with which he is born, which he loses and finds again at the brink of death. Pao Yu's father, Chi Cheng, the embodiment of patriarchal legalism, presides over the waking world with iron rigor and unrelenting contempt for his son and all his ways; but the dramatic pivots of the novel are a series of dreams, apparitions of the true world in which doubled images of the girls who love and hate Pao Yu function as moral determinants, presided over by the great matriarch, the grandmother of the family.

It is the metaphysical modesty of Taoism that gives *The Dream of the Red Chamber* its style, that modesty which is the necessary ingredient of the very greatest style in any art. The most profound human relationships; the deepest psychological insights; the most intense drama; the revelation of the moral universe in trivial human action, in the simple narrative of ordinary happenings—greatness of heart, magnanimity ("human-heartedness" is the Chinese term) is the substance from which the narrative is carved.

Reading *The Tale of Genji*, you are always conscious of the ethereal refinement of the characters, the profundity of the issues, the skill of the author. In *Red Chamber* you are conscious only of what is happening. Lady Murasaki's Japanese courtiers seldom eat or drink, and never move their bowels. *The Dream of the Red Chamber* is haunted by the faint odor of night soil from which a hundred flowers spring.

When you first read about all these people with strange names doing curious things in an exotic setting, you get lost. Then gradually the sheer human mass of Chinese fiction, a mass whose components are all highly individuated, envelops and entrances you. You realize yourself as part of a universe of human beings endless as the dust of nebulae visible in the Mount Palomar telescope, and you are left with the significance of a human kinship powerful as flowing water and standing stone.

From the date of writing, the mid-eighteenth century, until our time, *The Dream of the Red Chamber* was anonymous. In 1921, Hu Shih, after immense research, ascribed the first eighty chapters to Tsao Hsueh Chin and the remaining forty chapters to Kao Ngoh, one of the editors of the 1791 edition. Evidence later discovered would indicate that Kao himself had worked from first drafts by Tsao.

Hu Shih believed the novel to be autobiographical, but it is significant that until the twentieth century no one bothered to disturb its anonymity. Like Gothic cathedrals, which sufficient research can usually demonstrate were built by somebody, the great

Chinese fictions are more anonymous and communal than *The Iliad*. The *Ching Ping Mei* (*Golden Lotus*), *The Water Margin* (*All Men Are Brothers*), *The Romance of Three Kingdoms* are end products of the accretion of hundreds of tales by street-corner story-tellers, and their luxuriance of natural growth is characteristic of the Chinese novel even today.

If completely translated, *The Dream of the Red Chamber* would require about a million words. The European versions are all drastic abridgments. Bancroft Joly's version (Kelly and Walsh, Hong Kong, 1892–93), two large volumes, was only the first third of the original. Chi Chen Wang's (Routledge, London, 1929) was drastically cut, simplified, and secularized until not much more than a Balzacian domestic epic remained. The English of Florence and Isabel McHugh, from the German of Franz Kuhn (Pantheon, New York, 1958), preserves the Taoist otherworldly emphasis which surely was all-important to the author. Chi Chen Wang's (Twayne, New York, 1958; Anchor Books paperback, 1958) is a new translation greatly expanded and improved and, so to speak, desecularized.

Giacomo Casanova
History of My Life

Purity, simplicity, definition, impact—these qualities of Homer are those of Casanova too. In addition, he has a special talent for giving the impression of complete candor. Only when we escape from the swiftness of his narrative and recollect his adventures in tranquillity do we ever suspect that he is not telling the strict truth. Candor is the essence of the art of autobiography. Proust, Pepys, Rousseau, Madame Rolland, Saint Augustine and Henry Adams—as long as we are carried along we cannot help believing them.

The greatest of adventurers in an age of adventurers, from Catherine and Frederick to Saint Germain and Mirabeau, from throne rooms to brothels, Casanova is the most credible of a century of *incroyables*. Perhaps there is a deeper social kinship to Homer. The breakup of feudalism, the loss of Christian belief, the accelerating economic change created a social chaos in the eighteenth century like a barbarian invasion. The new classes and their parasites were predators in a Viking age of satin breeches and powdered hair—an age of transformation, a Heroic Age, the ideal environment for those blessed with inordinate love of life, for the superlatively healthy amoral animals who gamble away earldoms and seduce countesses and chambermaids and all in the same night, as the Berserkers burned monasteries and raped nuns. Casanova is natural man living at the highest pitch, loving a life made of nothing whatever but a leonine physiology and the wits of a fox—a self-made man.

People have argued about the transition from "shame culture" to "guilt culture" during the Heroic Age. Casanova is a freebooter to whom these terms are meaningless. With its hundreds of sexual capers, his narrative has no prurience whatsoever and no monotony. It has no malevolence, either, and Casonova's Italianate vengeances are without petty malice. He is always being ruined by his naïve good nature. He falls in love with adventuresses more unscrupulous than himself who tease him with sisterly kisses and beggar him betimes. He falls for the most hackneyed confidence games, if only they involve a pretty woman. He hoodwinks an old codger with a magic conjuration to raise an imaginary treasure. Instead, he raises a terrifying lightning storm and cowers within his own magic circle, praying for mercy. Always in his love affairs he seeks first the pleasure, sexual and otherwise, of the girl. This talent made him adored in a brutal time by countless women of all ages and conditions from Moscow to Portugal.

Sometimes his giddiness pays. Down to his last three gold coins, headed east in Poland into the unknown, he tips a waitress with the lot and immediately establishes his credit as a prodigal millionaire. Most gamblers are like arsonists—addicted to the exquisite, guilty thrills of tempting destruction. Casanova gambled as children gambol, for the pure love of the great chance of living.

Whatever Casanova does, he assumes responsibility for consequences in the act of doing. So he never looks back on his life with regret, except for one moment of irresponsible gossip which damaged the career of a man who was hardly a friend—and the abiding regret that it is all over. "When I was young I was very fond of sailor's hardtack. I had thirty-two beautiful teeth. Now I have only two left and can no longer enjoy it." Conscience, even introspective curiosity, are foreign to Casanova. Nonetheless, the long tale is told with a scarcely audible but persistent note of melancholy. Men who live like Casanova are seldom interested in themselves; their egocentricity does not give them time for egotism. Neither was Casanova, probably, until old age and loneliness came over him—once the king of bohemians, exiled to a castle in Bohemia.

Time and its ruining passage color all the book. His sense of his own imminent death lurks in the dark background of every brilliantly lit lusty and bawdy tableau. After all, Casanova's memoirs are not a diary but an aged man's memories of his youth. Saint Augustine's *Confessions* are the confession of the betrayal of his own youth because he was in love with eternity. Casanova was passionately in love with a perishing present that long since had perished. The gavel of mortality raps steadily and beats out a moral judgment of life—the most fundamental judgment, the judgment of the amoral.

Cellini is an immoral healthy animal, and disagreeable because actually sick in some irrelevant way. Restif de la Bretonne is a moral imbecile. Casanova is a man without interiority except for a profound awareness of the vanity of human wishes. Proust seeks for the meaning of time. Casanova knows it has none. Since this is one of the major conclusions that wisdom can form from the facts of existence, the book has a peculiar naked profundity certainly lacking in those other adventurers, Cellini and Restif. Havelock Ellis said of him that he was the consummate master of the dignified narration of undignified experience.

It is the wisdom of the doomed flesh that is responsible for Casanova's redeeming dignity. He has equals but no superiors in the art of direct factual narrative. Chinese adventure novels and the greatest modern detective stories do not surpass him. From the very beginning, the simple facts of his childhood and youth roll along like the wheels of an express train. The narrative carries all before it and carries the most indifferent reader with it. This is action writing at the highest pitch—pre-emptory story-telling.

When we pause for breath, we notice other qualities that Casanova shares with detective stories. We feel that we are always skirting the edges of a mystery. Something seems to be going on that we are not being told about. This isn't true; it is a tone, which is due to the fact that Casanova was at the very center of the mystifying occult Freemasonry of the mid-eighteenth century with its mixture of eroticism, mathematics, deism, and international espionage. Unlike Saint Germain, who pretended to be immortal, to speak all languages, and to have unlimited wealth; unlike Cagliostro, whose speculations must have astonished him whenever they accidentally escaped from total charlatanism, Casanova had no need to pretend. His life was illuminated by the glamour of liberated sensual devotion—the mystery of flesh and blood and nerves and bones in action.

The most mysterious thing about this apparition is that it comes out of nowhere and returns to nothing. The loving human body hurtles through time like a thrown battle-axe. "Eminently rapid, plain, direct in thought, expression, syntax, words, matter, ideas," said Arnold of Homer, "and eminently noble." Everyone would agree that all these terms apply to Casanova, except the last, which many would change to "eminently ignoble." Is this true? One meaning of the word "noble" is "descended from the chiefs of the Visigoths, Ostrogoths, Lombards, or Burgundians." It is this blood relation to the epic hero which distinguishes Casanova from the other rascals of literature.

Henry Fielding
Tom Jones

Tom Jones has been compared to Odysseus and Huck Finn. Huck he somewhat resembles; Odysseus not at all. He is more like a compound of Don Quixote and Sancho Panza—not a mixture, but a chemical compound of antagonistic qualities and virtues which has produced a new being. You do not read far in the novel before you become aware that Fielding is constructing a character to demonstrate a thesis. He is not preaching. Tom is not a dummy or a stereotype on which proofs are hung like clothes. On the contrary: the thesis is precisely his humanity; but Fielding's is a special vision of man—common enough now, especially in America, but strange to English fiction in his day.

If the novel were simply the portrayal of an ideal human type, it would have soon become unreadable. It is, of course, an immense panorama of mid-eighteenth-century England, as populous as any novel of Tolstoy's or Dostoievsky's. Comparison, however, with a work like *War and Peace* immediately reveals a profound difference. The plot of *Tom Jones* is not a "real life" story but a fairy tale, a *Märchen*, disguised with realism. Nor are the subsidiary characters fleshed out like the minor characters of the major Russian novelists. Fielding carefully subordinates all other characters to Tom and Sophie in a graded series of realization. The nearer and more important they are to the principals, the more complex they are, but they are never very complex. Blifil and Squire Allworthy are scarcely more rounded out than the characters of Ben Jonson's Theatre of Humours. The minor figures are reduced to bare essentials— quickly drawn stereotypes.

The fairy-tale plot is spun out and complicated endlessly, but it never becomes complex. All its situations are simple. They are pervaded with a mocking double irony by the ambiguous comments of the omniscient author. The relations between the characters constantly lapse into farce. This all gives the book an air of quiet madness. Life is seen in an imperceptibly warped mirror or through a telescope with an abnormally sharp definition—the clarity and distortion of myth.

Fielding is not only an omniscient narrator—he constantly tells you that you are reading a novel, that these people are all fictions. This is the alienation that Brecht made a catchword in our day, like that of the burlesque comedian who turns to the audience and says, "This is me, climbing the ladder to her room." Or the nineteenth-century Shakespearean actor who delivered the soliloquies directly to the audience as sermons on his own action. Most people today, raised on an illusionistic realism of narration, find it difficult to adjust to Fielding or anyone—Thackeray, for instance—who adopted the same author's authority. But *Tom Jones* is not naturalism, and it is realism only in the broadest sense. It is an immensely complicated farce.

The plot and the thesis are one: Tom is that universal hero of folk tale and myth, the foundling prince, the king's son raised by wolves, Moses in the bullrushes, whose princely qualities shine out in all his acts and eventually determine events so that his true heritage is revealed. Fielding is defining a gentleman. The fact that many of the characters are as well born as Tom or better born does not disturb the logic. They are the bad aristocrats. He is a natural gentleman—but not a noble savage, rather a noble fallen amongst savages, a savage noble, actually not a noble but a gentleman— quite a different concept from Rousseau's.

Hardly an episode does not demonstrate Tom's gentlemanliness. Fielding defines gentlemanliness as generosity of soul. Sin he may, but always for others' good. His relations with women are always motivated by the desire to please or help. When he is seduced by an old rip like Mrs. Waters, he responds with gratitude—the reaction of a generous man to generosity. This response overwhelms Mrs. Waters, and she responds at the crucial moment with a generosity that literally saves Tom's life. Unlike modern novelists, Fielding assumes that people enjoy sex.

Tom is the Good Natured Man, but by this Fielding means more than his contemporaries meant by the eighteenth-century catch phrase—something very like the "human-heartedness" of Confucius. Several times Fielding interpolates little lectures on good nature that sound exactly like translations from the Chinese. I have no idea whether he read the French translations, or the Latin, of the Jesuit renditions of the Chinese classics that were then so popular amongst French intellectuals. If not, the convergence is remarkable. Tom is very much the typical Chinese hero, and the novel could easily be restated in Chinese terms and setting.

Not least of its Chinese characteristics is its decorum. Fielding wrote *Tom Jones* against the lachrymose soul-probing of Richardson's heroines, as a protest against bad manners. Fielding has been criticized again and again by a psychologistic age for his characters' total lack of interiority. Whenever they so much as reflect, the omniscient author makes fun of them and always points out that they are deluding themselves.

This is part of the thesis: actions speak louder than words—and words than thoughts, especially about oneself. When his characters become unruly, violate his special concept of the etiquette of human-heartedness, Fielding intrudes and admits that they are creations of his imagination and he can make them do as he wishes—and then usually comments that they have taken on a certain autonomy that escapes his control.

This horrified Henry James, who considered it artistic treason and said he would be no more shocked to find such admissions in the histories of Gibbon and Macaulay. Of course, Fielding's point—the double point of his double irony—is that it is precisely such personal historians who should make such admissions. Ultimately, the decorum of Brechtian alienation is a judgment on real, undecorous life.

The blubbery self-revelations of Richardson's novels, says Fielding, are lies. He would doubtless consider those of Proust or James lifelong evasion on the part of their authors. What he thought of the novel of objective revelation of character, of Defoe and his descendants, I do not know. The evidence is that Tom himself is patterned on Defoe—but the other characters, not. Defoe, however, wrote false documents—novels presented as actual memoirs. Fielding did the opposite. As the novel approaches the conviction of reality, Fielding always pulls the reader back—"this is not real." What is not real? Our judgments of "real life"? This is the essence of his irony. The omniscient author hoaxes the reader into believing *he* is omniscient and then pulls the throne from under him. Richardson, James, and Proust, on the other hand, really believed they had revealed the essences of human behavior.

Tom Jones is Fielding's conception of optimum man—but seen entirely from the outside. You feel, reflecting on the novel after long familiarity, that his imperviousness to probing and lack of interest in self-probing were, to Fielding's mind, an essential part of the optimum. Behind Rousseau's new and revolutionary concept of man at his best lies the inward-turning eye of Descartes's *Cogito ergo sum*. Behind Fielding's Tom lie the clear and definite external sense data

of John Locke, and he is an equally revolutionary type of person.
Out of one came the endlessly self-questioning continental radical
intellectual. Out of the other came the active pragmatic man of
whom Jefferson is probably the best exemplar, if the truth be told—
a man who probably resembled Tom in more ways than one.

Laurence Sterne

The Life and Opinions
of Tristram Shandy, Gent.

Historians of civilization when they come to the eighteenth century
almost always devote most space to France. The Age of Enlightenment is usually considered the period in which French thought
dominated European culture. This is certainly true in a quantitative
sense: Voltaire or Diderot must have been read by the greatest
number of people, and we spontaneously think of eighteenth-century painting as represented by Boucher, Fragonard, or, at the best,
Chardin—this in spite of the fact that the Tiepolos, father and son,
are greater painters. As philosophers the French *philosophes* seem
pretty thin today, essentially popularizers. Their foundations go
back to the seventeenth century, and not primarily to the French-
man Descartes but to the Englishmen Locke and Newton.

Similarly with the novel. Nothing would appear in France to
compare with the great English novels of the eighteenth century
until Choderlos de Laclos's *Les Liaisons Dangereuses*, which was
not an expression of the Age of Enlightenment, but its obituary.

Modern taste, corrupted by the undemanding narratives of televi-
sion, the movies, and commercial fiction, may find Fielding, Smollett, and especially Richardson hard to read, but Laurence Sterne's
Tristram Shandy retains a wide measure of popularity. It may not
be as popular today as *David Copperfield*, but it is certainly more

popular than most other classic English fiction or than those favorites of our grandparents, *Vanity Fair* and *Ivanhoe.*

Dozens of books have been called "the first modern novel." As expressions of the modern sensibility of alienation, the best claimants are doubtless the novels of Laclos and Stendhal; but in a most important way *Tristram Shandy* is modern, so modern that a very long time would elapse before anything else like it would appear.

If Webster's *The Duchess of Malfi* can be called a play which assumes that the characters are performing not outside the mind but within it, *Tristram Shandy* is a drama of the mind itself.

It is a bucolic—rather, a provincial-town—comedy. It has often been pointed out that it is the very distillate of life in York—still the regional capital that it had been in the Middle Ages, with its own circle of intellectuals, its own "power structure," its own coffee houses and magazines, and its own cultural originality and autonomy. As such, the novel is a mirror of the greater London or Paris— the great reflected in the little, and more sharply refined, as in a reducing glass. But it is more than this. It is, as Sterne said it was, in the face of hostile critics who have gone on to this very day accusing him of being a lewd and neurotic country clergyman, indeed a philosophical and moral work, and one of very considerable profundity.

As Sterne saw the workings of the mind, it functioned according to the philosophy of Locke as modified by the atomism of Newton. There was nothing in the mind that was not first in sensation, and each primitive sensation was a kind of atom. The sensations entered the mind through the senses and were combined to reach ever-ascending levels of complexity and abstraction. If this process could only be as orderly as the sorting mechanism of the mind itself, what would result would be a universe of strictly deductive logic, a kind of immense and even more closely structured Euclid's *Elements* or Aquinas's *Summa Contra Gentiles.*

But the atoms of experience, the primitive sense data, do not occur at the option of the mind; nor, since the mind is ultimately itself formed of its own material, is the process so logically efficient. In fact, it is all extraordinarily random. Sensation is fed to us in the most helter-skelter fashion. At the lower levels of mental activity we are at the mercy of the chances of association. We may well be even at the highest levels, even though we do not realize it. This is an elementary, psychologistic, definition of comedy itself. It is certainly very funny, the way we put together our individual pictures of the universe, and the way we go through the experience we call "experience," and the way we emerge at the end.

Sterne's contribution, and it is a very important one to psychology and epistemology, is the realization that the essence of the comedy of epistemology, the profound humor of what we call knowledge of reality, is the ungovernable disorder of Time. If Locke's sense data came to us marching one-two-three-four through our sense organs into our brains, as Newton's atoms move in matter or his planets go around the sun, Time would be simple, linear, and comprehensible—but of course, they do not. We cannot measure experience by looking at the clock. Later philosophers were to distinguish something they call Organic Time; but this is a knowledge of process far more orderly than the comic disorder of Sterne's narrative.

Joseph Conrad's favorite narrator, Marlow, tells his tales with the natural switching and shifting of time of someone telling a story as it occurs to willed memory. In Proust, time dissolves and slows. Even the narrator, Marcel, is a character in a brain that is constantly trying to return the temporal process to its sources. James Joyce's *Ulysses* takes place in a day. *Finnegans Wake* takes place in a single troubled dream, and all of Joyce's experience is reflected and refracted in the brief circuits of a few revolving mirrors and prisms. But most of *The Life and Opinions of Tristram Shandy, Gent.* occur before he has any opinions, and a third before he has any life. He isn't born until far on in the book. Chapter after chapter goes by while the author struggles helplessly, in an inconsequential sequence in the narrative, to get two characters downstairs.

It was in discussing Sterne that Coleridge elaborated his famous definition of humor as the juxtaposition of the immense and important and the trivial and tiny in the real, in that reality which is always overshadowed by the infinite. Although he was offended, or at least said he was, by Sterne's bawdry, he was well aware of its significance.

One famous and often analyzed passage is a case in point. It is a sentimental set piece far more effective than almost anything in the novels of Richardson or the paintings of Greuze, and it ends with mockery. Tristram is on his way by coach to Moulins and encounters the beautiful, blind, and brokenhearted Maria "sitting upon a bank, playing her vespers upon her pipe, with her little goat beside her," driven mad with sorrow. Overcome with sentiment, Tristram stops the coach and seats himself beside the girl.

"Maria look'd wistfully for some time at me, and then at her goat—and then at me—and then at her goat again, and so on, alternately—

"Well, Maria, said I softly—What resemblance do you find?"

All through this touching narrative, so full of melancholy, we know that Tristram has been getting sexually excited unbeknown to himself, and the climax of the excitement is the sharp realization of the absurdity of the act of procreation. Small wonder Coleridge picked this passage. He was acutely aware of the ridiculousness of "coming to be and passing away." Coleridge's private notebooks contain descriptions in the language of "Kubla Khan" of the colors and perfumes of his morning's chamber pot. Tristram's father's discourse on the white bear is a thoroughly modern poem on the absurdity of our knowledge of the world.

CHAPTER XLIII

My father took a single turn across the room, then sat down, and finished the chapter.

The verbs auxiliary we are concerned in here, continued my father, are, am; was; have; had; do; did; make; made; suffer; shall; should; will; would; can; could; owe; ought; used; or is wont.—And these varied with tenses, present, past, future, and conjugated with the verb see,—or with these questions added to them;—Is it? Was it? Will it be? Would it be? May it be? Might it be? And these again put negatively, Is it not? Was it not? Ought it not?—Or affirmatively,—It is; It was; It ought to be. Or chronologically,—Has it been always? Lately? How long ago?—Or hypothetically,—If it was? If it was not? What would follow?—If the French should beat the English? If the Sun go out of the Zodiac?

Now, by the right use and application of these, continued my father, in which a child's memory should be exercised, there is no one idea can enter his brain, how barren soever, but a magazine of conceptions and conclusions may be drawn forth from it.—Didst thou

ever see a white bear? cried my father, turning his head round to Trim,
who stood at the back of his chair:—No, an' please your honour,
replied the corporal.—But thou couldst discourse about one, Trim,
said my father, in case of need?—How is it possible, brother, quoth my
uncle Toby, if the corporal never saw one?—'Tis the fact I want,
replied my father,—and the possibility of it is as follows.

A white bear! Very well. Have I ever seen one? Might I ever have
seen one? Am I ever to see one? Ought I ever to have seen one? Or can
I ever see one?

Would I had seen a white bear! (for how can I imagine it?)

If I should see a white bear, what should I say? If I should never see
a white bear, what then?

If I never have, can, must, or shall see a white bear alive; have I ever
seen the skin of one? Did I ever see one painted?—described? Have I
never dreamed of one?

Did my father, mother, uncle, aunt, brothers or sisters, ever see a
white bear? What would they give? How would they behave? How
would the white bear have behaved? Is he wild? Tame? Terrible?
Rough? Smooth?

—Is the white bear worth seeing?—

—Is there no sin in it?—

Is it better than a black one?

There is no essential difference between the circumstantial picture of the human condition in Sterne and that in the most anguished Existentialist, except that Sterne's portrayal is far more
elaborate and accurate, and he thinks it's funny. There is an important distinction here, that between comedy and humor. There is
nothing funny about the final aesthetic experience we get from
Machiavelli's *Mandragola* or Ben Jonson's *Volpone*, any more than
there is in the one we get from *No Exit*. There is an immense
amount of funny business along the way in the two older plays; but
all three are comedies, and their look into chaos is bleak.

There is all sorts of pathos along the way in *Tristram Shandy*—
the saddest the death of Le Fever, where Sterne unquestionably
surpasses Richardson or even Fielding, that great anti-sentimental-
ist. But Sterne, looking out like the Prince of the Fallen Angels over
the chaos of the world, does what Satan could never do: he laughs,
as Buddha laughed long before him at the vision of the compound
infinitudes of universes in the *Lankavatara Sutra*. Certainly most

people would think the conjunction of Sterne and Buddha as incongruous as anything in the novels of one or the sermons of the other; but the conclusion of the English country clergyman and provincial *philosophe* was the same as that of the founder of a world religion: an all-suffering compassion.

That is precisely what Sterne says is the message of *Tristram Shandy.* It is the constantly reiterated theme of his now-unread sermons, which were unique in a time when the pulpit in England was not distinguished for the identification of the clergy with the sufferings and the absurdities of the lives of the humble.

Restif de la Bretonne
Monsieur Nicolas

It is not cricket to review books that are unobtainable, and it annoys booksellers, but so it must be. I can only hope to stimulate interest on the part of one of the many firms that publish reprints of the world's important books.

There are few French critics today who would rank Rousseau's *Confessions* above *Monsieur Nicolas,* and there are few people left who read Rousseau solely for pleasure. In France, Restif is a genuinely popular author, in fact, something of a fad, only a little less fashionable with the sophisticated than Sade—a writer who, it happens, Restif despised and felt himself specially called to attack. His influence has been enormous.

Henry Miller might be called Monsieur Nicolas transliterated into early-twentieth-century American terms, and Céline a sour and crazed Restif. Restif was the inventor of the unbridled confession, real or imaginary, that is the dominant form of the modern novel. He is the master of the utterly convincing implausible; but in spite of obvious fantasy which sometimes borders on the confabulations of mild lunacy, *Monsieur Nicolas* is a priceless historical document for the best years of Louis XV; the scarcely perceptible slide into total social disorder under Louis XVI; the hidden, domestic, and personal living that went on behind the historical extravagance of Revolution and Empire.

Restif was a fantasist of reality. It is doubtful whether anyone could sleep with all the women he says he did, although this activity takes less time than the chaste imagine. But when he describes a quiet orgy on the sylvan banks of the Marne with two shopgirls, he tells us what they wore, how much the chickens and wine cost, and what the riverside inn and its host and hostess were like.

Probably the reason the beautiful John Rodker edition (in six volumes, translated by R. Crowdy Mathers with an introduction by Havelock Ellis) has never been reprinted is that it is too long to warrant the risk with an author almost unknown in the English-speaking world. This is a great pity. Restif took a section of *Monsieur Nicolas*, altered it enough to form a novel, and published it as *Sara, The Last Love Affair of a Man of Forty-Five*. The original English edition, also published by Rodker, on cottage-made Auvergne paper, is one of the most beautiful books of modern times. By itself it is a wonderfully coherent novel, as pathetic and ironic a story of sexual exploitation, of middle-aged folly and female guile, as the ridiculous Miss Charpillon episode in Casanova, and it is more moving because more shameless. The comic irony with which Casanova viewed himself always gives him a final, occult control of the situation. Restif may be the only major writer utterly devoid of irony or any sense of the ridiculous. He is always at the mercy of the reader.

Like the memoirs of Casanova, *Monsieur Nicolas* is not a book but a drug. It is impossible to put it down, impossible to escape from it. The novels of Defoe are false documents, written with the silent sarcasm of a counterfeiter. Restif is a Defoe narrator come to life. This is the way Moll or Roxanna would have written: irresistibly.

Restif is something almost unknown until recent times, and uncommon even now: an actual working-class writer. The working class in French fiction from Scarron to Hugo, with the exception of Eugène Sue, are servants, actors, prostitutes, criminals—the poor whose business it is to mix with the rich. Restif was a journeyman printer who often composed his books in type at the press, and he wrote of the working class who work—the artisans, journeymen, and petty shopkeepers who are known only to one another. A statistical abstract of the works of Restif would be an excellent introduction to the study of eighteenth-century economics and sociology. This is the base of the pyramid of the *ancien régime*, written by an articulate foundation stone.

It is interesting to note that the French working class were never better off than in the reign of Louis XV until the reign of Napoleon III. The mold of French culture was determined in the reigns of those two disgraceful and wasteful men, who have been so misrepresented in history because no political party likes them. So likewise the French spoken language assumed its final form in the days of Restif, but it would be impossible to deduce this from the writings of his contemporaries. His own style strikes one, after a reading of his contemporary Diderot, as a kind of hypertrophied pidgin French, especially if read in his own odd reformed spelling; but it is a language of power and plasticity, capable of transforming into candid and convincing speech great ranges of experience never known to literature before.

Restif's prose has an inescapable quality peculiar to itself. His greatest passages resemble the elementary textbook version of *Sans Famille* and have the same naked cogency. This is writing past the ivory walls of literature, and today our greatest writers, whatever else they may be, are anti-literary. Restif is the inventor of anti-literary literature, a method that is itself a philosophy of life. Candor that forces willful suspension of incredulity is the essence of the art of autobiography. Even at his silliest, poking into the petticoats of a cornered chambermaid, we accept Restif as we never can accept Rousseau at his most sincere—perhaps then least of all.

Like those of Blake and Henry Miller, Restif's head was full of the piled-up baggage of the intellectual underworld, the orthodoxy of the heterodox which probably does go back to the Stone Age. He had schemes to reform everything, many of them less foolish than the functioning programs of the Social Lie. He was a fetishist. He was a squaw man who hated the wife he ruthlessly exploited—who seems, like Baudelaire's unfortunate mistress, Jeanne Duval, to have been a most estimable woman. His sexual life begins to take on the character of overexcited senility in early youth. At least, it does not have the ignorance of physiology shown by his modern avatar, Henry Miller, nor is it perverted. We may not believe the number of Restif's affairs, but we never doubt that they were exactly as he described. He was mindless of good taste in life or letters, yet we accept him as we accept no one else from this period but Choderlos de Laclos; and we accept him with a deep personal love, as we might a shameful, talented, and shiftless member of our own family.

It is this ability to establish complete intimacy, however embarrassing, that makes Restif one of the great autobiographers. We do not read far in the book before we are tempted to write him an avuncular letter and offer to lend him money—something no one in his senses would be moved to do for Rousseau.

Edward Gibbon

The Decline and Fall of the Roman Empire

"It was at Rome, on the 15th of October, 1764, as I sat musing amidst the ruins of the Capitol, while the barefooted friars were singing vespers in the Temple of Jupiter, that the idea of writing the decline and fall of the city first started to my mind."

Scarcely a sentence from all the autobiographical literature of the world has been more often quoted, and hardly a historian of note in all the years since the publication of his great work but has written something of Gibbon, if no more than in a preface. It would be possible to fill a book with the wise things they have said and a sequel with the foolish ones. The most often repeated, the most vulgar but at the same time the most perceptive, is that, in his *Autobiography*, "he wrote of himself as if he was the Roman Empire." The secret of Gibbon lies in the reverse of this proposition. He wrote of the Empire as if it had been himself.

The Decline and Fall has a hero—the man of reason. Its thesis is that the life of the man of reason in history is tragic by nature. It has been said again and again that Gibbon's history is the perfect expression and fulfillment of the Age of Reason, the eighteenth century—greater than anything of Voltaire's, greater than Tiepolo or Watteau, greater than any of the noble domestic architecture. Certainly Voltaire's *History of Charles XII* does not stand comparison with any major connected narrative in *The Decline and Fall of the Roman Empire*, much less with the work as a whole. The reason is simple. The Augustan intellects of the eighteenth century prided themselves on their aloofness. Voltaire is never overcommitted.

One of the greatest stories, true or fictional, in all literature is Gibbon's account of the life and martyrdom of Boethius under the Ostrogoth Theodoric. Senator, poet, philosopher, man of reason, he was the last of his kind in all these categories. The story is an incomparable masterpiece of prose. From the opening sentence, "The Senator Boethius is the last of the Romans whom Cato or Tully could have acknowledged for their countryman," Gibbon builds a mighty organ toccata. He always seems to see ahead to every echo and resonance and inversion of rhythm, through the idyllic description of *The Consolation of Philosophy* to the terrible climax—the philosopher garroted and clubbed to death in the last gloomy hours of Theodoric, followed by the swift cadence, and the coda of the martyrdom of his fellow Senator Symmachus—four crowded pages of the most solemn music. Each man speaks in his own style. Gibbon speaks with such sublimity because, sitting in his quiet study, he was totally involved in the defense of reason against the triumph of barbarism and superstition and the ruin of all bright things.

At the beginning of the fall of Rome, Saint Augustine wrote *The City of God*; and Gibbon, looking back in his book from the walls of burning Constantinople in the final fall, on the eve of a new age of enlightenment, is in fact committed to the same interpretation of history as Augustine. Against the destructive irrationality of circumstance and the folly of mankind stands the community of the elect. In Augustine it is the community of faith; in Gibbon the elect of reason, a society that transcends history. The ideal Rome that Gibbon describes in his opening chapters on the Antonines is a passing avatar of the enduring City of Enlightenment. This, after all, is the subject of all tragedy: the defeat of the ideal by the real, of being by existence.

Even more than Toynbee's work, Gibbon's is a judgment, but a judgment achieved by the presentation of an integral work of art, the magnificent progress of a great story and the scenic aspect of marvelous events. Although scholarly research, most especially in Byzantine and Islamic studies, has undergone several revolutions since Gibbon's day, all but an insignificant few of his facts still stand. His carping critics have quarreled with his accuracy only as a cover for their objections to his dramatic thesis. In an age of scientific history when the art was turned over to committees of specialists, J. B. Bury—the editor of the *Cambridge Medieval History* volumes that cover the decline and fall of the Roman Empire and the history of the Byzantine Empire and the Christian heresies and councils and the rise of Islam—also edited *The Decline and Fall* and could find nothing in it to correct except trivial failures of information. The recent new edition of the Byzantine volumes of the *Cambridge Medieval History* are extraordinarily difficult reading, and they certainly supply little information that cannot be found in Gibbon. Laying aside the massive volumes, you know that no one of the committee of authors was personally involved.

The quarrel between history as art and history as science has often been interpreted as a matter of stylistic felicities. So for instance does C. V. Wedgewood in her essay on Gibbon. She is wrong. Why should not history be interpreted in terms of good and evil? She thinks the quarrel with the pure-science advocates is over inordinate attention to the embellishment of style. It certainly is not. The question is: is the historian a value-neuter investigator, as the physicist and the etymologist claim to be?

The great histories of the world—those of Thucydides, Su Ma Ch'ien, Gibbon, Ibn Khaldun, Tacitus, Livy, Herodotus—and those of lesser figures like Commines and Froissart or Hume and Macaulay have all been integral works of art. They have been so not because of their pretty prose but because of their objective dramatic presentation of the great truth that history, like life, is neither optimistic nor pessimistic but tragic. All values wear out at last or at once in the attrition of the passage of the world of facts. Gibbon's millennium-long drama is a tragedy presented with a good humor peculiar to himself. His story is of the decay of civilization, with the loss of self-determination and control of the human environment. He presents it with a maximum of civilized determination and self-control.

Pedantic minds have found his Byzantine chapters the least interesting, although certainly the majority of his readers have liked them best. He is accused of depreciating the Byzantine achievement. Does he? Not as much as Procopius, or Anna Comnena, or Psellus. He is remarkably like the most urbane Byzantine historians who were his sources. Panoplied and ceremonial chaos, ideological warfare, and silken barbarity are described with balance and deliberation, with quiet wit and malice, and with devastating understated footnotes, where necessary "relegated to the decent obscurity of a learned language."

In his own time, Gibbon's Latinate antithetical style already sounded archaic, yet it is still today eminently suited to his solemn subject. How else is one to describe the beauty, lechery, and political malevolence of Theodora, or the economic folly of her husband, Justinian, than in a quiet language derived from the letters of Cicero, the most ironic passages of Thucydides, and the innuendos of Tacitus? For the Muse of History appears like the child Theodora in the arena, dancing naked on the head of a bear, more often than she appears as the noble goddess of Livy's and Plutarch's mythologies. What better response to the spectacle than the caustic caution and gentlemanly calm, the prudent incredulity Gibbon developed in meditation on a thousand years of the slow triumph of disorder—meditation by the orderly Swiss lake of Voltaire's exile?

Stendhal

The Red and the Black

"I rose and fell with Napoleon," said Henri Beyle, who called himself Stendhal. If the Revolution put the middle class into power in France, Napoleon attempted to make it heroic and internationalize it, as the aristocracy of the Almanach de Gotha are international, and once claimed heroic virtues. *The Red and the Black* is the story of an inglorious Napoleon, a man of energy without a chance. Stendhal's hero, Julien Sorel, is the Revolutionary adventurer trapped in the Restoration—as, of course, was Stendhal himself. The novelist differs from his character in insight. He is always aware that he in his youth had liberated himself from the mediocrity that oppressed him.

Philosophes and Jacobins had hoped to make the middle class intelligent and heroic. Stendhal had given up that hope. Again and again he spoke of his work as a lottery ticket that would pay off in fifty or a hundred years. No one ever wrote more masculine novels. He knew that they would be read in his time mostly by idle women—spoiled duchesses and disappointed wives of businessmen: exactly the women who destroy his hero, Julien. So the violent arrogance of *The Red and the Black* is a kind of seduction, an assault on the spurious chastity of its public. For fifty years he was read only by such women and by the few intellectuals who shared his sensuous scorn. Then his reputation began to grow. He took his place easily with the radical critics of modern life of the end of the century. By the hundredth anniversary of the publication of *The Red and the Black* he was acknowledged as the greatest of French novelists.

Hypertrophied or dissociated, the style he invented is still dominant in French fiction. Popular writers as diverse as Mrs. Voynich and Simenon have modeled themselves directly on him. More significant, *The Red and the Black* established the type and fixed the pattern of the novel as black comedy. In his youth Stendhal longed to be the Molière of the nineteenth century, a great comic poet. He couldn't write proper French verse, so he thought he had failed. He had not. *The Red and the Black* is the first modern overturned tragedy, the first black comedy. Julien Sorel is a comic Napoleon, a Bonaparte with frayed cuffs and patched shoes, mocked in Bartholomew Fair. To the immature readers of the last century, his story was a tragedy. To men of the world who read it in the twentieth, it is a comedy, but of the grimmest sort. "The world is a tragedy to those who feel, a comedy to those who think."

Hardly another man of letters has been as much a man of the

world as Stendhal. Henri Beyle—dragoon; grocer; Napoleon's governor of Brunswick; commissary officer on the retreat from Moscow; consul in Civita Vecchia, the port of Rome; wit of the salons of the Empire and terror of those of the Restoration; lover of actresses, courtesans, and noblewomen—this is a man to whom words were always instruments of action. So to his hero, Julien Sorel, ideas are a backwash of blocked action. He struggles to act and expresses his frustration in thought. His interior monologues are designed by Stendhal to ironically illuminate action, like the speeches of Thucydides, and never to impede it.

Julien's thoughts are Stendhal's irony. His own are expressed in Julien's acts. This is what gives his narrative its extraordinary pace and intensity, unique in its time and rare in any. There had been nothing like it before in any European language except Icelandic. Others had been colloquial and barbarous unwittingly. Stendhal strove always to write in the manner of urgent speech. From his youth he studied operative prose, witnesses in court, technical descriptions, dispatches, orders, the Civil Code, the language of people who meant business with words. He is an adult writing for adults. In a letter from burning Moscow he says, "I saw things sedentary authors would not see in a thousand years."

Everybody acts out in *The Red and the Black*—Julien, the hero of the armed will; Mathilde, the tragic Renaissance princess; Madame Renal, the helpless victim of a grand passion. Stendhal is very explicit in underlining their self-dramatizations. They are not, though they think they are, forced on by tragic necessity. On the contrary, their acts, including those of the final scenes, are gratuitous indulgences from which at any time they can withdraw. Their adventures are certainly sensational, but Stendhal preserves, in the face of the unbridled Romanticism of his characters, a more than Classicist imperturbability—Dumas in an iron mask. He is never the victim of his characters, never overthrown by the passions he creates. His is the armed will; he is the master of narrative Bonapartism.

In its sharp definition, breathless pace, crowded frames, melodrama, *The Red and the Black* anticipates the methods of the cinema—so much so that it is hard to understand why it has never been made into one of the classic motion pictures. But its characters are like so many modern people whose disasters are spread on the newspapers: they seem to have seen too many movies. As the novel progresses, their actions acquire an ever-increasing, ever more agonizing ridiculousness. Finally everything explodes in the black comedy of Julien's pistol shots, which, like Uncle Vanya's, kill nobody, and the novel ends in a denouement, a merciless crescendo, followed by a sarcastic anticlimax—the last role-playing of the Renaissance princess. The mercilessness is not that of tragedy, but that of the deepest comedy.

Julien Sorel is destroyed by the mean unreality of the world in which his Napoleonic campaigns of sex and ambition are planned. But he is destroyed before he starts. His battles must be fought not with armies, but with the limitless fraud of organized society. Stendhal keeps the fraudulent character of all his engagements steadily in view; this is the touchstone of all moral evaluation. *The Red and the Black* and his other great novel, *The Charterhouse of Parma*, are dramas of gamesmanship on a crooked table—one lost, the other won. "Molière," said young Stendhal, "ridiculed the vices that corrupt society. Today we must attack the vice of the spirit of society itself."

Fraud empties motive of content. As we follow the story and try to analyze the relationships of the characters, they recede from us and become masks which conceal appetites for power. The emptiness of their desires is the measure of their absurdity. The tale of charismatic personalities with nothing to do is the height and depth of comedy.

Stendhal could look back to the outburst of primitivism, the hour of revolt, the actual street fighting, and he identified himself with Napoleon, whose purported principles of intellectual integrity, rational imperative, honor, and the "career open to all the talents" was a freebooter's ethic, not a class one, least of all either bourgeois or aristocratic. Bonapartism is the religion of the New Man who rose from nothing to the greatest heights in history. A generation later, Julien Sorel is only an upstart, who carries his revolution about with him as Pascal did his abyss. This does not make him a tragic figure, but his reflection, backward into history, makes Napoleon a comic one.

The Red and the Black is far more than a charade of a philosophy of history or a sociological theory. It is first of all one of the most perfectly constructed and told novels. It establishes the novel securely in the place of the dramatic poem. It is further a great personal utterance. It is not only a judgment of the history Stendhal had lived through, but a subtle and ruthless judgment of himself. "I am Julien," he said. Like a Russian Nihilist, Julien seeks pure act and embraces the guillotine. As a man of ego and will, he struggles toward liberation from the principle of individuality. Stendhal called a term to action in the sensuous audacity of a life of planned moderation. His liberation was precisely his individuality.

Baudelaire

Poems

"Baudelaire is the greatest poet of the capitalist epoch." True or not, this statement, with its Marxist implications, is appropriate, because he is specially the poet of the society analyzed in *Capital* or described in *The Condition of the English Working-class.* His subject was the world of primitive accumulation, of the ruthless destruction of all values but the cash nexus by the new industrial and financial system—of bankers and their mistresses in sultry boudoirs; of the craze for diabolism, drugs, flagellation, barbarism; of gin-soaked poor dying in gutters, prostitutes dying under bridges, tubercular and syphilitic intellectuals; of the immense, incurable loneliness of the metropolis; of the birth of human self-alienation, as Marx called it—Baudelaire called it vaporization of the Ego—of the Communist Manifesto; and of revolution and revolution betrayed.

Baudelaire's Catholic apologists deny that he had an Oedipus complex. He is the archetype, a far more extreme example than Rousseau or Stendhal. Yet neither Marx nor Freud is an adequate guide to Baudelaire. They diagnose the illness of the nineteenth century in its own materialistic terms. Far more afflicted than they, Baudelaire transcends his century. His ultimate meanings are emerging only in the decline of the twentieth. He is the founder of the modern sensibility—not just of that of its first century, but of a special character that will, as far as we can see ahead, endure throughout the age of the breakdown of our civilization. Some learn to cope with this sensibility. He was at its mercy, because he embodied it totally. He lived in a permanent crisis of the moral nervous system. His conviction that social relationships were one immense lie was physiological.

The Romantics had a rhetoric of secession; Baudelaire had a life commitment, an organic divorce. Further, he was literally outcast— expelled from his caste. Few men have ever had a stronger conviction of their clerisy, of their belonging to the clerkly caste of the responsibles. Yet because of the terms of his wardship, he was continually dispossessed, forced to recognize his loss and shame every time he had to beg from his mother or his guardian. His writing, which he looked on as prophetic utterance, he was forced to sell as a cheap commodity. At the end of his life he told a friend he had received a total of about three thousand dollars from all the writing he had ever done.

He spent his life in a state of demoralization, and his work is a relentless attack on that demoralization. Much of his life and most of his poetry are tortured by a consciousness of sin. He thought of sin as the corruption of the will to vision. Only very rarely does he ever seem to realize that it is the corruption of the organ of reciprocity. His human relationships are all charades.

It has been said that Baudelaire chose the life he lived, that nobody has to live like that. True, but what did he choose? He did not choose his degrading trust fund, his Hamletic relation with his mother, his obsessive ritualized oral sex and masochism, or his syphilis, all of which worked together to multiply his guilt, to close to him person-to-person relations with women, and to turn women into melodramatic actresses in his own internal theater of frustration. Nor did he choose a debilitating oral opium addiction; in youth he chose the ecstasies of drugs before he realized the consequences—not just painful addiction, but destruction of the will, and a *vaporisation de Moi* worse than that caused by the dehumanizations of a commercial society.

He chose to place himself at the disposal of experience, and he chose to place his experience at the mercy of a conscience conceived as an instrument of mystery and a key to the enigma of being. Transports, ecstasies, orgies—what is the *secret*? The poet, says Baudelaire, is a decipherer, a Kabbalist of reality, a decoder. Ordinary life, if it is not a message in code, a system of symbols for something else, is unacceptable. It must be a cryptogram; it can't be what it seems. The poet's task is to decode the incomprehensible obvious. His life becomes a deliberately constructed paranoia, as Rimbaud, Breton, Artaud were to say generations later.

As we read him we discover that Baudelaire believes in the charm, the incantation, the cryptogram, but he ceases to believe in the *secret*. The spirits have not risen. The code says nothing. This is the mystery concealed by the disorder of the world. The visionary experience ends in itself; the light of the illuminated comes only from and falls only on himself. This is not unlike Buddhism in its starkest form, the end result of a rigorous religious empiricism— which is why similar minds find him so congenial today.

Baudelaire liked to call his verse Classical, and gullible modern critics echo him. It is not, although it is so Latinate as to begin the corruption of logical syntax that reaches its culmination in Mallarmé and Reverdy. It is ritualistic; the tonic patterns of French verse are flattened out, and a reverberating sonority of vowel music as in English or Medieval Latin takes their place. A poem like "La Cloche Fêlée" is written Gregorian chant—"*media vitae*, in the midst of life we are in death."

Nor is Baudelaire the poet of the modern megalopolis in any realistic sense. Corpses spilling worms in the ditch, ancient courtesans cackling over gaming tables in the dawn, boulevards lit with prostitutes, Negresses lost in the winter fog, sweaty lesbians in beds dizzy with perfume, a wounded soldier dying under a heap of dead—is this everyday life in the modern city? It is the city as the mother of hallucinations of the alienated. He presents it with the utmost tension of abstract and concrete, "in a noble, distant, superior manner," said Laforgue—a hieratic manner, the manner of a priest. He claimed the power of transubstantiation—"Paris, you gave me mud, and I turned it to gold and gave it back to you."

It has been said that Baudelaire, like Blake, had no philosophy, or had to make one up out of himself. Like Blake, he states his philosophy clearly enough. It is the orthodoxy of the heterodox, older far than Aquinas or even Plato. Correspondences, the doubled world, the doctrine of signatures, the ambivalence of microcosm and macrocosm—he found all these notions in Swedenborg; some in Coleridge; some in Poe; all in Blake, whom he may have read; and all worked out in vulgarized detail by his friend Eliphas Lévi, the founder of modern occultism.

More sophisticated, more desperate than his masters, Baudelaire uses his gnosticism in an anti-gnostic sense, to contradict itself. Man is not saved by knowledge; *gnosis* does not produce *ecstasis*, but vice versa. Vision produces the knowledge of the irrelevance of knowledge, a state of being beyond the vaporized ego, beyond the temporal order, an end in itself. This is the secret of clerisy, of the *sanior pars*, the saving remnant of doom. It is the substance of a new ordination.

In youth he called the disengaged man of conscience the Dandy. As he grew older, the Dandy merged with a new kind of priest or shaman. His clerkly role explains his distinctive dress, his strange caste standards, far more strict than those prevailing amongst *les autres*, peculiar to the clergy—"benefit of clergy"—a people set apart.

He chose the life that enabled him to do what he did. Above all other writers, poetry was to him a vocation, a calling to a new kind of holy orders. So to the degree to which he could manage it, his life was monastic—like the celibacy of the brothel: an almost complete sacrifice of domesticity and the amenities of secular man to the liberation and refinement of a sensibility and a conscience that he considered synonymous. He insists on the poet and artist as *vates*; as the visionary eye of the body politic, as he says explicitly; as the priest who sacrifices himself and atones vicariously for The Others.

There are no satisfactory verse translations of Baudelaire. The best way to read him if you have no French is with a prose pony, as in the Penguin edition by Francis Scarfe. There are excellent translations of the prose, which should all be read—there's not so much.

Karl Marx

The Communist Manifesto

Is Marx a classic? Most economists and sociologists today, including many serious Marxists, consider the theoretical system of Karl Marx, as a scientific structure, either a failure or no longer relevant. Yet more people live under Marxism as official state-established doctrine than live under all other orthodoxies put together. More men live in Marxist states today than had lived in all organized states from the Neolithic period to the birth of Marx.

The number of adherents to a doctrine does not make its basic documents classics. We do not consider the multiplication table or the metric system a classic. Where Marx competes with mathematics, history, to which he made his appeal, has proved his axioms, propositions, and assumptions false as a coherent system. In the economically more advanced capitalist societies, the material misery of the working class has not increased. The workers have not become more revolutionary. Economic crises of ever-increasing frequency and severity have not occurred for a generation. *Laissez faire* has disappeared, and even minor economic relationships are subject to government and corporation planning.

The more industrially advanced societies have been, the less their labor movements have been influenced significantly by Marxism and the more rapidly they have moved away from class conflict. The economic interpretation of history or of current events has been successful only when modified by so many qualifications as no longer to be the comparatively simple tool Marx and Engels imagined they had forged. The simple triadic structure of the Hegelian dialectic has been abandoned by all but the most naïve dialectical materialists as verbalism more sterile than scholastic logic. Even orthodox Marxists obviously think pluralistically, polyvalently, and then cast their ideas into the grammar of dialectic. In

the Marxist states, the working class has not established the dictatorship of the proletariat. On the contrary, their workers have less
influence on government than do those in the United States or
Great Britain.

It is true that there are Marxist arguments which explain away
each of these dilemmas separately. If only one or two points were
apparently false, it might be possible to save the entire system by
doctoring them. But when all have become so evidently dubious to
the unprejudiced observer, the structure has obviously disintegrated.
Marxism is not classic in the sense in which the works of Darwin,
Newton, or Euclid are classic. Yet Marxism is not only enforced by
law over a third of the earth's surface; it is passionately believed in
by millions who are subject to no coercion whatever.

I suppose a classic, in the common sense of the word, is a literary
work that is universally accepted for its aesthetic merits, moral
insight, relevance to the human condition. It is in this stricter sense
that *Capital* or the *Communist Manifesto* is a classic. Significantly,
as brute facts moving in the course of history have invalidated much
Marxist economics as science, the defense of Marxism has shifted to
the writings of the young Marx—particularly to the *Economic and
Philosophical Notebooks of 1844*. As critics have pointed out that the
socialization of production and distribution in the Communist
countries has not done away with alienation but, on the contrary,
seems to be increasing it even over that which prevails in the
capitalist countries, the defense of Marxism has shifted to the doctrine of alienation itself. Alienation as Marx held it in his youth is an
aesthetic concept, and the great documents of later Marxism are
aesthetic realizations of it.

The Communist Manifesto is far from being a practicable program for today. As a friend of mine once said, Hitler immediately
realized all the emergency programs of the *Manifesto* and in addition made May Day a legal holiday. The *Manifesto* is relevant
because it is a symbolic criticism of values. Its appeal is of the same
nature as that of a poem or play. It is a dramatic objectification of
conflicts and dilemmas and denouements that are interior.

The irreducible structure of the Marxist myth is self-evidently
that: a myth, a final eschatology—the Fire of Revolution, the Judgment of Proletarian Dictatorship and Terror, the Second Coming,
when the Golden Age of primitive communism will return unimag-

inably glorified in a new kingdom of brotherly love and divinization of man.

Marx is compared to the Hebrew prophets. He is much more like
the writers of apocalypse. One of the characteristics of organized
Marxism is its melodramatization of life. The faithful live in a state
of subjective apocalypse, an interior vision, which transforms all
exterior reality, so that man seems to be, in the most trivial affairs, in
boring and inefficient meetings and humdrum tasks, an active
participant in the conflict of immense metaphysical entities incarnated in himself, his comrades, and their enemies.

It is impossible to understand the literature of the capitalist epoch
without understanding the alienation that is characteristic of it and
is shared by all its major writers. Marx, Nietzsche, Kierkegaard,
Dostoievsky deal most explicitly with the alienation that finds symbolic expression in Baudelaire, Rimbaud, Mallarmé, Stendhal, Flaubert, Henry James.

The young Marx started with the assumption that all labor is
alienated and that genuine self-activity liberated by revolution
would be a manifold aesthetic creativity surpassing ultimately for
each and every man that of the greatest artists.

On the eve of the 1848 revolutions he dropped the term, because
of its Hegelian metaphysical connections. From the cash-nexus
passage of *The Communist Manifesto* onward, alienation is identified with commodity production for the competitive market and
with the moral consequences of the industrial process under capitalism, but the term itself is abandoned.

Marx's revolution is a vision of the transformation of a metaphysical quality of the abstraction "Man." Man the hypostasis, never
each separate unique human individual, will cease to be self-
alienated and become divinized in a great apocalypse in which the
contradictions between all the antitheses—essence and existence,
act and knowledge, form and content, being and becoming—will be
consumed in a great synthesis.

The forces of classical economics are turned into the figures of
Classical tragedy and the great beasts of the Hebraic visions of the
end of history. The dry abstractions of "the dismal science"—
constant and variable capital, labor power, surplus value, the falling
rate of profit—are inflamed with irresistible moral imperative and
become dramatic personalities. Scientific necessity turns into *hubris*

and *nemesis*. Fallacies of scientific analysis are overwhelmed by the convincingness of the *Manifesto* or the great passages of *Capital* as objectifications of spiritual conflict. The reader is swept up and put on the stage. He becomes an actor in a plot of which the motor, the hidden all-pervading concern—human self-alienation—is the same existential absurdity that reverberates behind the clash of battle, of pride and shame, comradeship and treachery, in *The Iliad*, that sociological document Simone Weil called "The Poem of Force."

A reading list for Marx is not easy to compile, because of the extreme tendentiousness of editors and translators. The best general life is Franz Mehring, *Karl Marx*, now in Ann Arbor Paperbacks, University of Michigan Press. The appendices are by the German Stalinist editor of the posthumous edition and are false and misleading. The best current discussion of contemporary post-Bolshevik Marxism is George Lichtheim, *Marxism in Modern France*, Columbia University Press. It has an extensive and reliable bibliography.

There are many editions of selected writings, the minor works, and the first volume of *Capital*. The complete *Capital*, three volumes in the authorized translation, is published by Charles Kerr. Almost everything else is published by International Publishers. The books popular with the "New Marxists" are *Early Writings*, McGraw-Hill. By far the best general introduction in English is Karl Korsch, *Karl Marx*, Wiley. It is the only one that is uncorrupted by some sort of sectarianism.

Walt Whitman
Leaves of Grass

Our civilization is the only one in history whose major artists have rejected all its values. Baudelaire, Mallarmé, Rimbaud, Stendhal, Flaubert, Dostoievsky, Melville, Mark Twain—all are self-alienated outcasts. One nineteenth-century writer of world importance successfully refused alienation, yet still speaks significantly to us: Walt Whitman, the polar opposite of Baudelaire.

Most intellectuals of our generation think of America as the apotheosis of commercial, competitive middle-class society. Because Whitman found within it an abundance of just those qualities which it seems today most to lack, the sophisticated read him little and are inclined to dismiss him as fraudulent or foolish. The realization of the American Dream as an apocalypse, an eschatological event which would give the life of man its ultimate significance, was an invention of Whitman's.

In our own day, when the term is a badly soiled shibboleth, it is difficult to take it seriously. Other religions have been founded on the promise of the Community of Love, the Abode of Peace, the Kingdom of God. Whitman identified it with his own Nation-State. We excuse such ideas only when they began three thousand years ago in the Levantine desert. In our own time we suspect them of dangerous malevolence. Yet Whitman's vision exposes and explodes all the frauds that pass for the American Way of Life. It is the last and greatest vision of the American potential.

Today, when intellectuals and politicians hold each other in supreme contempt, few remember that America was founded by, and for three generations ruled by, intellectuals. As they were driven from power in the years before the Civil War, their vision of a practicable utopia diffused out into society; went underground; surfaced again in co-operative colonies, free-love societies, labor banks, vegetarianism, feminism, Owenites, Fourierists, Saint-Simonians, Anarchists, dozens of religious communal sects.

Whitman was formed in this environment. Whenever he found it convenient, he spoke of himself as a Quaker and used Quaker language. Much of his strange lingo is not the stilted rhetoric of the self-taught but simply Quaker talk. Most of his ideas were commonplaces in the radical and pietistic circles and the Abolition Movement. This was the first American Left, for whom the Civil War was a revolutionary war and who after it was over refused to believe that it was not a won revolution.

Unfortunately for us, as is usually the case in won revolutions, their language turned into a kind of Newspeak. The vocabulary of Whitman's moral epic has been debauched by a hundred years of editorials and political speeches. Still, there are two faces to the coin of Newspeak: the counterfeit symbol of power and the golden face of liberty. The American Dream that is the subject of *Leaves of Grass* is again becoming believable as the predatory society that has intervened between us and Whitman passes away.

Walt Whitman's democracy is utterly different from the society of free rational contractual relationships inaugurated by the French Revolution. It is a community of men related by organic satisfactions, in work, love, play, the family, comradeship—a social order whose essence is the liberation and universalization of selfhood. *Leaves of Grass* is not a great work of art just because it has a great program, but it does offer point-by-point alternatives to the predatory society, as well as to the systematic doctrine of alienation from it that has developed from Baudelaire and Kierkegaard to the present.

In all of Whitman's many celebrations of labor, abstract relations are never mentioned. Money appears only to be scorned. Sailors, carpenters, longshoremen, bookkeepers, seamstresses, engineers, artists—all seem to be working for "nothing," participants in a universal creative effort in which each discovers his ultimate individuation. The day's work over, they loaf and admire the world singly on summer hillsides, blowing on leaves of grass; or strolling the quiet First Day streets of Manhattan, arms about each other's broad shoulders; or making love in religious ecstasy. Unlike almost all other ideal societies, Whitman's utopia, which he calls "these states," is not a projection of the virtues of an idealized past into the future, but an attempt to extrapolate the future into the American present. His is a realized eschatology.

The Middle Ages called hope a theological virtue. They meant that, with faith and love, it was essential to the characteristic being of mankind. Now hope is joy in the presence of the future in the present. On this joy creative effort depends, because creation relates past, present, and future in concrete acts which result in enduring objects and experiences. Beyond the consideration of time, Whitman asserts the same principle of being, the focusing of the macrocosm in the microcosm—or its reverse, which is the same thing—as the source of individuation. Again and again he identifies himself with a transfigured America, the community of work in love and love in work; this community with the meaning of the universe; the vesture of God; a great chain of being which begins, or ends, in Walt Whitman, or his reader—Adam-Kadmon, who contains all things—ruled in order by love.

Whitman's philosophy may resemble that of the *Upanishads* as rewritten by Thomas Jefferson. What differentiates it is the immediacy of substantial vision, the intensity of the wedding of image and moral meaning. Although Whitman is a philosophical poet, almost always concerned with his message, he is at the same time a master of Blake's "minute particulars," one of the clearest and most dramatic imagists in literature. Blake himself, in the philosophical-mythological epics in which he confronts the same problems and seeks the same solutions as Whitman, is graphic enough, but the details of his invented cosmogony are not sufficiently believable and so soon become boring. Whitman found his cosmogony under his heel, all about him in the most believable details of mundane existence. So his endless lists of the facts of life, which we expect to be tedious, are instead exhilarating, especially if read aloud.

Not least of the factors of Whitman's greatness is his extraordinary verse. He was influenced, it is true, by Isaiah, Ossian, and all the other sources discovered by scholarship. His has influenced all the cadenced verse that has come after it. Yet in fact there has never been anything like Whitman's verse before or since. It was original and remains inimitable. It is the perfect medium for poetic homilies on the divinization of man.

Only recently it was fashionable to dismiss Whitman as foolish and dated, a believer in the myth of progress and the preacher of an absurd patriotism. Today we know that it is Whitman's vision or nothing. "Mankind, the spirit of the Earth, the paradoxical conciliation of the element with the whole and of unity with multitude—all these are called utopian, and yet they are biologically necessary. For them to be incarnated in the world, all we may need is to imagine our power of loving developing until it embraces the total of man and of the earth." So said Teilhard de Chardin; or as Whitman says in the great mystical poems that are the climax of his book, contemplation is the highest form and the ultimate source of all moral activity, because it views all things in their timeless aspect, through the eyes of love.

Dostoievsky
The Brothers Karamazov

A generation ago, most critics of competence would have agreed that *The Brothers Karamazov* was the greatest novel ever written and that Dostoievsky was one of the world's great philosophers. For over fifty years young intellectuals everywhere were weaned on the book, brought out into the universe of general ideas through its soul-wracking conversations. Today this is no longer true and Dostoievsky is rather at a discount. His characters, taken at their own evaluations, pass from moral crisis to moral crisis. Each roomful of excited people, each dialogue over tea and cherry jam, appears to be a dramatic microcosm of the general crisis of nineteenth-century civilization. Once you have read enough Dostoievsky, you come to realize that these scenes are highly formalized rituals as abstract in their way as the Commedia dell' Arte.

Russian intellectuals have always been puzzled by the great popularity of Dostoievsky in the West, and they point out that the English and French translations erase the newspaper-serial vulgarity of his prose style and disguise the formlessness of his narrative. The great issues that agitate his characters have passed away. The moral dilemmas of Ivan Karamazov have been dissolved rather than solved by time. The piety of Alyosha is a special development of a culture that no longer exists, like that of a Sioux medicine man. Furthermore, the troubled souls of Dostoievsky's novels are not grown men. They talk endlessly about things that adults learn it is better to keep quiet about. Tragedy ceases to be impressive when it is so garrulously articulate, and at last even to be believable.

If, as Aristotle held, a slave cannot be ethical because he has no will of his own, and a lowborn man cannot be the hero of a tragedy because his choices are not important, certainly the disasters that overwhelm those whose minds are unformed and whose wills are always ineffective are not tragedies. This is true: the novels of Dostoievsky are not tragedies; they are enormously complicated farces. Dostoievsky is the first major novelist to make a literary virtue of the incorrigible immaturity of his people. It is true too that he is styleless in the sense in which Flaubert used the word style, and that he modeled his narratives on dubious exemplars whom he greatly admired—Dickens and Eugène Sue, for instance.

But if the tireless refining of his sentences turned Flaubert from a broad satirist or a writer of sentimental love stories into a great ironist, the stylelessness of Dostoievsky; the pressure of serial deadlines, gambling debts, sickness, female trouble; his general buffle-headedness; and his utmost naïveté when confronted with general ideas, all conspired to release in Dostoievsky an irony of stylelessness, a literary subconscious that behind all the intellectual sentimentality and moral melodrama truly comprehended the simple absurdity of the human condition.

Superficially, the various conflicting "messages" of Dostoievsky, considered as he was for so long as a philosophical novelist, are the opposite of wisdom; they are general ideas reduced to foolishness and hysteria. So the relations of the Karamazov brothers and their father are not tragic, but embarrassing. We are not embarrassed when we discover that Oedipus has lain with his mother, but we are always embarrassed when the secrets of Dostoievsky's characters are revealed. Smerdyakov is the literary embodiment of pure embarrassment.

Yet something happens. Slowly, out of all the shambles, out of the profundity of a bottomless marsh, a formal vision emerges; life is reduced to the simplest terms, relationships to stark matter of fact, motives to behavior. When we go back and read one of the major novels over—*The Brothers Karamazov*, *The Idiot*, *The Possessed*— we discover that Dostoievsky has been mocking us, and himself, from the beginning. After all, *The Brothers Karamazov* opens with the scandal of the death of a saint whose holy corpse stinks with the comic odor of corruption.

This self-mockery is consistent, and once we recognize it, we see it everywhere. It is most obvious in a novel seldom read nowadays, which the most perceptive critics, beginning with Meier-Graefe, have called the revelation of Dostoievsky's method—*A Raw Youth*.

It is almost a parody of *David Copperfield*; but it is also a comic variety show of all of Dostoievsky's own favorite characters and situations. Yet it is far from being a caricature—in fact, it has been called his greatest novel. The method of Dostoievsky, and he did have a method, becomes conscious and explicit; the messages dissolve, and the dilemmas along with them.

For a generation after it was written critics debated, "Who is the hero of *The Brothers Karamazov*?" That, of course, is the point. It is a tragedy without a hero—as it is a detective story without detectives, without a murderer, and without a murder. Ivan Karamazov's guilt and Smerdyakov's shame cancel each other out. Each is reduced to inconsequence. Alyosha evaporates from the novel altogether, like the spirit that troubles the waters and then departs. His saintliness is consistently ineffective. All it does is disturb the patterns as they move to climax, to the final formal resolution. But there is no formal resolution in the sense of an ultimate charade. The novel does not end in a sculptural set piece like the Laocoon— which fascinated Dostoievsky as he was writing it—just as it does not end in a hero. It ends in a man who does what has to be done.

Dmitri acts—by shrugging his shoulders and accepting reality. Only he and Grushenka ever really act in all the tumult, and so it is only around them that true conflict ever occurs; the rest is confusion. But this is life. This is a far more profound truth than the midnight lucubrations and confessions of Ivan or the distilled Orthodox piety of Alyosha. "Grushenka!" whispers Dmitri to himself as his tortured virgin goes off on a train and he hunches into his greatcoat and drives away through the winter night to an overheated room full of drunks stumbling around a wild girl dancing on a table.

And what is the solution of the detective story? Nobody knows. The trial is the greatest absurdity in all the book. Who killed the old man? Maybe Dmitri; he certainly needed killing. Maybe nobody. Whatever they did, certainly neither Smerdyakov nor Ivan, because they could not act. I once had an ingenious friend who proved to his own satisfaction that it was Alyosha. Maybe. It doesn't matter. All that matters is that death is absurd, and against its absurdity the unadorned affirmation of the flesh is only just a little less so.

This is no message—it is tragic awareness; and it is the final statement of Dostoievsky, that man of many messages, a man in whom the flesh was always troubled and sick and whose head was full of dying ideologies—at last the sun in the sky, the hot smell of a woman, the grass on the earth, the human meat on the bone, the farce of death.

Gustave Flaubert
A *Sentimental Education*

As we turn over the pages of nineteenth-century literature, we are constantly confronted with the question of alienation. Baudelaire, Marx, Kierkegaard, Chateaubriand, Cardinal Newman—it does not matter whether the voice comes from the Left or the Right; all are agreed in their rejection of the values of the prevailing ethic. Yet we never get a clear definition of alienation: what is man alienated from, and why? Perhaps it is precisely the democratic society, the growing affluence and education, that have revealed the natural state of man—much as the development of medicine has enabled greater accuracy of diagnosis, with the resultant tremendous increase in the record of certain diseases. Perhaps the discovery of human self-alienation was simply a statistical refinement made possible by the spread of the privileges of culture to the middle classes.

Flaubert, of all the century's major novelists, most emphatically did not believe this. *Madame Bovary, A Sentimental Education, Bouvard and Pécuchet* were conceived as head-on attacks on middle-class life in all its aspects, its ideals as well as its realities. *The Temptation of Saint Anthony, Salammbô* are sensation-drugged reveries for an anti-bourgeois elite. Yet what happens? Flaubert was a tireless craftsman, and as he reworked his sentences, seeking always the ultimate precision of a surgical instrument, the simplicity of his approach yielded before an irony of which he never became fully conscious. There are as many definitions of great prose as there are

examples—from Apuleius or De Quincey to Swift or Defoe. Flaubert had a vision, a model, of how words should function, and he
ground down each phrase until it fitted that model, a kind of
abstract template that did not merely shape rhythm and image, but
revealed a fundamental quality of the sensibility. The grindstone
revealed the iron.

A *Sentimental Education* is a step forward in time from Stendhal's *The Red and the Black*, and a step downward in the decline of
human nobility. Julien Sorel, Stendhal's hero, is the hero of a tragic
farce, a village Bonaparte who never got a chance; but even though
his life, and its end, are acted out with mock heroics, the vestiges of
nobility still cling to him and to his two foolish women. He dies for
glory as he conceives it. There is nothing heroic about Frédéric, the
hero of *A Sentimental Education*. He is a man of the Forties, of the
reign of Louis Philippe—the bourgeois parody of a king who fell
before a bourgeois parody of an emperor. Julien Sorel was motivated
by an unfulfillable lust for power; Frédéric is motivated by greed.
Julien forces his life to its tragic denouement, a Romantic re-
enactment of a Classic end. A generation later, Frédéric lives in a
world in which Romantic solutions are no longer available. He
simply runs down.

The plot of *The Red and the Black* still preserves something of the
self-sufficiency of Racine or Sophocles. The people live in a world
determined by their own interrelationships. A *Sentimental Education* is a social and historical panorama; Frédéric is the narrative
focus of a people and a time. He is mass man, nearer the top of the
mass than the bottom. Julien is, or at least wishes to be, man against
the mass. Today they would be called other-directed and inner-
directed.

If in any sense *The Red and the Black* is a *roman à clef*, its
deciphering adds nothing to the fiction. A *Sentimental Education* is
full of deadly caricatures of actual people. It was written under the
Second Empire, when the forces it analyzes had realized their
potential, and many of the characters are in fact Flaubert's contemporaries at the period of writing, moved back ten or twelve years. So
the book is a mirror-image of the first volumes of the *Goncourt
Journal*.

"Enrich yourselves!" was the slogan of Louis Philippe's rule, and
in A *Sentimental Education* we can watch an elite, a clerkly class,

abdicate finally all claim to being the "responsibles" and get down and scramble at the trough of the *nouveaux riches.* Julien, in a time of transition, strove to hammer content into his poor life. Frédéric's life, says Flaubert, has no content, and when content offers itself he avoids it or, if necessary, destroys it.

It was in these years that Proudhon said, "Property is theft," and reading this novel we can see why he did. It is the story of a den of thieves, busy stealing counterfeit coin from one another. This is the salient characteristic of Flaubert's portrayal of covetousness and distinguishes it sharply from the simple greed that motivates so many of Balzac's characters. There are greedy men like those of Balzac in Greek and Latin comedy and all through Medieval literature. The covetousness of Flaubert's people is the special nine-teenth-century, capitalist, hypertrophy of covetousness specifi-cally—that sin so heinous as to be forbidden by two of the Com-mandments.

Flaubert's change of focus is accompanied by a change in style, a change in the very meaning of style. Balzac and, in a more profound way, Stendhal adopted for literary purposes the language of the documents and dispatches of Napoleon. They made a subtle literary instrument out of an anti-literary direct communication which was new to spoken as well as written French. Flaubert worked in a completely opposite way. He is artistic. He persuades himself that style is an end in itself and that communication is to be shaped by a rhetoric that may be the antithesis of the rhetoric of either Cicero or Chateaubriand, but that is rhetoric nonetheless.

All this is a kind of occupational delusion. If there is a hero of the *Goncourt Journal,* it is Flaubert. He enters a young Viking in a berserker rage of literary creation. He leaves an old man mad about writing. Café conversations and little dinners of gossip, petty politics and grave discussions of the merits of sundry tarts he turns into pursuits of "the just word," conversational fox hunts that end in assays of the sound of sensibility—a mixed metaphor that may convey something of the excitement.

Amongst the painters Courbet, Manet, Degas, and then all the Impressionists, nature was being illuminated with a new kind of light, never seen before. For sheer brilliance of direct vision, Flau-bert's prose surpasses any of them, and has yet to be equaled by any of his disciples. All the manifold details of life, of nature, of still life, glow with an internal fire, the fire of burning prose that has been distilled to a perfect transparency. This is quite unlike Stendhal's mirror loitering down a pathway—he hoped we would forget we are reading. Flaubert wants us to be always excruciatingly conscious of the craftiness of his art. "It is with a strange malice that I distort the world," said Wallace Stevens. So Flaubert is distorted, by irony, by artifice.

If this were all, he would be only another Huysmans, only the founder of Art for Art's Sake. But behind the irony is a terrible pity. Frédéric with his sentimental covetousness, the crooked revolutionaries, the literary impostors and whores, the women exhausted with bad dreams, the treacherous friends—all the cast of A *Sentimental Education*, as immense as that of a Russian novel, are finally brought to judgment and let go. The novel is not, as Flaubert thought it was, a pure work of art devoid of any moral. Pity and terror, said Aristotle, were the essence of tragic response. At the end we look back over the generation that enriched itself and share with Flaubert a sad, calm terror at the pity of the human condition. This is all it ever comes to; the Last Judgment is not the melodrama of the flames of Hell mounting toward Heaven, but only two emotionally ruined old men, all lust and covetousness used up, like prisoners paroled in old age after serving thirty years of a life sentence.

Tolstoy
War and Peace

What most impressed his contemporaries about *War and Peace* was Tolstoy's enormous skill. On superficial examination, this would seem to be a mistaken judgment. *War and Peace* is full of what Creative Writing teachers call unforgivable faults: long passages that a publisher's editor would insist on cutting out; dozens of scenes that would vanish in a movie "treatment"—as indeed they have.

When the book came out, reviewers did object to the exhortation and propaganda—most especially to the lengthy philosophizing about history that ends the book. Tolstoy thought of *War and Peace* as a thesis novel. As so often occurs in the history of the novel, the thesis is not the one intended.

Midway in his life, Tolstoy was a determinist. He hoped his book would demonstrate the impossibility of free will and the lack of importance of individuals, much less of generals and rulers, in history. Most of Tolstoy's arguments seem dated today, but they are at least as sound as those of any spokesman of the rationalistic enlightenments of either the eighteenth or the nineteenth century. They are unanswerable on the plane on which they operate, and one can overcome them only by transcending them.

This is what Tolstoy himself did. His great novel anticipates his own conversion, as its dramatic architecture takes form under his creating hands. *War and Peace* is above all other things an immense drama of the power of the human spirit. At every crux in the narrative, it is the autonomous moral will that determines value. Kutuzov's decision not to defend Moscow or the Rostovs' decision to abandon their luxurious chattels and use their thirty wagons to transport the wounded from the doomed city are alike significant ethically. It is conscience that acts on the grandest or the most trivial scale, and Tolstoy's point is that the scale does not matter. The determinism, the mid-Victorian materialism, underlines the narrative with the ancient irony of random circumstance. History, as this drama of a major historical event demonstrates, is not the arena of moral action.

The strange thing about Tolstoy's editorializing is that even his severest critics seem to have read it, and his most perceptive made little objection to it. Even today, readers who have worked through *War and Peace*, climax and anticlimax, go on through the last thirty-six pages of philosophizing to the end, and this in a time when the tendentious novels of a generation ago have become unreadable. This is the masterful skill that amazed aesthetes like Turgenev and Henry James—Tolstoy could get the reader to pay attention to anything he wished.

We are liable to confuse this readability with the slick digestibility of the commercial fiction of our time—which, when it handles large-scale narrative, certainly owes as much to Tolstoy as to any other classic novelist. Again, like the commercial writer and unlike almost every other important literary figure since the eighteenth century, Tolstoy is not alienated. None of his characters reflect a pathological relationship between their author and the society from which he came and which provided him with audience and subjects.

Not only are his people living in the world, but the issues that concern them, and that redeem—or destroy—their lives are those which concern the mature. *War and Peace* is a panorama of the real tragedies and real comedies that make up what is called the Real World. Since the Real World we are asked to face up to when we become adults is a hoax and the phrase is only a cliché of the Social Lie, it is very easy for the immature to confuse *War and Peace* with the serial novels that used to appear in the magazines given away in grocery stores or with the historical-moral fictions uttered by spokesmen for the English Establishment.

How does one distinguish? The criteria are gained only by maturity, but the sheer force of Tolstoy's artistry effects a willed suspension of immaturity in the reader. Any talented decadent can make unreality believable. To make reality convincing is another matter, a matter for only the greatest masters.

The startling thing about Tolstoy is precisely that he was completely unalienated and at the same time disbelieved utterly in all the principles that were the foundations of his society—or rather, of the conflicting societies in which, as a nineteenth-century Russian, he had to live. He did not believe in feudalism, the Czar, or the church. He did not believe in capitalism or in Socialist revolution. Neither did he believe in the special subculture of the international artistic community in revolt against bourgeois culture.

The great *aliénés* of the nineteenth century—Baudelaire, Stendhal, Flaubert—never cease to shock us with their reactionary or, worse, simply conventional opinions. Flaubert had the social attitudes of a provincial advocate. Tolstoy disbelieved in the Social Lie whatever form it took. He was able to do this in what might be called a nonpathological manner because he had power where Baudelaire had none. The society was his society, and he had the right—the right that comes with might—to object to it. He knew it from the inside, from the top down.

War and Peace is the story of those people high enough in the social structure for their decisions to make a difference. Yet the "responsibles" of society, caught in a vast catastrophe, discover that decisions break down in the material world and are redeemed only through transcendence. People so placed are privileged to exercise their full humanity, an opportunity more common in the nobler dramas than in everyday existence. A special dramatic isolation—that limited, clearly defined scene so essential to dramatic conviction—distinguishes *War and Peace*. The confined Classical "Unity of Place" takes on the appearance of the whole world.

It is this vast expansion of dramatic intensity that gives us the illusion that Tolstoy's characters are fully developed, well rounded, in a way in which those in most novels are not. So much is concentrated on them that they stand out with a terrible clarity. Thousands of people are raised to the power of the characters of *Seven Against Thebes*.

Seen in this light, all men are justified. It is a glare not unlike that of the Last Judgment—the light of mercy. Tolstoy was an extraordinarily intolerant individual and difficult to get along with. He had plenty of excuse to be at odds with the world and man. Yet above all other novelists he is distinguished by an all-forgiving mercy. This makes his characters more human than they might have been in reality. Fiction presents simulacra like Egyptian painting, and we accept its characters as artistic constructs; but Prince Andrey, Pierre Bezuchov, Natasha Rostov, Platon Karatayev seem to be living in the flesh in a world more real than our own which Tolstoy has structured into an illimitable architecture. The prevailing spirit of the book is a passionate joy in living, a reflection of his happy domestic life at Yasnaya Polyana. As he said of his life there in those days, "Happy people have no history." It is this statement and its converse that are the theses for *War and Peace*.

Astonishing literary skill, stylistic smoothness, rejection of alienation, grown-up characters, complex and absorbing plot, inexhaustible tolerance—listing these virtues reveals them as the hoaxes of the most dishonest money writing. That is why they are the pretended virtues of Ananias, the False Artist. In Tolstoy they are not hoaxes. Of all literary artists he is distinguished by his unflinching integrity. There is nothing so stunning as to encounter the actual virtues claimed by hypocrites. Finally, those ideas which he came to preach so passionately in the years after *War and Peace* and which are the emerging intellectual forces behind the novel, and which even his most favorable literary critics once dismissed as the notions of a crank, have turned out to be right.

Organized society is a lethal fraud, and men must learn to live simply and at peace, in mutual respect and love, or the species will not last out this century. This is obvious to everyone now. Or is it?

Rimbaud

Poems

"Les Phares" they have been called, the lighthouses that guide the course of modern poetry and, following poetry, all the other arts. They are Blake, Hölderlin, Poe, Baudelaire, Whitman, Rimbaud, Mallarmé, Apollinaire, Reverdy, Breton, Artaud. Most of them are slightly mad. Some—notably Poe, Breton, and Artaud—are not even very good poets. Most of them were incapable of competing with the world on its own terms. They were not competent in any accepted definition of the word. Whitman was sane and healthy enough, even normal—if one is not a prig—although he was a little foolish at times. Only Rimbaud and Apollinaire were supremely competent, able to make their own way against all comers whatever the circumstances, and Apollinaire was much the lesser man. He was a successful hack, as Poe was an unsuccessful one, a kind of petty-bourgeois adventurer in letters—alongside a career as a great poet.

Rimbaud was cut from a far vaster cloth—another Clive or Cecil Rhodes, a robber baron like the men who ruthlessly hurled railroads across the mountains and deserts of America. That he failed was not his fault. He chose, unwittingly, to operate in a theater of impossible conditions. The regions from the Red Sea to Addis Ababa were

intrinsically incapable of being developed like South Africa or
Australia or the Far West, and have remained so to this day.
Rimbaud did not fail as a capitalist adventurer in Africa. He was
defeated by a mistake in geography and then was brought low by
cancer. Had he not died in what after all was still late youth, he
might well have a rebel republic in the heart of Africa named after
him today. Great mathematicians do their best work in early youth,
because the intellectual lures of mathematics wear out after a few
years. Entrepreneurs and imperialists usually develop late. It takes
time to become as wily as a fox, as impervious as a turtle, and as
supple as a snake. All who met Rimbaud in Africa agree that he had
learned his lessons superlatively when death seized him by the knee.

Almost all the books on Rimbaud, and there are about six
hundred in French and English alone, autobiographize, if the barbarism may be forgiven, his poetry. The books are written by writers,
and Rimbaud's life shocks writers. He grew up in a drab provincial
town in the worst part of France. He was a brilliant and unruly
child, no worse and no better than any other boy with brains fallen
amongst the brainless. The only opportunity for escape in such a
place was the public library. There he discovered not just poetry,
but the extraordinary claims of the poetics of late Romanticism.

He immediately applied the recipes to himself, and since he took
them literally and acted on them with superlative vigor and intelligence, the results were astonishing. Not only were they epoch-
making—they are still making epochs. The reason is simple: no one
before had ever really believed the claims of the poets, and no poet
had ever before had either the brains or the muscle to act on such
impossibilist claims if he had believed them.

After a brief correspondence with the poets he admired and
believed—alas, stuffed shirts like Théodore de Banville and debauched amateur nuns like Verlaine—Rimbaud ran off three different times to make his way amongst the great in Paris. He succeeded
only in embarrassing and frightening them. The first time, he was
arrested and returned in ignominy to his home. His second visit
coincided with the fall of France and the arrival of the German
armies; his third, with the Commune. Like Whitman's adventures
in the Civil War, Rimbaud's in the Commune seem to be largely
imaginary. But he did see through the Commune. He came to it
believing all its rhetorical pretensions; he left totally disillusioned.

This was April, 1871. In May he had transferred all these apocalyptic, eschatological hopes and visions to poetry. This is the month in which he wrote his two "Letters of a Visionary," to his teacher Izambard and his friend Demeny. They are the most extreme statement of the prophetic, shamanistic, vatic role of the poet in the literature of any language to that date. It would be most illuminating to see the vanished answers from these two small, provincial people—both letters anticipate the answers that must have come. They are not only aesthetic programs; they are apocalyptic visions and calls to action. Rimbaud attacks with all the fury of the visionary who sees an onrushing apocalypse that his contemporaries refuse to even notice. "Judgment, and after the Judgment, the Fire." He seduced the will-less and witless Verlaine, and for two years tried to make him the poet he claimed to be—by the sheer exercise of erotic force.

Within three years Rimbaud was to learn that he had been the victim of a hoax. The poets he met were not Isaiahs but drunken Scribes and Pharisees. The apocalypse was delayed, and its omens died away. Poetry turned out not to be a sufficient vehicle for a total overturn of the human consciousness and a transvaluation of reality. So Rimbaud turned away from poetry as an insufficient vehicle of his ambitions. He was twenty years old.

No one else has ever had the faith, the hope, and the lack of charity to attack poetry the way Rimbaud did. No one else with so much strength and intelligence has ever had the innocence to take all of its most extravagant claims with complete seriousness. Rimbaud tried to do to and with poetry what others only pretended—when talking to adoring women and other customers—to be able to do. Poetry has never recovered. To say it has never been the same since is not slang, but simple fact.

Baudelaire may have founded modern poetry, but his work is assimilable to the past—to Coleridge, or Maurice Scève, or Catullus, or Petronius, or Webster, or Marlowe, or whom you will. With Rimbaud, the connections are snapped. The only poetry like Rimbaud's is to be found amongst primitive peoples who believe as did the boy Rimbaud, really and truly, that the poet is an all-powerful shaman and seer, capable of altering the very nature of reality. It does no good to hunt for other Rimbauds amongst the more deranged Romantics; they are to be found amongst the Eskimos, the Kwakiutls, the Chukchis, the Kamchatals; amongst the founders of ecstatic cults in China and Japan, where some poetry of this sort has made its way into literature; and amongst a very few, far fewer than you would think, Medieval European ecstatics, like Saint Hildegarde of Bingen and Saint Mechtild of Magdeburg.

What did Rimbaud accomplish in poetry? He developed, refined, and pushed to its final forms the basic technique of all verse that has been written since in the idiom of international modernism—the radical disassociation, analysis, and recombination of all the material elements of poetry. This means all, not just the syntactical structure. True, the logical pattern of Western European thought and language begins to break down. The basic form—subject, verb, object, and their modifiers—dissolves. The prosody dissolves too, into doggerel, free verse, and a new kind of incantatory prose quite unlike Baudelaire's. The whole tendency of the prosody is toward hypnotic incantation and invocation of delusion—acoustic magic.

More important by far, however, the ultimate materials, psychological, descriptive, dramatic—the things the poetry is "about"—are shattered beyond recognition and recombined into forms that establish the conviction of a new and different order of reality. The subject and the poetic situation are liquidated. It is impossible to say who the actors in the room are, or where they are, or what is happening to them—not in terms of any pattern of the real world brought to the poem from previous experience. The poem is closed within its own dramaturgy.

This is why most critics insist on interpreting Rimbaud's poetry in terms of his own life. Superficially, this often works. Certainly "Bateau Ivre" is a poem of an adolescent boy with his head full of cowboys and Indians, pirates and cannibals. Certainly it is possible to read, with the help of a little vulgar Freudianism, most of the erotic poems as records of the visions and disappointments of masturbation.

All this is too easy and produces an easy Rimbaud. Best to take the poems at face value, to forget about the struggles with Verlaine when reading "Une Saison en Enfer" or the sodomizing cannoneers of the Commune in their rowdy barracks when reading the bitter, cryptically obscene poems and the "Illumination" called "Democratie." Rimbaud may never have seen the Commune and may well not have had any genuine homosexual affair with Verlaine. The poems are all about something else. "*Je suis un autre*," said Rimbaud.

By the time we get to the paintings of Juan Gris, or the poems of Pierre Reverdy, Rimbaud's philosophy of composition has been brought under cool control. It has, so to speak, entered the period of Plato, Aristotle, or even Aquinas. But behind Plato lies the demonic Socrates, whom nobody could understand, but only systematize. Rimbaud is stout Cortes, not silent on a peak in Darien, but walking into the streets and plazas of Tenochtitlán, into a universe of wonder.

To achieve the dissolution and dissociation of all the elements of poetry, it was necessary for Rimbaud to undertake a forced dissociation of the personality—under the strict control of a powerful will and reason. This is the "reasoned derangement of the senses" which has become a byword of all modern art.

In Rimbaud it is commonly accompanied, and always in his best poems, by the phenomena of dissolution of the personality that are found in natural mysticism and in trance states that result from toxins—whether drugs, or the products of fasting, or manipulation of the breath and the autonomic nervous system. Cyclones, explosions, blue lights, shattering crystals, colored snow, whirling sparks, shipwrecks, whirlpools, the looming of an alternative reality behind the fiction of the real, the sense of estrangement of the self. "The true life is absent." "I am another."

It is this vocabulary which is common to Saint Hildegard, Baudelaire, and Mallarmé, which has led so many to worship Rimbaud as a diabolic saint, just as it has led so many in our time to confuse the similar effects of hallucinogenic drugs with mystical visions of ultimate reality.

Rimbaud did not see the Absolute, or try to become an angel, or any of the other things his worshipers attribute to him. He very simply tried to take the pretensions of poetry seriously and to reform art so that it could alter the experienced meaning of reality. He decided that this was a hoax and an activity beneath the dignity of grown men, and he turned to what he considered more interesting activities. However, he almost succeeded, and poetry will never be the same again.

The translations and the books about Rimbaud in English are of doubtful guidance. They are all weakened by adherence to one or another of the Rimbaud myths. We badly need a translation of the devastating critique of Étiemble. Best read two or more *face en face* translations and puzzle out the French with a dictionary. Wallace Fowlie's recent critical book is pretty much a repetition of the now very dated pseudo-Thomist criticism of Jacques Maritain. However, his translation is usually trustworthy, and it is complete.

Edmond and Jules de Goncourt
Journal

On December 2, 1851, as their first book went on sale, the brothers Edmond and Jules de Goncourt began a diary—written down by Jules at the dictation of them both, as were all their other works. This date, the anniversary of the battle of Austerlitz, coincided with the seizure of power by the Prince-President of the Second Republic, Louis Napoleon, who dissolved the National Assembly, arrested the leaders of the Royalist and Republican parties, and had himself made dictator of France. On January 20, 1870, Jules died, and Edmond, who at first decided to discontinue the entries, went on, writing a subtly changed journal until 1896.

These dates are of great importance. The second half, but especially the third quarter, of the nineteenth century saw the growth of a new kind of culture in France, of a sort never seen before. There had been founders and forerunners of the modern sensibility, increasing in number for a century, but these were the years of its establishment amongst whole classes of the population.

They were also the years when France once again assumed the leadership of the world in the arts and literature, when the poems and novels were written and the pictures were painted that would shape the responses of civilized men to life until the final breakdown of this synthesis in the First War. Many of the social forms and customs of French life would persist unchanged and unchallenged until after the Second War: what we still think of as characteristically French in dress; food; art; wine; women; "Society," or high life, as well as low life. A special taste was consolidated, like a conquering army, and in itself became a historical force.

The Journal of the Brothers Goncourt is the most illuminating revelation of this taste, this consensus in important responses to life. We can watch it evolve in action, reach its highest point, and begin to decline or change into a different historical style. The Goncourts wrote the case history of the style of an epoch. They did more. The ironies of history, worked over by their own personal ironies, created a drama, if not an epic, of the rise and fall of a way of life.

Baudelaire; Gautier; Hugo; Flaubert; Dumas, *père* and *fils*; Daudet; Zola; Mallarmé; Degas; Gavarni; Guys; Courbet; all the great hostesses, all the great tarts, from the mistresses of the Emperor to part-time actresses; banquets and funerals; wars and revolutions; the new Napoleon at the beginning, Bismarck and the Paris Commune at the end of the joint diary; the new century four years away at the end of Edmond's, with the notorious Montesquieu, the Charlus of Proust's novel, in the last entry. The age had its own comic and bitter structure. It was so complete and so complex a world, and it produced so many of the great works of art on which our own period is still nourished, that we seldom realize that it has passed utterly away. In brief entries of the *Journal* it is all about us, rustling and shimmering like a whirlwind of dead leaves.

None of the other great diarists of literature ever made so telling an instrument of the single entry. Beside the Goncourt brothers Samuel Pepys seems artless indeed. Each entry tells, not only in itself, but as part of a whole. It is as though they had known what was going to happen for half a century before they ever sat down to write. Characters appear and disappear, grow or decline, but always change. Sometimes there are startling reversals. One of the most poignant entries is the description of the death of their aged nurse, who had cared for them as babies and who continued with them into their own middle age. They mark the day of her passing with a prose elegy of tender gratitude for a life lived in devoted love. In the next entry they have discovered that she was a nymphomaniac who stole from them to pay ragamuffins and thugs to sleep with her, right up to the time of her death.

The eroticism that underscores the narrative everywhere is as special as the culture it describes. The Goncourts have been called scabrous, malicious, spiteful. For at least the years when they worked on their journal together, the reverse is true. It soon becomes obvious to the reader that they could have told much more shocking tales had they wished merely to shock. They were interested in revealing the motives and relationships that truly were operating in the society about them, not in scandal for its own sake. The intimacy is shameless, but the final result is profound pity for the weaknesses and follies and wastes that occupy most of the time and energy of even the greatest lives. A kind of sharp, rutting lust pervades all society and erupts suddenly in the most unexpected places, much as it does in Simenon's novels, the last great chronicles of a way of life now vanishing.

We can watch little tarts work their way up the ladder of important beds until they are completely accepted socially. Against them is counterpointed a contrary movement: writers and generals and ministers age, lose control, decline, and fall. The Goncourts were the Gibbon of the brothels, boudoirs, and salons of the Second Empire. They are almost the Toynbee, because a philosophy of history certainly emerges from what at first seems only a random diary: men are brought low by the wars of lust and pride. It was a time when the newly rich flourished, but they seldom appear. The Goncourts were concerned only with the people who count, who determine a social order and a culture. It is their lives as lived that determine history, not the details of politics and war, and as far as the record is concerned, these lives are usually lived in secret.

This is the latter half of the nineteenth century, and the painted facade, the official myth, of society was at least as self-righteous in France as in Victorian England. The Goncourts scarcely bother to notice the Social Lie, except where its enforcers move to prosecute or threaten their books and those of their friends. They simply assume that "everybody knows this is what life is really like." So today they still horrify people who do not know or pretend they don't.

The Goncourt brothers themselves were certainly a special case.

They lived and worked together far more closely than man and wife, with a love surpassing that of brothers and with no record of important quarrels or disagreements. Both had mistresses, but neither seems ever to have entered a close or deep love relationship, or ever permitted the other sex to come close at all. Long after Jules's death, Edmond wrote a story of two acrobats who "joined their nervous systems to master an impossible trick"—and so they did. Their novels, but even more remarkable, their intimate diary, are the records of one sensibility.

After the death of Jules, the *Journal* changes. Edmond never ceases to be sharply conscious that he is an amputee. Half the author, half the experiencer, of the diary is missing. Jules died in 1870; the first volume was not published until 1887, and the next two in the following year. It is probable that the brothers originally planned not to permit publication until long after they were both dead. But for the last ten years of his life, Edmond more or less made a career of the *Journal*.

As 1870 opened, the age seemed to be at its apogee, the brothers Goncourt at the height of their career. Month by month their world fell apart. Jules died of syphilis; Bismarck rolled over France; the Emperor abdicated; the Commune rolled over Paris, and the white terror over the Commune, in the first of the immense massacres of classes or whole peoples that are characteristic of our own modern world. Edmond's modern world was totally overturned, and a schism was opened up in French society that has never healed. His detailed, on-the-spot descriptions of the Commune have an unsurpassable immediacy, and for all his loathing of the lower classes, a sympathy with their agony and a dim understanding of what its results would be. The rest of the volumes are essentially the story of those results—the running down to death of one of the great ages of man, as the narrator runs down alongside.

There is an excellent translation of selections from the final eleven-volume manuscript, published in 1956–59; *Pages from the Goncourt Journal,* edited and translated by Robert Baldick (Oxford University Press, 1962).

Mark Twain
Huckleberry Finn

At the very beginning of Western literature stands an epic and a romance of travel that have never been bettered. Greece is only a tiny lighted area in a vast darkness peopled with monsters, monstrous humans, and malignant personified forces of nature. Odysseus travels through their hostile world carrying with him on his little boat, and finally only with his own sea-tossed body, the Greek community of reason, order, and ingenuity—Odysseus of many devices—the symbolic embodiment of thousands of merchant-adventurers who wandered from the Atlantic coasts of Morocco and Spain to the shores of the Caucasus and returned to the marketplaces of their bright little city-states where crowds gathered who spent their time in nothing else but either to tell or to hear some new thing.

Odysseus, merchant-adventurer, moving like a tiny dot of light over the dark map of the Mediterranean, the representative of a civilization, reason and order, confronting the irrationality and disorder of the natural world—hostile, valueless, chthonic, and strangely decadent. Circe, Calypso, Polyphemus—we are always conscious of the fact that these creatures, as personifications of an older world, know secretly, instinctively, that their day is done. They are the old order, ultimately powerless against the craftiness of this agile representative of a new world, who eventually conquers even Poseidon and the chaotic, many-voiced sea.

Twenty-five hundred years later an American was to write a kind of anti-Odyssey, the story of two comrades drifting on a flood without motor or sail, past civilization—a civilization hostile, haunted, valueless, and early-decadent. Except for a sweep that uses the current to avoid snags and whirlpools, they are at the mercy of flowing water—like the water that flows through the *Tao Te Ching*. Odysseus fights Poseidon with oar and sail. Jim and Huckleberry Finn co-operate with the Mississippi or yield to it passively. The enemy lurks ashore, in the towns of the frontier, in a way of life not very unlike that of the city-states of Homeric Greece.

Mark Twain's judgment of that life is very different from Homer's, and not unlike that of Saint Paul in the *Book of the Acts of the Apostles*—if Saint Paul had been an atheist.

The Adventures of Huckleberry Finn is not modeled on the *Odyssey* the way Joyce's *Ulysses* is, but it would have been quite impossible for Mark Twain not to have Homer constantly in mind, as he must also have had *Robinson Crusoe, The Pilgrim's Progress*, and the travels of Peter and Paul and of dozens of others, not least Marco Polo. He carefully contradicts them all.

Huck and Jim are obviously Crusoe and Friday reborn; but it is Jim who is sane, knowledgeable, always resourceful, and guided by a simply defined, incorruptible morality—not a "system," but a natural aptitude and a lifelong habitude. Crusoe's island is a miniature of civilization, populated by one Whig early-industrial "projector" and his embodiment of "labor power," quite untroubled by conflict or competition. Crusoe and Friday are civilization.

The raft is a passive vehicle of natural forces carrying the integrity of unalienated comradeship. Each member is himself, the embodiment of the integrity of selfhood; and the raft carries them through a universe of moral chaos—if not safe and sound, at least undestroyed. Beyond the all-dissolving flood on which they float, man is invariably wolf to man.

Each episode of *The Odyssey* is a triumph of reason; each episode of the odyssey of Huck and Jim is another perspective into chaos: "The best lack all conviction and the worst are full of passionate intensity." Honor is a pretext for mass murder in the feud between the Grangerfords and Shepherdsons. History is a cruel hoax—all Dukes and Dauphins are like the frauds who invade the raft. The King and Duke capture the raft, but they never, in any way, ever penetrate its little community of two. When they are gone, in spite of the damage they have done, it is as though they had never been.

Past Kings and Dukes and murdering gentlemen of honor sweeps the mob swirling like maggots in the belly of a dead dog.

Twain yields one point to his enemy Sir Walter Scott. Above the chaos, like peaks above the icefields of Greenland, rise a few pure and noble women—logical flaws in Mark Twain's sociology of relentless alienation, his weakness in actual life, and the doom of his full achievement as an artist. Stendhal had no such illusions. They are the good fairies and princesses in Mark Twain's fairy tale, the relief in an otherwise unrelieved nightmare of violence and fraud and hypocrisy.

All passes—the characters of the epic fade like figures of nightmare. The great River, the stream of Tao, is reality; the rest is dream. "He had a dream and it shot him," says Huck. "Singular dream," says the voice of civilization.

In the end, the dream prevails. Huck and Jim become dislocated from their community of mutual aid and stumble unaware into the world of Tom Sawyer—the world of the business ethic tricked out in the romantic gawds of public relations fantasy. It is remarkable how much Mark Twain's analysis of the predatory society resembles Thorstein Veblen's. Tom is free enterprise as defined by Veblen, disguised as a little boy, and a horrible thing he is.

Unperceptive critics have objected to the ending of the novel— but it is the capture of Huck and Jim by the world from which they fled that turns the novel into black comedy, into the Theater of Cruelty. The Social Lie wins again against the brotherhood of man. The King and Duke, the bloody feud of the Grangerfords and Shepherdsons are gone like evil dreams. But Tom Sawyer and Aunt Sally are not dreams; they are "reality," and they will abide. They may be more unreal than the naked, obscenely painted Dauphin, but they will never go away. "A book for children" indeed—like *Gulliver's Travels!* But maybe it is; perhaps every American child should read it and ponder its lesson. To judge by the papers, many of them have.

Mark Twain had a hard time giving up his own illusions. Pure womanhood, young and old—mom and sis and daughters—rising above the foulness of "the system" was one. Pure women pivot and close the plot of *Huckleberry Finn*. The frontier was another. Huck's last words are, "But I reckon I got to light out for the Territory ahead of the rest." These myths distorted his life and his personality. The River was another. He returned in middle life to the River to find it emptied of meaning. On the frontier he found the same fraud he had left—even a fraudulent Mark Twain: one Bret Harte. Brotherhood was another. His brother Orion was a lifelong nuisance and a great expense. Pure and noble women did their best to bring him down and almost succeeded.

Huckleberry Finn sets the tone and pattern for hundreds of American novels after it. No other civilization in history has been so totally rejected by its literary artists. Mark Twain is far more at odds with the values of his society than Stendhal, Baudelaire, or Flaubert, and yet he is far more a part of it. In many ways he was the typical educated—self-educated, usually—American male of his day. He was also enormously successful, one of the most popular American writers who has ever lived. Significantly, his hack work was less popular than *Huckleberry*, and even his blackest, bitterest books sold very well—and still do. Perhaps the typical American male is secretly far less the optimist than he would have the world believe; but the lies he rejects and the myths he believes are still those whose contradictions tortured Mark Twain.

We tend to assume that a work which involves the deepest symbolic levels of the human mind must be learned, intellectual, obscure—but quite the opposite should be true. The voyage of Huck and Jim is a simple tale of the adventures of simple people. It has been compared to the underworld journey of Osiris—but Osiris was Everyman. Likewise we forget, misled by contemporary practice, that black comedy is broad comedy, and it has usually been as hilariously funny as the fraudulent universe that Tom Sawyer constructs around Huck and Jim in their final captivity. The basic comedy—as has so often been true—lies in the contrast between an individual with no individuality, no personal center, and two people who cling to their integrity in spite of all.

There is something quite commonplace-American in all this. Twain's novel occupies the same symbolic universe as Whitman's "Passage to India." Huck's reveries in the illimitable night on the boundless flux are those of the boy in "Out of the Cradle, Endlessly Rocking." The son of a lawyer and judge; migratory worker and adventurer in early youth; unsuccessful businessman in middle age; his life ruled by pure women; raconteur; political cynic; in love with his work; man of the world—there have been millions of Americans like Mark Twain, and their dreams too have echoed Lao Tse, or Osiris, or Don Quixote, unaware. That is his power. Power—Waley translated *Tao Te Ching* as *The Way and Its Power*, and it could well be the title of *The Adventures of Huckleberry Finn.*

Chekhov
Plays

It comes as a bit of a shock to sit yourself down and deliberately think, "In the first half of the twentieth century, the position once occupied in ancient Greece by Aeschylus, Sophocles, and Euripides was held, in the estimation of those who sought serious satisfaction in the modern theater, by Ibsen, Strindberg, and Chekhov." What had happened in two thousand years? Had it happened to the audiences, or to the playwrights, or to the self-evolving art of drama? Or was the change more profound than this, more profound even than a change in the meaning of civilization—was it a change in the very nature of man? We still say we enjoy *Antigone*; but if we go directly from a performance of that play to Chekhov's *Three Sisters*, it is difficult not to believe that the men of Classic times were different from us, a different kind of men.

In certain plays, both Ibsen and Strindberg set out deliberately to compete with the great past, with Shakespeare or Schiller or Sophocles or Aeschylus. The results are hardly competition. *Peer Gynt* or *Damascus* bears little resemblance to the past, though certain Strindberg plays do contain distorted reflections of Euripides. But Chekhov—what would the Greeks have made of *The Sea Gull*? They would have classed it with Menander, with the New Comedy of domestic conflict and absurd situation. So did Chekhov. We seldom pay attention to half-titles in "Collected Plays," but there it says, right on the page—"*The Sea Gull*, A Comedy in Four Acts." *Ivanov* is called "a drama"; *Uncle Vanya*, "scenes of country life"; *Three Sisters*, a "drama"; *The Cherry Orchard*, certainly the saddest of all, "A comedy."

So simply Chekhov states his aesthetic, and with it a philosophy of life. If we take these heartbreaking plays as tragedies in the sense in which *Oedipus the King* is a tragedy, we are self-convicted of sentimentality. No one has ever had a more delicate sentiment, a more careful sensibility, when it comes to portraying, and so judging, the lives of more-than-ordinary men and women—but no one was ever less a sentimentalist—than Chekhov. This is why he outraged a swashbuckling sentimentalist like D. H. Lawrence, who hated him and who couldn't understand why he didn't come down hard on the right side and plump for the Good Guys and The Life Force.

Chekhov always insisted that the five plays of his maturity that his audiences insisted were tragedies were simply developments, precisely in maturity, of the hilarious short farces of his youth. But if Uncle Vanya's impotent pistol shots and Irina's "Moscow, Moscow, we'll never see Moscow now!" are not tragic, then Chekhov is mocking us, and his characters—and, not least, his actors—too. No. Chekhov is the master of an art of such highly refined modesty that he can present his people in their simplicity on a stage and let life itself do the mocking.

He wanted a new theater, a theater that would tell it the way it really was. There has been plenty of realist and naturalist theater in Russia in his day and since, but there is only one Chekhov. The naturalist theater uses a whole armamentarium of devices to create an illusion of "real life" and then drive home its points, all derived from the storehouse of literary and dramatic morality.

There have been many more lifelike plays than Chekhov's. His is not a circumstantial naturalism of décor and talk and event—it is a moral naturalism. These lost people, off in the vast provinces of Russia, frustrated, aimless, hopeless, or full of utopian unrealizable hopes, all alike coming to trivial ends, actually make up a highly stylized theater of their own, as formal or classic as the Commedia dell' Arte or Plautus and Terence.

What is realistic, or naturalistic? What is "life as it really is"? This is the silent moral commentary that underlines every speech, like an unheard organ pedal. Is it a judgment? In the sense in which "Judge not lest ye be judged" is a judgment.

There is something intrinsically ridiculous about all the people in all the plays. Chekhov's is truly a theater of the absurd. Yet we never think of them as very funny—and we don't think of them as very sad, either. The play as a whole may sadden us, as life saddens us with all the massive pathos of mortality, but Chekhov's people we simply accept.

We do not judge Uncle Vanya to be a fool or Irina to be a silly girl or Trigorin to be an ass and a cad, although they certainly say foolish and silly and asinine things. And when that recurrent character who always says, "Some day life will be splendid, and people in those far-off days will look back on us and pity us in our filth and misery and thank us for having endured our agonies for them, so that they might be" speaks his recurrent part, we neither laugh nor sigh nor believe, but at the most think, "Perhaps. Not likely. It won't matter."

Chekhov would have been horrified if anyone had cold-bloodedly accused him of teaching a moral—but so he does. We accept these tragic comedies, these sorrowful farces of Chekhov's the way we would accept life itself if we were gifted with sudden wisdom. Chekhov places us in a situation, confronting the behavior of a number of human beings in what seems to them, at least, an important crisis. We are so placed, so situated and informed, that we can afford to be wise. We can regard the affairs of men as they should be regarded, in the aspect of timelessness. But this is what Sophocles does.

Once we accept both the idiom of Chekhov and the idiom of Sophocles we can compare them, and we can see very clearly the great precision and economy with which Chekhov works. His plays are pre-eminently, in modern times, playwright's plays, a joy for a fellow craftsman to see or read. How right everything is! How little time or speech is wasted! How much every line is saturated with action! Sophocles, Molière, Racine—very few other playwrights have been as accurate and as economical.

It is this genius for stating only the simplest truth as simply as can be that makes Chekhov inexhaustible—like life. We can see him for the hundredth time when we are sick of everything else in the theater, just as we can read his stories when everything else, even detectives and science fiction, bores us. We are not bored because we do not feel we are being manipulated. We are, of course, but manipulated to respond, "That's the way it is." Since the professional manipulators of the mind never have this response in view, we are quite unconscious of Chekhov's craftiness—that he is always interfering on the side of suspended judgment.

Quite unlike those of Ibsen and Strindberg, who were tireless preachers and manipulators, Chekhov's people are not alienated. They have trouble, as men have always had, communicating, but the cast of each play forms a community nonetheless. They would all like to live in a society of mutual aid if only they could define the means and ends of aid itself. One feels that Ibsen and Strindberg didn't like any of their casts very much and made them up of people who wouldn't listen to Ibsen and Strindberg. Chekhov doesn't want to be listened to. He isn't there. He is out of sight, in the last row of the balcony, listening. "I imagine people so they can tell me things about themselves." This is an unusual, but certainly an unusually effective, credo for a playwright.

It is easy to accept Orestes or Hamlet as an archetype. Hundreds of books are written analyzing the new pantheon of heroes who make up the inner dramas of our unconscious. They are very spectacular personages, these. It is hard at first to believe a playwright who comes to us and says, "The schoolteacher and the two stenographers next door to where you live in Fort Dodge—these are the real archetypes." But until we have learned this—and most of us will never learn it, however many Chekhov plays we see; not really, not deep in the bowels of compassion, but only as we learn things in books—we will never learn to approach life with the beginnings of wisdom: with that wisdom so characteristic of Sophocles.

Afterword
by Bradford Morrow

"Axes of reference," was Pound's phrase in *How to Read*. Confucius, Homer, Sappho . . . Stendhal, Flaubert, Rimbaud. Axes that together form a constellatory framework for all literary experience. Pound and Rexroth—two of the most opinionated polymaths of the Modernist movement—independently compiled lists of classics, and while there are obvious divergences (Tennyson and Virgil would be excoriated from Pound's list) there is more accord than might be expected. Intended purposes of these compilations are similar for both poets. Pound: "After this inoculation he could be 'with safety exposed' to modernity or anything else in literature"— *he* of course being the great *We* who, with or without a liberal education behind us, may always benefit from reappraisal of literary values, whether our occupation is university professor, computer programmer, ditch digger. For Rexroth, this is understood; further, he takes the controversial position, dismissed more than ever in our academies where the self-referentiality of all lingual constructs stands at the center of so many critical arguments, that art has its utilitarian side insofar as he believes a masterpiece may be spirit-healing. About Tu Fu: "He has made me a better man, a more sensitive perceiving organism, as well as, I hope, a better poet. His poetry answers out of hand the question that worries aestheticians and critics, 'What is poetry for?' What his poetry does superlatively is what is the purpose of all art."

In March 1983, ten months after Kenneth Rexroth passed away, I flew to Santa Barbara to go through his massive personal library, collect and collate all the manuscripts he had left behind. His widow, Carol Tinker, and I ferreted out more material that we might have expected. Besides the unfinished sequel to *An Autobiographical Novel*, which he was working on at the time of his death, were typescripts of full-length books—*Camping in the Western Mountains* (written for the W.P.A. during the 1930s), *The Poetry of Pre-Literate Peoples* (an ethnopoetics anthology intended to complement Jerome Rothenberg's *Technicians of the Sacred*), and *A Lantern and a Shadow*, which now has been verified as the author's first book of poems. Underneath a nest of proofs tentatively held in place by a rigging of cobwebs and cantilevered cardboard on the top of the tall reference shelf was a blue ring-binder marked "Miscellaneous Essays Unpublished." Reviews, synopses, articles, part of a ballet; not the least intriguing of the forty-eight pieces in the binder was a list entitled "Projected Classics Revisited," clearly an outline for another volume of *Classics Revisited*. (*The Elastic Retort*, published by Seabury in 1973, has a section entitled "More Classics Revisited," with twenty-nine essays similar in format to those in the present book. Interestingly, those "classics" coincide with these listed below in only one instance: H. G. Wells.)

The list, first (not chronological, but roughly alphabetical, as given): "*Anna Karenina*, Henry Adams, *Arabian Nights*, Aristophanes, Augustine *Confessions*, the Epic Books of the Bible, Boethius *Consolation*, Boswell—Johnson, etc., Charlotte Brontë *Jane Eyre*, Emily Brontë *Wuthering Heights*, Buddha, *Charterhouse of Parma*, Confucius, Conrad *Victory*, Dante *La Vita Nuova* (first), Donne, Froissart, *Golden Lotus*, *Hamlet*, Hardy, Hawthorne, Histories—Shakespeare as English Epic, Horace, Hugo *Les Miserables*, Smollett *Humphrey Clinker*, Ibsen, James *Wings of a Dove*, Johnson, Joyce, Lear, Rochefoucauld, Lawrence, *Bovary*, Mallarmé, Clerk Maxwell, Melville, Mill *Autobiography*, etc., Milton, Molière, Sophocles *Oedipus* cycle, Pascal, Pepys, Plautus, Poe, Prescott, *Princesse de Cleves*, Proust, *Ramayana*, Strindberg, Tennyson, Terence, Thackeray, *Upanishads*, Vasari, Vauvenargues, *Water Margin* (*All Men Are Brothers*), Wells, Zola, de Tocqueville, Thoreau, *Winter's Tale, one piece*: Morris/Ruskin/Kropotkin, *one piece*: Bashkiertsieff/Barbellion/Amiel/Hinton, Richard Jefferies, etc.—nineteenth-century nature writers." At the end of the list Rexroth has written:

"These group bits would only occur very widely spaced—the series should be single books or at most single authors with hardly any exception. The lesser known people have been selected because they make interesting copy. Of course they are all still read."

Granted, there are some selections on this secondary list which seem at first glance eccentric, or must have been grudgingly made. Rexroth commented to me in interview in 1981: "James Joyce's books, which are all autobiographical, reveal a man of insufferable conceit. Unlike Gertrude Stein, his syntactical and technical devices are unusable. Anyway, I, for one, cannot take seriously a man who insisted that only Italian be spoken at his dinner table in the very week a new glory was born in a Dublin post office." Yet Joyce is included, in entirety. St. Augustine's sermons on the Psalms and his commentary on Job—not the *Confessions*—Rexroth venerates in *Classics Revisited*. Some authors Rexroth has already prepared apologias for. Clerk Maxwell, for example, is cited in *The Pilgrim's Progress* chapter: "In the nineteenth century, this quality [modestly exerted power] passes from the art of literature to the literature of science and reaches its culmination in the crystalline, utterly unselfconscious prose of physicist Clerk Maxwell. It is the reflection of greatness of soul." There are also matters of interpretation. Lear must be Edward Lear not *King Lear*. "*La Vita Nuova* (first)" means: to be read before the *Comedy*. Surely he would not have us read all of Thackeray, but *Henry Esmond* and *Vanity Fair* are givens. Pound provided for these judgmental differences. "For practical class work the instructor should try, and incite his students to try, to pry out some element that I have included and to substitute for it something more valid." This is an invitation Rexroth also would offer. But an even more rewarding approach might be to accept these parameters as proposed, and find in their design what personal *Zeitgeist* lies within. Far beyond literary merit or culminations of form, "greatness of soul" emerges as the key to this curriculum. One could do worse than reading first in this book the chapter on Izaak Walton's *The Compleat Angler*: from it tracings of a grander design become evident.

The note at the end of the secondary list suggests Rexroth had some plan of inaugurating a series not unlike the Harvard Classics, or a cosmopolitan La Pléiade or Library of America. The format chosen for the *Classics Revisited* appraisals—brief, lively, learned, unstodgy critiques—would have worked well as introductions to individual volumes. His appendices limn out particularly authoritative editions and best translations for the would-be publisher to adopt. If Rexroth actively looked for a house willing to undertake the project, he found none.

Perceptive lucidity, goodness of soul, integrity, mastery of literary expression, abiding witness to both the nobility and sheer ordinariness of the human heart, its tragedy, its comedy—these are present in degrees in all of Rexroth's classics. Rexroth was fond of quoting Horace Walpole's letter to the Countess of Upper Ossory, "This world is a comedy to those that think, a tragedy to those that feel." The crucial epistomological question seems now to be whether, in a society increasingly ignorant of the foundations and history of its literature and thought, the very capacity for thought and feeling is threatened, and with it any sense in the terms comedy and tragedy. Those *Saturday Reviews*, in which most of the essays in this book were first serialized beginning in April 1965, seem so impossibly distant as to exist in another culture altogether. Cogent and fresh as the essays are, one wonders what popular magazine editor would be willing to "risk" them on a large audience now. It is nothing prophetical to surmise the potential readership for such work remains much larger than arbiters of popular taste imagine.

Classics Revisited ought not remain alone on its readers' shelves. This is a workbook, and its author's faith rested in its energy to stimulate consequences.

October, 1985
New York City